Forked Tongues

'Forked Tongues;

Speech, Writing and Representation in North American Indian Texts

David Murray

Indiana University Press
Bloomington and Indianapolis

Manufactured in Great Britain

Library of Congress Cataloging-in-Publication Data

Murray, David.
    Forked tongues: speech, writing, and representation in American
Indian texts/by David Murray.
        p.   cm.
    ISBN 0-253-33942-1.   ISBN 0-253-20650-2 (pbk.)
    1. Indians of North America—Languages—Translating.
    2. Intercultural communication—North America.   3. Ethnology—
Authorship.   4. Indians of North America—Public opinion.
    5. Public opinion—North America.   I. Title.
    PM218.M8   1990
    497—dc20   90-49156

1 2 3 4 5   95 94 93 92 91

Contents

Acknowledgements

Earlier versions of parts of Chapters 5 and 6 have appeared in *European Journal of Native American Studies* (1986), P.B. Messent (ed.) *The Occult: a Collection of Critical Essays*, Englewood Cliffs, NJ, Prentice Hall, 1981, and A.R. Lee (ed.) *First Person Singular: Studies in Native American Autobiography*, London, Vision, 1983.

Parts of the research for this book were undertaken at the University of British Columbia (funded by the Canadian High Commission), University of Washington, Seattle (financial aid from US Embassy and a grant from Nottingham University), and the J.F. Kennedy Institute, Berlin (funded by Volkswagen Foundation). My thanks to these institutions and donors, and to the staff of the Newberry Library, Chicago and Nottingham University Library.

My colleagues and friends in the American Studies Department at Nottingham have given me constant support and stimulus. Peter Messent's careful reading of the whole thing was invaluable, and individual sections were read and constructively criticised by Richard King, Tim Youngs, Nick Foxton, Mick Gidley (University of Exeter), and Don Fixico (University of Wisconsin, Milwaukee). To all these people, to Eric Mottram, who got me started, and to many others not named, for conversations, ideas and encouragement, my heartfelt thanks.

Introduction

In the Art Institute of Chicago hangs a picture showing a meeting of whites and Indians, out in the open, with a backdrop of mountains. Gifts, or objects of trade are being unpacked and examined, but it is not clear whether the meeting is to make peace, agree a treaty or to trade. At the centre of the scene stands a man, who is the focus of attention for both sides, and for us too, since they are all facing him, with their backs to us, so that we follow their gaze. He in turn, though, is pointing to a young man on horseback on the left of the picture. When we consult the title of this striking painting, the significance of the central figure becomes clearer, since Frederic Remington has called it *The Interpreter Waved at the Youth*. The painting has its origins in an illustration for a short story, 'The Way of an Indian',[1] and we learn from it that the interpreter is a half-breed, but apart from that we know nothing of him. In this way the *story* is characteristic of accounts of Indian-white contact in ignoring this crucial mediating figure, but the *painting* is unusual, and serves as an appropriate starting point for this book, in making the interpreter the centre of attention. But even here the very composition of the painting, as well as the title, draws us beyond this central figure to the man he is pointing at, so that the painting can be used to characterise the curious role of the interpreter, who is the centre of attention, only in order that he may efface himself. One of the main aims of this book is to demonstrate the complex and various ways in which the process of translation, cultural as well as linguistic is obscured or effaced in a wide variety of texts which claim to be representing or describing Indians, and what cultural and ideological assumptions underlie such effacement.

By paying attention to the mediator or interpreter, rather than what he is pointing to, or in other words by concentrating on the various forms of cultural and linguistic mediation which are always taking place, we reduce the danger of making the space between the two sides into an unbridgeable chasm, or of turning differences into Otherness. Any temptation to imagine an archetypal pristine moment of confrontation between absolute others needs to be tempered by the almost ubiquitous presence on the scene of someone, usually an Indian, or, as here, a mixed-blood, who had already made the connection, and who could act as mediator. The role of Squanto, who conveniently appears, speaking English, to help the Plymouth colonists on their arrival, is a good example, in that he had already been to Europe, having been captured, sold into slavery in Spain and then lived in England for several years,[2] and the fact that the presence of such figures at early (often described as first) encounters is often ignored or effaced can play a crucial part in the *essentialising* of difference, with all that this culturally and politically entails.

This effacement enables the production of two absolutely opposed mythical moments of encounter, which reappear implicitly in the presentation of Indians; the meeting with untouched and unknowable otherness, beyond the reach of language; and the rapport of unproblematic translatability, and of transparency of language. These two mythic moments operate in a whole series of forms, as reference points in many of the texts to be examined in this book, and I hope that an examination of their relation to a set of assumptions about language and nature, and the relation of speech to writing can offer a way of locating one aspect of what could perhaps be called a 'discourse of Indianness', which is available to Indians writing in English, as well as to whites.

To talk of a discourse in this way is inevitably to invoke the work of Michel Foucault, and the Edward Said of *Orientalism*. Towards the end of his study of the representation of 'the Orient' in Western texts Said asks, 'How does one *represent* other cultures? What is *another* culture? Is the notion of a distinct culture (or race, religion, civilisation) a useful one?' (1978: 324). I shall be arguing that an examination of the representation of Indians and Indianness in a self-sustaining discourse over several centuries offers a way of developing, if not answering his questions. Said's approach has been criticised for its tendency to present the discourse of Orientalism, spread across a wide range of disciplines and cultural forms, as not just self-sustaining but as almost inescapable.[3] In his book he deliberately refuses to set up an 'actual' Orient to counteract the discourses he is examining, thereby avoiding the usual rather flat-footed assumptions in studies of stereotyping, that 'fact' can be invoked to dispel 'fiction'. Since the languages of science and factuality are as much discourses as those of imaginative writing, and since knowledge in its formation and dispersal is intimately related to power, it can no longer be seen as neutral and non-ideological, as part of the solution rather than part of the problem. The rhetorical approaches to history of Hayden White (1973, 1978, 1987), and a series of critical approaches to anthropology (Marcus and Cushman 1982; Clifford 1983b; Clifford and Marcus 1986), have shown the usefulness of treating factual writing *as* writing and subjecting it to the same sort of rhetorical analysis as fiction, and we should by now be fully aware of the problems involved in claiming to represent another culture or time.

At the same time, though, we do need to be aware of the risk, in tending to seal off cultures or historical periods or epistemes from each other, of reinforcing and mystifying that very sense of 'otherness' which we would want to question rather than accept. Clearly, to argue for the power of cultural and ideological assumptions and our capacity to project our needs and fears on to our representations of others need not be *in itself* to deny the existence of the others, or the political realities of our relationship with them. It would probably be true to say that most of the work of this sort in the field of colonialist discourse is informed by strong political beliefs in the validity and right to autonomy, of other cultures. Nevertheless, the *effect* of a Foucauldian approach can be to deal with the other only as a creation of *this* culture.[4]

In terms of the material I am dealing with the danger can be described as that of textualising the Indians out of existence. In trying to avoid the colonialist assumption of an ability to comprehend (in the sense of encompass, as well as understand) Indian cultures and their difference, we could modestly confine ourselves to examining the accounts and representations of Indians, not to judge their accuracy but to reveal what they say about white ideological investments. It could be argued that this is the correct political and intellectual agenda in a situation of cultural and political inequality, in that it leaves Indians to represent themselves. It also, though, raises a whole other set of questions in its assumption of the *primacy* of cultural difference rather than similarities or shared concerns. Once difference has been asserted as a given, and the past effacement and denial of it, under the banner of an ethnocentric universalism, has been rejected, it is difficult to see what sorts of political or intellectual positions can follow, unless this difference, rather than being essentialised, is seen to be in constant interplay with *cross*-cultural unities and continuities. We must therefore have a view of translation and communication which can take us between the Scylla of universalism, and the Charybdis of absolute relativism. We need as Arnold Krupat, puts it, 'not to overthrow the Tower of Babel, but, as it were, to install a simultaneous translation system in it; not to homogenize human or literary differences but to make them at least mutually intelligible'(1989:216).

The work of Mikhail Bakhtin and his ideas of dialogue and polyphony have been increasingly invoked as a model for such a simultaneous translation system, and while I share many of the reservations expressed by Krupat and others, about quite what these terms might be made to imply[5] it is important to locate Bakhtin's ideas as an important potential resource in countering the idea of self-sealing discourses in which Said and Foucault might potentially trap us. This book deals with a very wide range of texts each of which raises the question, in its own way, of the representation and expression of Indian difference within the available intellectual and artistic discourses of the time, and my intention is to show the instability of each of these overlapping discourses, and how they can be dialogised by using one discourse against another, or by locating points of contradiction or hesitation in the text. These moments of contradiction can occur either where one set of assumptions collides with another within the text or where we bring to bear upon the finished text the circumstances of its production.

Each chapter can be seen as addressing a particular question. Chapter 1 explores the ideological investments in the idea of translation, its ease, or impossibility, while Chapter 2 concentrates on mainly nineteenth century discussions of Indian languages, and shows the implicit use of a natural/ civilised opposition running through them. This opposition, and the supposed place of Indian languages, and Indians within it, is then shown in Chapter 3 to be at work in the textual presentation of Indian speeches. The extent to which Indians, as writers as well as speakers, are not simply passive subjects of representation but subjects in their own right, is explored in Chapter 4, which deals mainly with the Christian Indians Samson Occom and William Apes, and in Chapter 5, on Indian autobiography and self-expression. The last two chapters move to the representation within ethnographic texts of Indian myths and culture, and try to show the role of a pervasive model of cultural and interpretive totality, and of rhetorical strategies in the making of ethnographic texts. A final discussion of the possibility, and potential usefulness of a dialogical anthropology tries to bring together the issues of power and language which run through the book.

Notes

1. See Remington (1905).
2. For a useful account of Squanto see Sweet and Nash (1981:228–46).
3. See essays in Barker et al. (1985), and Clifford's review of *Orientalism* (1980).
4. The gap between the Said of *Orientalism* and his political writings, let alone his active political role in the Palestinian cause, has often been remarked upon. The relation of Foucault's writings on power to his work for prison reform can similarly be seen as further evidence of the difficulty of relating Foucaldian theory to political action.
5. Most problematic is the ease with which the issue of power and the inequality of power relations which are central to Bakhtin, can be turned into a generalised faith in a pluralism which turns out to bear a striking resemblance to American liberalism (see Murray 1987 and Krupat 1989). The whole question of the scope of Bakhtin's claims is developed further in Chapter 7.

CHAPTER ONE

Translation

Communication between whites and Indians involved the learning of foreign languages, and in some cases sign languages, or the use of interpreters. There have always been whites who have learned to speak particular Indian languages, either from missionary zeal like John Eliot and the French Jesuits in Canada, or sheer proximity and necessity, like captives, traders, or children living close to Indian communities. Later, too, there developed a specifically scholarly interest in learning Indian languages, and some of these will be dealt with in the next chapter, which is devoted to Indian languages and language uses. It is important to remember, though, that the great *bulk* of language learning and translation was being carried out by Indians, this reflecting, of course the wider situation, in which Indians were also the ones involved, willingly or otherwise, in *cultural* translation. As Ulli Bitterli has pointed out in an examination of the failure of the Jesuit mission to the Hurons, the initial willingness to learn Indian languages did not include the necessary cultural openness or adaptability:

> It was not enough to extract an Indian word from the half-understood utterance in which it had occurred, and to declare it synonymous with a French word: the real task was to trace the complex ties between the Indian word and its entire cultural background. The missionaries would have had to adjust their conceptual language to this cultural framework, even at the considerable risk of distorting the very essence of their message. (1989:101)

This is a risk not usually taken, of course, and it is the disparity between this failure and the impression given by a wide variety of written accounts, which regularly pass over or obscure the issue of language and translation, that interests me.

I referred in the introduction to the myth of a totally pristine encounter with the other, and I will be returning to the ideological investments which have been made in the Indian as representing this possibility, but the diametrically opposed myth to this is that of the transparency of language, and the effacement of problems of translation. This too has powerful ideological implications, as Eric Cheyfitz points out in an article which combines discussion of early Indian–white relations, Tarzan of the Apes and American foreign policy. In a situation of mutual agreement and equality of power, adaptation and translation can be a two-way process. In a situation of dominance, the cultural translation is all one-way, and the penalty to the subordinate group for not adapting to the demands of the dominant group is to cease to exist. Knowledge of the *processes* of this translation, though, must be repressed by the dominant side, in favour of a reassuring image of mutual intelligibility which does not register as significant who has had to 'translate'. As Cheyfitz points out, we can see this in European travel narratives, 'where what were necessarily the difficulties, discords, indeed, absences of translation are displaced into fictive accords of communication' (1989:343). By seeing communication as a problem for 'them' rather than 'us', ethnocentrism can be preserved in the feelings of superiority engendered by any failures of translation. Grammatical mistakes, or incongruities of behaviour – Indian adaptations of white behaviour or dress to 'inappropriate' effect, for instance – can be put down to their native naivety or inadequacy, thereby reinforcing that sense of cultural superiority on the part of the whites which they saw as justifying them as forcing the Indians to change in the first place. 'The failure of dialogue,' as Cheyfitz puts it, 'figured as a genetic failure in the other, rather than as a problem of cultural difference, is the imperial alibi for domination' (1989:352).[1]

In its most extreme form this superiority is expressed in the idea that the Indians did not even *have* a language. Stephen Greenblatt points out that although the first kidnapping by Columbus was to gain interpreters (meaning that 'the primal crime in the New World was committed in the interest of language'), Columbus' own justification was 'that they may learn to speak'. Columbus must have known, says Greenblatt, that the Indians could speak, but 'the idiom has a life of its own; it implies that the Indians had no language at all' (Greenblatt 1976:563). This idiom, though, depends on a set of assumptions about language and about civilisation and its boundaries, according to which to speak a language which is utterly alien is the equivalent of speaking no language at all. Greenblatt suggests that the difficulty in representing a language barrier in the sixteenth century was that 'embodied in the narrative convention of the period was a powerful, unspoken belief in the isomorphic relationship between language and reality' (1976:572).

Early Christian missionary enterprises set a great deal of store on being able to communicate with the Indians, and Puritanism, with its rigorous intellectual standards, could not contemplate the idea of conversion without full theological understanding. As a result there were early, though shortlived, efforts to learn the language of the natives, the best publicised of which was that of John Eliot, known as the 'Apostle to the Indians'. Eliot learned enough Massachusett to be able eventually to preach the Gospel, and to translate and publish religious texts in it, but his attitude to language learning was totally instrumental; he saw it as a necessary step on the road to the Christianisation of the Indians. As Raoul Smith has pointed out, once Christianity had achieved a foothold (or, if we adopt Francis Jennings' more sceptical view, once white economic and political power was thoroughly established under the mantle of Christianity), the inequality of power was itself enough to ensure that the translations were all in one direction, and printed texts in Massachusett are seen as unnecessary (see Smith 1979; Jennings 1976). I shall be dealing in detail with Eliot and his textualisation of Indian speech and the effacement of translation and dialogue in the next chapter, but it is worth noting here how the actual accounts of Eliot's mastery of Massachusett anticipate the later systematic playing down of Indian interpreters. These men were indispensable to Eliot, and W.W. Tooker has reconstructed a history of Eliot's first interpreter, who is described, though not named, by Eliot: 'This Indian is ingenious, can read, and I taught him to write, which he quickly learnt..... He was the first I made use of to teach me words and to be my interpreter' (quoted in Tooker 1896:12).

Even when Eliot manages to give a sermon to the Indians in their own language he cannot manage questions, and describes himself 'borrowing now and then some small help from the Interpreter whom we brought with us, and who could oftentimes expresse our minds more distinctly than any of us could' (Tooker 1896:15). This interpreter, whom Tooker identifies as Cockenoe, and who appears later as interpreter in a series of Indian land transfers, is later replaced by Job Nesutan, but neither of them is given any real attention in comparison with Eliot, with the result that the encounters are presented as a heroic case of cultural adaptation by Eliot, while the bulk of the adaptation and translation was from the Indian side.

I am using the case of Eliot here to represent a characteristic white approach, which is to emphasise translation as an issue only when whites choose, or are forced, to do it, and to ignore it otherwise. Apart from the representation of speeches and oratory, which is the subject of Chapter 3, Indian attempts at speaking English are either ignored or patronised. One important reason for this, as well as the ideological ones I have outlined, would be the absence of an appropriate form in which to represent such speech until the development of literary conventions in which to express the vernacular, which were not available even to express English dialects. Indians, therefore, could speak like the educated white men who were writing, or they could not be represented as speaking at all. As the literary and popular conventions develop, so do the possibilities of a stereotyped inarticulateness, full of 'um's and 'How's, as Ralph W. Steadman has exhaustively shown, but it is important to note that what we have here are Indians speaking a new language. In other words they are doing something culturally more

sophisticated than the whites can manage, but it is being used as evidence of
their lack of civilisation. Evidence for this may be found in the fact that in his
account of the development of Indian lingua francas Allan R. Taylor describes
some of the characteristics of pidgin English as 'omission of the verb *be*, the use
of *um* to mark a transitive verb' (1981:180). The idea that non-standard English
may not be failed English, but something else altogether will need to be
returned to in discussion of Red English and translation in Chapter 6, but for
now it is enough to note the way that such representations can feed
assumptions about Indian inferiority.

Given this perceived inferiority, the tendency, when translation difficulties
do occur is to explain them by invoking the limited and primitive nature of
Indian languages, which by the nineteenth century are seen in relation to an
evolutionary scale. Only with the development of ideas of linguistic relativity
later in the nineteenth century do we begin to find the distinctive characters
of languages seen in terms of a complete system of difference, which marks a
significant potential shift from evolutionary assumptions. Daniel Brinton was
one of the earliest and most influential proponents of the ideas of Wilhelm
von Humboldt, and he applied them directly to Indian languages. Whereas
evolutionary approaches would put the emphasis on *continuity* between
languages, seen as being at different stages, Humboldt would stress the
organic unity and separateness of each language, constituting a whole
'thought-world in tones' (quoted by Brinton, 1885:311). Since the nineteenth-
century hierarchy of races and languages remains unchanged, under this new
scheme, it is a moot point whether from the Indian point of view it was any
better to be viewed as being at a retarded stage of development, or in
possession of a language which sealed you off from progress altogether.
Certainly Brinton is in no doubt about their limitations:

> Those peoples who are born to the modes of thought and expression enforced by
> some languages can never forge to the front in the struggle for supremacy; they
> are fatally handicapped in the race for the highest life. (1894:4)

Just in case there should be any lingering doubt about which races and
languages were 'fatally' deficient and which were not, Brinton describes
Humboldt approvingly as 'willing to call it an innate creative genius which
endowed our Aryan forefathers with a richly inflected speech' (1885:318).
Thus a linguistic characteristic such as inflection or incorporation, by its role
in 'moulding the intellect or depressing it' (1894:4) affects the historical
development of a race, and one of the notable characteristics of Indian
languages is their resistance to change: 'they manifest the utmost refractori-
ness both to external influence and to internal modifications' (1885:319).
Since it is unlikely that Brinton would actually have hard evidence for this (in
fact he comments elsewhere on their great facility with other languages –

1883:12) this seems much more of an ideological than a linguistic judgement. If the Vanishing American is vanishing, his language must be 'fatally' at fault, in fixing him at a certain stage of development.

This particular use of Humboldt's ideas to fix languages in unequal relations to each other is not the only possible one, of course. A stress on difference rather than continuity of cultures and languages can have quite other ideological ramifications, and it is worth following up briefly one of these, which has used particular Indian languages in ways which are very relevant to the issue of translation. The development of a Romantic and organic view of culture, which saw each culture as a separate entity, held together by language, tradition and sometimes more mystical bonds, meant that the ground was laid for individual languages to be seen as unique, and this anti-universalist approach has been traced by Julia Penn (1972) from Hamann and Herder right through Humboldt to Boas and eventually to Sapir and Whorf, where it takes on particular relevance for American Indian languages. Clearly, on the way it changes its nature quite markedly, and the complex interplay of possibilities within the argument over uniformity versus diversity within ethnolinguistics has been lucidly schematised by Dell Hymes (1966:115ff.). In its most striking form this anti-universalism is well known as the Sapir-Whorf hypothesis of linguistic relativity, and while this now seems to have become rather a stale issue in linguistics and philosophy, and perhaps of more interest to 'outsiders' (though see Silverstein 1979 and Friedrich 1986), it is worth looking at in some detail, not just because its arguments were supported from Indian languages but because of its implications for the idea of translation in general.

First of all it is necessary to distinguish the separate issues that are involved in the claims about linguistic relativity. In its strongest form it is a claim that the formal properties of a language, its grammatical categories and so on *determine* the ways in which its speakers conceive of the world they live in. Within a language we find already ordained 'the forms and categories by which the personality not only communicates, but also analyzes nature, notices or neglects types of relationship and phenomena, channels his reasoning, and builds the house of his consciousness' (Whorf 1956: 252). As a result, since languages differ the implication is that different groups live in different conceptual universes shaped by the language they use. According to Edward Sapir

> the 'real world' is to a large extent unconsciously built up on the language habits of the group. No two languages are ever sufficiently similar to be considered as representing the same social reality. The worlds in which different societies live are distinct worlds, not merely the same world with different labels attached.
> (Sapir 1951:162)

Modifying and qualifying this extreme form are a number of different formulations which argue for degrees of influence rather than determination. Even in its extreme formulation, though, the hypothesis never claims that speakers of one language cannot understand, or be made to understand, anything said in any other language. What Rossi-Landi (1973:63–5) refers to as the self-extensive or generative power of language allows it to reconstruct an equivalent of anything expressed in any other language. The concern is more with habitual, and even unconscious, ways of seeing the world, to which a language predisposes us. Once the case is put in this more cautious way it becomes both less provocative and harder to test experimentally (see Lenneberg and Roberts 1956; Carroll and Casagrande 1966; Fishman 1966; among many others), but it is in its more extreme forms that the argument is interesting as a cultural phenomenon.

It has been taken up in connection with a more general argument in favour of the greater wisdom, naturalness or rootedness of primitive people and their language, which is a sort of mirror-image of the negative racist views of the last century. At first sight this may look like a distortion of the argument, given the idea of relativity, and lack of an absolute standard, which seems to be at its core, but this would be to leave out of account, in the case of Whorf, the religious views which had earlier led him to write an occult novel and which supported his belief that there was a God-guaranteed right way of conceiving of the universe which modern rational and technological society had lost. His use of the Hopi, one of the most remote and traditionally oriented tribes, is of a piece with the use of Pueblo Indians in general by whites, ranging back to Cushing and the Zuni (to be dealt with in Chapter 7) through Lawrence and the use of Taos, and it could be regarded, therefore as entirely appropriate that this theory should be generated out of a study of one of their languages. Rossi-Landi, for instance, sees both the 'invitation to better understanding them, to avoid overwhelming them metaphysically, and the defence of their *Weltanschauungen* from scientific progress' as a manifestation of white guilt towards the destruction of Indian cultures. This is, I think, too crude an explanation, and it also omits another important element in the response to the idea of linguistic relativity, which could be said to be a particular modern form of primitivism, or at least something allied to it.

It is possible to see the theory as offering a cultural *frisson*, either what Fishman refers to, interestingly as the 'horror of helplessness' (1966: 513), at being trapped in our language, or an excitement at the idea of a genuine otherness beyond our capacity to understand. This combination can be seen as a modern version of the sublime, about which I will have more to say elsewhere, in its use of the idea of an otherness which is not a spiritual absolute (God, Nature) but a breakdown of our ability to represent. The sublime may always have been the unspeakable, but in Romantic thought this pointed to a spiritual presence. Once this presence disappears what we are left with is a psychological *effect* created in the gap between signifier and signified (see Weiskel 1976; White 1987:58–82). This is not to say that the modern and post-Romantic fascination with the other and the primitive does not ascribe to others the possibility and reality of belief, but to say that *our* sublime, our *frisson* is derived from the otherness and incommunicability of it. In terms of Whorf's ideas, then, what is important is not so much whether they can be verified as the very idea that they can't, and I will try to show later in Chapter 7, in looking at a number of examples of a particular sort of failed dialogue in the work of Castaneda and Edmondson, how this continues to operate.[2]

This whole question of what can be translated and what cannot, and what this implies about the relation of language to mind, quickly moves into philosophy, but it is interesting to note that even in the work of Quine, whose influential views on translation go well beyond my concerns and certainly beyond my competence, we find a culturally rather revealing use of the idea of the incommensurability of cultures. Arguing against the idea that a good translation preserves meaning because a sentence in one language can express the same proposition as that expressed in another language, Quine argues that most of the time we are in fact translating either between 'cognate languages, e.g., Frisian and English' where we are 'aided by resemblance of cognate word forms', or between unrelated languages we are relying on 'traditional equations that have evolved in step with a shared culture' (1960:28). In other words we are not translating propositions but attitudes, or 'present dispositions to verbal behaviour', and the continuities between cultures

> encourage an illusion of subject matter: an illusion that our so readily intertranslatable sentences are diverse verbal embodiments of some intercultural proposition or meaning, when they are better seen as the merest variants of one and the same intracultural verbalism. (1960:76)

He wants to argue, in fact, for the indeterminacy of translation,[3] and to develop this he invents the figure of the radical translator, who has to deal with the language of 'a hitherto untouched people'. As he acknowledges, this is improbable, in that in practice 'a chain of interpreters of a sort can be recruited of marginal persons across the darkest archipelago'.

Clearly this invented confrontation is being used by Quine as a test case, a sort of end or limit point, and his overall concern is not with radically other cultures or even with translation in its normal sense, since his general argument ultimately applies to sentences in the same language, but the invocation here of this pristine and absolutely other people, and the colonialist situation of what he later calls 'our jungle linguist' begs some interesting questions. While Quine himself has no interest in exploring the implications of such an encounter, and would probably scorn such a literal use of his metaphorical device, it does have an anthropological and even a political dimension. Commentators on Quine seem to deal with the idea in purely philosophical terms,[4] and it is quite striking to see the almost complete absence of reference to any ethnolinguistic work, but Quine himself refers briefly to work done in response to Whorf, and interestingly to Malinowski,

Lévy-Bruhl and the problem which the prelogical or primitive could pose for
translation:

> to take the extreme case, let us suppose that certain natives are said to accept as
> true certain sentences translatable in the form 'p and not p'. Now this claim is
> absurd under our semantic criteria.... Wanton translation can make natives sound
> as queer as one pleases. Better translation imposes our logic upon them, and
> would beg the question of prelogicality if there were a question to beg. (1960:58).

But the use of this material, already outdated when he was writing, hardly constitutes much of an ethnographic interest, as his final remark indicates. Nevertheless, this invocation of the idea of the untouched tribe can be seen to carry
political implications, in its assumption that, as Simon Blackburn has put it,

> understanding is gained by translation back into a home medium which the
> outsider brings with him. Like Fodor's infant an interpreter is a cognitive
> imperialist, who imports his own compound of categories and concepts, beliefs
> and principles, into which he retreats while he ponders the significance of native
> carryings-on. (1984:58)

There is the invocation of the idea of the radically other, but also the
assumption that the only way of coming to terms with it is on our terms. The
obscuring of the practical implications of this coming to terms can be seen in
George W. Grace's revealingly literal reading of Quine. He sees the
possibilities of a radical translation in Quine's terms as 'practically
unobtainable in the world of today'. Western culture 'has expanded to
embrace almost the whole world', so that we live in a world of 'shared subject
matters and shared ways of talking about them, i.e. ways of talking about
them which are diffused in large part by calquing from one language to
another' (Grace 1987:70). Here he is both dismissing the present possibility
and implicitly accepting the past reality of the idea of radically different
cultures, but he is also presenting a particular ideologically informed view of
the present relation of cultures. The 'embrace' of the West which creates a
'shared' experience sounds like an equitable enough affair, but it obscures the
relative imbalances of power and knowledge between cultures in ways which
return us to the starting point of this chapter, and the effacement of the issues
of power in relation to translation.

Notes

1. See Homi Bhabha's use of the ideas of 'white but not quite' (1984b).
2. One of the most interesting and wide-ranging applications of the Sapir–Whorf
   hypothesis is Paul Friedrich's *The Language Parallax*, which uses the language of

poetry and dreams to explore the ways in which languages order reality, but also the different *extent* of ordering involved in different sorts of language. He also invokes Gödel's principle, to the effect that 'any formal system – and any language, for grammar is to a degree a formal system – can predicate or generate propositions that contravene its usual output or implications' (Friedrich 1986:144). This principle implies that no system can be self-sealing, and one way of taking this would seem to allow for the possibility of translation, in that any system can express things which are, strictly speaking, outside it. This can lead us back to the area often labelled as the sublime, or the area of poetry, which exploits disorder as well as order in language. A quite different extrapolation from Gödel is to be found in Suzette Haden Elgin's science fiction novel *Native Tongue*. Elgin, a linguistics professor specialising in Indian languages, portrays a world in which women are specially trained as translators, but are a suppressed group. Some of the aliens, though, are *so* alien, that it is impossible for the human mind to imagine itself into their reality. Even to try is to risk absolute destruction, since according to Haden's two reformulations of Gödel, 'For any language, there are perceptions which it cannot express because they would result in its indirect self-destruction', and 'for any culture, there are languages which it cannot use because they would result in its indirect self-destruction'(Elgin 1985:145). Elgin is here using Gödel, or her version of him, to extend the implications of Whorf, and using the licence of science fiction to make literal what was a theoretical *reductio ad absurdum*. In her novel a baby put in contact with an alien to try to take on its world-view is physically destroyed, literally turned inside out, and the oppressed women painstakingly work towards a language which will by its different forms liberate them. (For a similar use of the interaction of language and physical reality, see Delaney (1966).

3. Deconstructive approaches to translation are also relevant here, in their concern to demonstrate the moments of undecidability in translation as a way of revealing traditional assumptions about meaning and language in general. For a brief indication of the deconstructive engagement with earlier important theories of translation in Heidegger and Walter Benjamin, see Silverman and Aylesworth (1990:164–202). For a useful sample of recent work in translation theory, see Bassnett and Lefevere (1990).

4. See Robert Kirk (1986:250) for a detailed argument against Quine's doctrine of the indeterminacy of translation. In acknowledging the persistence of the belief, he refers to it in terms that could also be applied to the reception of Whorf. 'Like all sceptical doctrines, it feeds our craving for radically disturbing, mystifying ideas. It takes us to an abyss where we cannot possibly know what others think or feel--'.

CHAPTER TWO

Languages

So far my argument has been that the two quintessential and mythical poles of Indian–white relations, those of encounter with the incomprehensibly other and of transparent intelligibility, need to be seen in both their linguistic and their more general cultural dimensions. I want here to examine what is at stake in a number of mainly nineteenth-century discussions and presentations of Indian languages, and the way that the perceptions of these languages have taken their place within a more general and pervasive discussion of the primitive and the civilised, in which issues of translation are also placed.

From the earliest encounters we can find scattered comments, and rather random collections of Indian words, sometimes reflecting particular beliefs about their Hebrew or Welsh connections, but almost always assuming that Indian languages were deficient or limited, and few raise issues of structure or syntax. Probably the most wide-ranging of these is Roger Williams' *A Key into the Language of America* (1643), which has been more widely used for the incidental information on Indians it supplies than for any specifically linguistic insights. In a way this is appropriate, in that Williams' word lists are designed, as part of his full title suggests, as 'an help to the Language of the Natives' rather like a modern phrasebook which allows one to 'get by' in a language rather than pay attention to the properties of the language itself. John Eliot's interest in language as such was, as I have shown, minimal, but one of the most interesting and accurate early accounts of an Indian language does arise out of a missionary situation similar to Eliot's, albeit as a strange by-product of it. When, more than a century later, the theologian Jonathan Edwards lived among, and ministered to the Indians at Stockbridge there was no pretence on his part of giving any ground to Indian ways – in fact it is quite astonishing how little is ever said by him or his commentators about his Indian context.[1] His son, though, was effectively bilingual as a child, since, as he tells us, 'out of my father's house I seldom heard any language spoken, beside the Indian'. In 1787 he wrote his *Observations on the Language of the Muhhekaneew Indians*, which contains some remarkably careful and detailed explanations of particular grammatical forms in Mohegan. In particular he explains how the absence of the verb 'to be' has good grammatical logic: 'As they have no adjectives, and as they turn their substantives into verbs on any occasion, they have no need for the substantive or auxiliary verb' (Edwards 1787:13).

Aware of the conclusions usually drawn from this absence, he is at pains to spell out that this 'accounts for their not using that verb, when they speak English. They say "I sick" &c'. He states very clearly that the Mohegan have 'all the eight parts of speech, to be found in other languages'. Furthermore

> It has been said also that savages never abstract, and have no abstract terms, which with regard to the Mohegans is another mistake.... I doubt not, but that there is in this language the full proportion of abstract, to concrete terms, which is also to be found in other languages. (1787:14–15)

I have given here some of Edwards' detailed observations not only because of the scarcity of such accounts but because Edwards is here already responding to, and rejecting a cluster of assumptions which had developed by the eighteenth century, about primitive languages in general and what they might reveal about our origins. Nevertheless, generations of writers and commentators on Indian languages later compensated for their lack of Edwards' detailed first-hand knowledge by recourse to these powerful and persuasive assumptions. Over the years, Enlightenment universalist assumptions about a common origin for mankind, with subsequent variations, and the possibilities for progress or degeneration, gradually give way to evolutionary thinking, and philology reflects these changes in thinking, with an emphasis on racial difference rather than environment and the search for common structures of mind revealed in a common grammar (see Bieder 1986; Edgerton 1944; Smith 1979). This larger intellectual movement, though, is shot through with inconsistencies, partly because of the variation in the amount actually known about Indian languages, and partly because, as I hope to show, each attempt to locate Indian languages within the prevailing intellectual framework of primitive and civilised, simple and complex, concrete and abstract, ran into profound contradictions. As a way of exploring these contradictions I propose to deal with a number of nineteenth-century accounts of Indian languages and 'writing' systems in terms of these oppositions, since there emerges, implicitly, a conception of a sort of spectrum, or, if seen in developmental or evolutionary terms, a sequence, which goes from silence through gestures and signs to spoken words, to picture-writing to syllabic and eventually to phonetic writing. But as soon as we look at the ways in which these forms have been opposed to each other, and the grounds for doing so, we find them overlapping and realigning in ways which undermine the claims for the existence of a spectrum or sequence.

Jacques Derrida's tracing of the relation between speech and writing in relation to a nature/culture opposition, and his idea of supplementarity is my starting point here, but I want to extend it by analysing some discussions of Indian sign languages as well as Indian speech and writing systems.

One of the most consistent claims made for primitive languages has been that they are simple, concrete and, like their speakers, inextricably linked to nature. In this way they connect us to an original language rooted in things rather than ideas, and without the slippages and ambiguities of civilised speech and writing. Derrida has followed up the contradictions in this idea of a natural language in Rousseau, and has seen it as an attempt to

> recapture a sort of happy pause, the instantaneity of a full language, the image stabilising what was no more than a point of pure passage: a language without discourse, a speech without sentence, without syntax, without parts, without grammar, a language of pure effusion, beyond the cry but short of the hinge that articulates, and at the same time disarticulates the immediate unity of meaning. (1976:279)

Any actual knowledge of how particular Indian languages work, such as that of Edwards, can make only limited headway against such widespread assumptions about their grammatical deficiencies, and the persistence of the paradoxical idea of a language of things and not signs, a language without syntax.

The idea of a language of fixed terms, rooted in a concrete reality is an image, as Derrida has suggested, of a restricted economy, where exchanges and substitutions are guaranteed by a universal standard.[2] In a general economy, where there is no fixed standard, slippages occur, and in the realm of language terms take their meaning not from any fixed system of signification but from the play of signifiers. If words could be fixed to things, just as if the value of things could be fixed to gold in a restricted economy, honesty and order could be guaranteed. Once paper money is seen to reflect exchange value, rather than to be an unequivocal signifier for gold, value becomes relational rather than fixed. Similarly, once the word becomes seen as separate from the thing, and its meaning defined by other words, any guarantee of meaning disappears, as one sign refers to another. The linguistic alternative of the gold standard here is the invocation of a natural and original state of affairs in which language is rooted in things, and this rootedness is threatened the more conventional or artificial the language or form of language becomes. Thus authenticity and self-presence seems to diminish as we move from gesture to speech to writing, but as Derrida has shown we are really involved in a process of supplementarity which throws this simple progression into question. He pinpoints the unspoken implications of Rousseau's ideas on language:

That substitution has always already begun; that imitation, principle of art, has always already interrupted natural plenitude; that, having to be a *discourse*, it has always already broached presence in differance; that in Nature it is always that which supplies Nature's lack, a voice that is substituted for the voice of Nature. (Derrida 1976: 215)

In looking at accounts of Indian languages I want to trace and demonstrate both the investment in the idea of the original and the natural, and the inevitability with which the very way that this is described in fact gives support to Derrida's deconstructive reading of Rousseau, and Rousseau's desire 'to separate originarity from supplementarity' (1976: 243).

The comparison between a language grounded in the concrete and without any play of signification, and a currency grounded in a guaranteed point of value (the circulation of signs and of money) is not one invented by Derrida, of course. Garrick Mallery, writing in 1881 on Indian languages, quotes approvingly from J. Hammond Trumbull, who sees it as a special property of such languages that

> every word shall be so framed as to admit of immediate resolution to its
> significant elements by the hearer. It must be thoroughly *self-defining*, for (as
> Max Müller has expressed it) 'it requires tradition, society, and literature to
> maintain words which can no longer be analyzed at once'. – In the ever-shifting
> state of a nomadic society no debased coin can be tolerated in language, no
> obscure legend accepted on trust. The metal must be pure and the legend
> distinct. (1881, rpt in Umiker-Sebeok and Sebeok 1978: 430)[3]

Mallery's main concern in the essay from which this is taken is actually Indian sign languages. The widespread use of these had always attracted comment, both admiring (a recognition of their flexibility and their operation as a lingua franca) and patronising (the common suggestion that Indian languages were so primitive that they needed to be helped out by gestures. Mallery's extensive work on them, as well as demonstrating an interesting early awareness of what are really issues of semiotics, constantly skirmishes with the notion of what is natural and what conventional. Gestures and signs were seen as the least mediated form of communication, and therefore closest to nature, and their absence of syntax and abstraction seemed to guarantee an immediacy and honesty.

Far from being a drawback, this lack of logical organisation gives sign language a universality, since it is based not on artificial constructions but on the operations of nature itself:

> Sign language is superior to all others in that it permits every one to find
> in nature an image to express his thoughts on the most needful matters
> intelligibly to any other person. The direct or substantial natural analogy
> peculiar to it prevents a confusion of ideas. (Mallery 1880 repr. in Umiker-
> Sebeok 1978:426)[4]

Coming from nature and not any particular culture it therefore partakes of language before Babel, and removes the spectre of an endless deferral of meaning. What Mallery refers to as its 'power of interpreting itself' (that is, presumably, its self-evidence, and lack of dependence on learned convention), gives it an advantage over other languages which 'can only be interpreted by means of some other spoken language' (1880:429). This has practical implications, in that sign language 'can be readily applied by travellers and officials so as to give them much independence of professional interpreters – a class dangerously deceitful and tricky' (Mallery 1881, repr. in Umiker-Sebeok 1978:6). The difficulties of translation, and the uneasy reliance on mixed-bloods and marginal individuals, which I argued earlier needed to be repressed, is here acknowledged, but only to be effaced again by the advantages of a truly natural language.

So far I have emphasised only one aspect of sign-language, in suggesting that commentators saw it as natural rather than conventional. In fact almost all of those who described it, including Mallery, were aware of the ways in which signs which may have stemmed from a natural object were then adapted to represent other and more abstract qualities. Some also comment on the fact that Indians would take their cue from whomever they were speaking to, and would accept the other person's sign, once they had interpreted it, and build it into that particular exchange. What this implies, of course, particularly the second instance, is an awareness of the conventional and provisional nature of the signs on the part of the users of the system, which allowed them to shift and adjust their system so smoothly that some observers were able to see it as a natural and spontaneous language. In their introduction to the best collection of writing on aboriginal sign language D.J. Umiker-Sebeok and T.Sebeok describe the languages as

> semantically open both in the sense that they may be used to formulate a potentially indefinite number of messages and that the lexicon may be enlarged to suit changing demands on the system (as in spoken languages). (1978:xv)

This is largely because these languages use and adapt conventional signs, though the Sebeoks do see 'iconic and indexical elements outweighing symbolic ones (the reverse of the hierarchy prevailing in spoken languages)' (1978:xv). Their use here of index, icon and symbol[5] offers a refinement of the natural/conventional polarity, and allows us to see the instability of any one element, and its ability to change function. This will be important to my argument in dealing with all the other elements of representation on my original spectrum, but as an indication of quite how interwoven these issues are, in their relation to ideas of the natural and the civilised for earlier observers of Indians, I want to look in detail at one particular account of sign language by Richard Dodge, which he gives on the basis of, to use part of the title of his 1882 book, '33 years personal experience among the red men of the great West'. My purpose here is not to criticise Dodge for confusion and inconsistency, but to use him as a particularly clear, but not unrepresentative, instance of the strength of the investment in the idea of the natural, and the way that different facets of Indian expression and representation are constantly played off against this term. At each stage what is presented as natural in relation to something else conventional or civilised can be shown already to contain the qualities of its opposite. In case this should seem to boil down to no more than an exercise in deconstructive cleverness, a demonstration of the slipperiness of language, it is worth insisting that assumptions about nature, civilisation and otherness were continually being translated into policies and actions involving political as well as cultural representation. Difference needed to be demonstrated and defined, even when, or especially when, the instability of the bases of difference was becoming more and more evident. Throughout the nineteenth century, for instance, the status of Indian tribes as independent entities was being destroyed, as they became 'domestic dependent nations' and their land was incorporated into the United States, but at the same time the development of scientific racism was ensuring that certain sorts of incorporation were not taking place, and that difference was preserved.[6]

Dodge is at pains to praise what he calls the 'wonderful expertness of Indian sign-talkers', and he gives an informed and sympathetic view of their adaptability and resourcefulness, but it is his way of relating this to more general categories which concerns me here. He sketches a narrative in which tribes initially unable to understand each other developed a way of using signs

> We may suppose that at first only signs most natural and expressive were used. By-and-by other signs were introduced, always conventional, but becoming more and more arbitrary, until there resulted a means of communication almost as perfect as if each understood and spoke the oral language of the other. (Umiker-Sebeok and Sebeok 1978: Vol 2. 4-5)

Here he recognises quite clearly the conventional nature of the fully developed sign language, but when he starts to compare it with oral speech we find a bewildering shifting of terms. On the one hand he sees speech as 'entirely arbitrary and conventional', whereas signs 'have their origin in feelings and emotions which are common to mankind'. As a result, like Mallery, he sees sign language as obviating the need for translation, since it requires 'on the one hand only so clear a conception of the idea or emotion as to make a sign expressive of its posture or effect, and on the other an equally clear conception, and a sufficient perceptive faculty' (1978:6). Within a few pages, though, we find the comparison going in the other direction. Noting the fact that not all Indians use signs with equal facility, he points to the *acquired* nature of it, and contrasts it with speech. 'Oral speech is natural, and all men use the language to which they were brought up with a certain degree of ease and force.' But how is it natural if one needs to be 'brought up' to it? Later he explains the superior sign-language abilities of the Plains Indians by the fact that 'in their own camps and families, this language is used so constantly that it becomes a natural and instinctive habit' (1978:8), which would seem to imply, confusingly, that instinct develops, comes from habit, rather than being inborn.

Like Mallery, quoted earlier, Dodge makes the connection between what he sees as the 'crude and imperfect' nature of Indian oral languages and the capacity for sign languages. The oral languages consist of

> nouns, verbs, adjectives, adverbs, lacking in case, number, tense, or mood, and run together in interminable strings, each of which presents, as it were, a word-picture, the whole giving a very definite idea of the facts sought to be communicated. This idiomatic mode of thought and expression offers peculiar facilities for the use of the sign language (1978:11).

But the very factors which make oral language crude and imperfect here are those which are praised as natural and expressive in sign language, and in other sets of oppositions we will in fact find Indian oral languages praised for these same qualities when set beside the language of civilised abstractions. It was not just in such theoretical discussions that signs, words and even pictures were impossible to keep separate. Sign language did, after all, accompany most speeches, to considerable rhetorical effect; they were 'graceful, as well as significant' as J.L. Humfreville put it (1978:70). For whites particularly, this would serve to emphasise the 'picturesque' or figurative elements of the speech, and the presence of signs may even go some way to explaining the constant description of Indian languages and especially oratory as *like* sign language (concrete, visual, figurative and non-syntactic), if the interpreters were partly taking their cues from the accompanying signs.

But as well as linking with speech, in one direction, sign language also pointed towards other forms of visual representation, in particular pictograms, and here again we find the seductive idea of a natural and unmediated representation making its appearance. The same pitfalls are lurking, though since, whether with gestures or with pictures, a semiotic system is invoked.[7] Mallery's view of the relation of gesture to picture is particularly interesting as an indication of the way that one form is invoked to represent the 'natural', and of the endless and unstable interchange of concrete and abstract. He claims that sign language can be particularly useful in helping the archaeologist to interpret 'native picture-writing', a subject which he also extensively researched (see Mallery 1888), and his reasons need quoting at length. Most importantly, he sees some elements in pictograms not as pictures, but as traces of a gesture:

> It was but one more step [from sign language] to fasten upon bark, skins, or rocks the evanescent air-pictures that still in pigments or carvings preserve

their skeleton outline, and in their ideography approach the rudiments of a phonetic alphabet. Gesture-writing is, in fact, not only a picture-language but is actual writing, though dissolving and sympathetic, and neither alphabetic nor phonetic. Though written characters are in our minds associated with speech, they are shown, by successful employment in hieroglyphics and by educated deaf-mutes, to be representative of ideas without the intervention of sounds, and so also are the outlines of signs. This will be more apparent if the motions expressing the most prominent feature, attribute, or function of an object are made, or supposed to be made, so as to leave a luminous track impressible to the eye, separate from the members producing it. The actual result is an immateriate graphic representation of visible objects and qualities which, invested with substance has become known to us as the *rebus*, and also appears in the form of heraldic blazonry styled punning or 'canting'. The reproduction of gesture-lines in the pictographs made by our Indians seems to have been most frequent in the attempt to convey those subjective ideas which were beyond the range of an artistic skill limited to the direct representation of objects, so that the part of the pictographs, which is still the most difficult of interpretation, is precisely the one which the study of sign-language is likely to elucidate. (Umiker-Sebeok and Sebeok 1978:8–9)

Like sign language, then, pictograms operate between the poles of the natural, which presents no problems of interpretation, and the symbolic, which needs some knowledge of the conventions of representation employed by those who created the pictogram. Mallery's intriguing suggestion here is that the symbolic elements are actually based on the path traced in the air by a gesture, which connects them once more to the natural rather than conventional, but he does want to claim it as 'actual writing'. It is hard to think of a better example of Derrida's idea of the trace, of writing whose presence actually depends on the absence of that which it stands for, and yet contains within it the implication that it is a part of what it represents.[8] As with sign language, then, picture-writing is uneasily located on the spectrum running from the natural to the conventional.

In another essay Mallery opposes picture-writing to the widely used mnemonic devices, because picture-writing is

the sole form in which [the Indians] recorded events and ideas that can ever be interpreted without the aid of a traditional key, such as is required for the signification of the wampum belts of the northeastern tribes and the *quippus* of Peru. (Umiker-Sebeok and Sebeok 1978: 421)

The need for a key certainly suggests the conventional rather than the natural here, though whether this qualifies such mnemonic devices as writing systems will need to be discussed. First, though, it is worth pointing out that Mallery is locating picture-writing in the same place as gesture:

It is one distinctive form of thought-writing without reference to sound, gesture being the other and probably earlier form. Whether remaining purely ideographic, or having become conventional, picture-writing is the direct and durable expression of ideas of which the gesture language gives the transient expession. Originally it was not connected with the words of any language. (1888:25-6).

The insistence here on a language prior to words, on something to occupy the gap between the natural and the conventional, represents part of a larger need generated by evolutionary thinking, to fill gaps, a need filled in a number of ways by the study of Indians and other 'primitives'. Once a nature-to-culture development has been asserted, places must be filled in order for that system of knowledge to function, and once it has been decided that not all human beings are equally cultural (and, for that matter, natural) in having language, and societies, then the idea of development becomes as much about drawing distinctions as about establishing continuities. In talking about the lack of symbolic uses of pictograms in North America, for instance, Mallery thinks it is 'futile to seek for that form of psychological exuberance in the stage of development' of most tribes, and all attempts to interpret them along the lines of Egyptian, Mexican or Mayan pictographs result in 'mooning mysticism' (1888:611). However much we might applaud that final judgement when applied to some of the large range of 'interpretations' which continue to appear, and which feed on the whole idea of mystery concerned with origins (see, for instance Fell, 1976, and for a general survey Wauchope, 1962), what we can constantly find in Mallery, along with scrupulous collecting and describing, and a genuinely semiotic awareness, are evolutionary distinctions on the basis of certain sorts of language use.

In the same year as Mallery was drawing these distinctions in relation to writing, Daniel G. Brinton was already pointing in another direction. Brinton had already acquired a formidable reputation for his knowledge of a huge range of languages and for his publication and advocacy of the disputed Lenape Algonkin text dealing with mythic origins and the historical past, the *Walam Olum*. In an article laying down criteria for judging the authenticity of pictographic texts he argues that

> The term 'picture-writing' as applied to this graphic material conveys an erroneous impression. These delineations were intended and are to be regarded as letters, not as pictures. The object of the artist was not to paint or draw but TO WRITE. (Brinton 1893:201)

While he inevitably shares many of Mallery's terms and assumptions, Brinton's reading in German philology meant that he began to diverge from prevailing evolutionary assumptions, and this distinctive blend and development of ideas can be seen by looking at a number of his shorter pieces. In 'the Language of Palaeolithic Man', a lecture delivered in 1888, he deduces the possession of language by early man from his high level of skills which imply an intellectual capacity, and then attempts to reconstruct early man's language from existing languages, 'especially those which have suffered little from admixture or by distant removals' (1888:5) Using examples from Indian languages , he tries to demonstrate that sounds are not arbitrary, but rather than making the usual case for onomatopoeic origins he connects them with ideas. In Athapaskan, 'labials express the ideas of time and space, as age, length, distance, and also whiteness, the last mentioned , perhaps, through association with the white hair of age, or the endless snowfields of winter' (1888:6).

To make the connection, though, between sound and idea, he has to have recourse to a visual image, which then undergoes metaphoric extension, and we can see the crucial role of metaphor (developed further in my next chapter) in allowing the movement from concrete to abstract. In the following passage we can see how in order to make his generalisation he depends implicitly on our acceptance of this movement:

> The analysis of American tongues leans decidedly toward classifying primitive man among the *visuaires*. His earliest significant sounds seem to have been expressive of motion and rest, energy and its absence, space and direction, color and form. (1888:15)

Energy and its absence would seem to have no very obvious visual, rather than auditory link, but it is the metaphorical capacity of the visual image that is being insisted on here.

A similar extrapolation from Indian languages is carried out in relation to their much-remarked polysynthetic character,[9] though Brinton prefers the broader term, 'incorporative'. Because of their supposed lack of inflections, rather than connecting up separate words by grammar Indian languages create great clusters of words, so that 'each clause tends to get expressed in one phonetic complex' (Brinton 1894:7). Brinton quotes Herder to the effect that primitive man, like a baby, wanted to say it all at once, and Humboldt to explain that its psychological origin is 'an exaltation of the imaginative over the intellectual elements of mind'(1885:327). This imaginative side is given more freedom of expression in the incorporative method because 'a thought presented in one word is more vivid and stimulating to the imagination, more individual and *picturesque* [my emphasis], than when narrated in a number of words' (1885:327).

It has the instant fusion of the metaphor, rather than the progression of an argument, it is 'presented' whole rather than 'narrated' in sequence. It is, in fact, Imagist poetry, not prose, and we can already see here the elements which were later to influence the presentation of Indian literature, in the study of which Brinton was also a pioneer, in his 1883 *Aboriginal American Authors and their Productions*.

So far I have tended to follow the various commentators on Indian

languages in talking about languages and their essential characteristics as
complete and static objects to be observed. One of the dangers of talking
about languages as complete systems, though, is that the actual role of
language within a society tends to be taken as a constant. Dell Hymes has
argued the necessity of seeing the particular role and function of language
within cultures as subject to variation. The significance of speaking within
certain situations and contexts, the importance given to language and its
particular forms in assertion of cultural values, may vary markedly, and to
collect language data 'in abstraction from contexts of use' is misleading
(Hymes 1966:157).[10] This relates importantly to my arguments about Indian
speeches in the next chapter, and to translation in general, but also to the oral-
literate issue, in that writing, too, must be seen as having a relative function
and value, and it is to writing that I want now to turn.

In tracing this far some of the ways in which Indian languages have been
seen within varying sets of assumptions about nature and culture, and identity
and difference, one of the key terms which has as yet been only skirted round is
writing, which within the framework I have been describing tends to be
evoked as an intellectual achievement, an index of development, rather than as
an actual range of diverse processes. It has now become more usual to make
natural/cultural distinctions, if anywhere, at the *point* of language itself rather
than its uses, though even this is of course problematic,[11] and this has allowed
discussion of writing to take place in less holistic and less evolutionary terms.
(The influence of Derrida in this respect has been complex. His brilliant and
profoundly influential deconstruction of the idea of the secondariness of
writing, and its relation to the idea of voice as unmediated presence is a
powerful aid in undermining any nature/culture opposition. In this context of
deconstruction, clearly, the word writing is being used to describe not a series
of actual practices, but something always already there in language. The
difficulty is that this can then lead to a short-circuiting of any detailed
examinations of specific oral and literate relationships, since we all know that
everything is 'writing' – not, presumably, something that Derrida himself,
with his careful reviews of Leroi-Gourhan and others would endorse.) I want
now to look selectively at the *role* of writing in some Indian groups, rather
than try to define its boundaries, and eventually to concentrate on the figure
of Sequoyah, who constitutes something of a scandal within the oppositions I
have been describing so far.

Most of the materials I have dealt with so far have tended to talk about
single *elements* in Indian languages, to demonstrate their concreteness or their
visual qualities, almost as if to argue for rootedness meant to describe a static
system rather than a process. A gesture, image or word related primarily to
something concrete 'out there', rather than to other elements within the sign
system. Writing about visual images written down, Jack Goody (1987:8)
makes an interesting distinction between single elements and sequences of
images which 'reproduce the flow of speech or of linguistically dominated

"thought" ', and sees the latter as a sort of embryonic writing. Goody's earlier works have themselves attracted criticisms (some of which he has accepted), of their ethnocentric and developmental assumptions about the liberating cognitive and even political effects of literacy (see Bloch 1989:15-18), and there is still here the idea of a move from something rudimentary to more developed phonetic conventions, even if his treatment of each 'stage' demonstrates very clearly how difficult it is to range them along any natural/conventional axis.

Mallery's distinction (see p. 21) between picture-writing and wampum, for instance, depends on the mnemonic role of wampum, rather than its representational elements, but Goody is careful to distinguish this conventionality from that of writing. Such mnemonic devices may be conventional signs used in sequence but he insists that 'they are not transcriptions of language, but rather a figurative shorthand, a mnemonic, which attempts to recall or prompt linguistic statements rather than to reproduce them' (1987:17). Certainly this is the way in which wampum is usually described, in the context of its ceremonial public display and exchange. When an Indian spokesman at one of the Carlisle treaties had to explain to a waiting audience that the Indian representatives 'have mislaid some Strings, which has put their Speeches into Disorder; these they will rectify, and speak to you in the Afternoon', it certainly suggests something close to notes for a speech. Sheehan, who cites this incident (1969: 351) interestingly refers to wampum's role here as 'a handy reminder for the Indian of the scheme of metaphor'. If we ask why metaphor, and not ideas or points in an argument, the answer suggests itself that Sheehan is assuming that Indians, (lacking ideas, or lacking an abstract language in which to express them?) think and express themselves by means of natural objects which are then used figuratively.

This issue will be developed in relation to oratory and figures of speech in the next chapter, but is of interest here in its view of wampum as pictographic rather than conventional. Clearly there is an important difference between the ability to repeat based on mnemonic structures grounded in common knowledge, memory and a shared context, and what Derrida describes as iterability, the way in which a statement can be separated from the context which apparently guaranteed it its meaning. Whether or not this disqualifies it as writing, or in what ways it might constitute a semiotic system of the same order as writing, whether syllabic or phonetic,[12] what does become clear from the accounts of the *uses* to which different forms of writing are put is that context remains a decisive issue. Early missionaries sometimes described their pupils as making marks on pieces of bark which they used as aids for learning, and the boundary between mnemonic aid and writing is not always clear in their accounts, though Mallery (1888:666-72) is insistent in line with his general evolutionary assumptions, that this is not writing (see also Walker 1984a). There is also evidence that phonetically written texts could still be *used* mnemonically long after the ability to 'read' had disappeared, as in

Willard Walker's accounts of the way that even now elderly Passamaquodies
use a book printed in their own language in the last century as 'a device that
triggers the accurate recitation of long-familiar texts. It is emphatically not a
graphic representation of the sounds of speech' (1984a:45). As Walker has
shown, how writing is *regarded* by Indian communities may be crucial to its
chances of implementation. If it is seen as an aid to the continuance of
traditional values it is more likely to be used and acquired. It is also more likely
to be seen as an adult matter rather than something to be acquired early on by
children. In other words, the assumption that literacy necessarily moved the
Indians across the great divide into abstract thought, and that their failure to
learn it was because of intellectual deficiency in this respect are thrown into
doubt by the rapid spread of writing in situations where it was fulfilling a
culturally conserving role. The fact that this has more often involved
syllabaries than a phonetic alphabet can also be explained by the lack of
'impediments to learning, like punctuation or spelling conventions or
capitalization or "proper" grammar' (Walker 1984b:163), which for whites
have been inseparable from the civilising process of literacy, as can be seen by
their comments on the deficiencies of their Indian pupils.

In the traditional schema which separates the oral from the literate, the
anomalous figure has always been Sequoyah, the illiterate inventor of his own
Cherokee syllabary. He has been represented as the Indian Cadmus, as an
exceptional and isolated genius, but also sometimes more as a borrower and
adaptor of the Roman alphabet. Mallery, for instance rather dismisses his
originality, (1888:663) in spite of the fact that his use of his chosen characters is
totally unrelated to their phonetic significance in the alphabet, and the
presence in his syllabary of many quite different characters. In any case he is
seen as someone who advanced the civilisation of the Cherokee nation, one of
the so-called Five Civilised Tribes. The widespread literacy and development
of printing which followed the introduction of his syllabary need to be seen,
however, in relation to the issues of cultural continuity outlined earlier.
William McLoughlin has pointed out that in fact Sequoyah's alphabet was
already too late to wed literacy in Cherokee to 'civilisation', which was already
established as involving the speaking of English:

> Acculturation had proceeded so far that the nation could not adopt
> [Sequoyah's discovery]. The mixed-blood leaders of the nation spoke English
> better than Cherokee, and English remained the official language of the nation.
> (1984:184)

Brought up as, and remaining, a traditionalist, in spite of his white ancestry,
Sequoyah saw his syllabary as a way of preserving the Cherokee values and
traditions, rather than an instrument of white civilisation, though most white
accounts acknowledge this role only obliquely and as an unfortunate by-
product. James Mooney, for instance, who collected a large number of
traditional writings for the Bureau of American Ethnology, comments that

What is perhaps strangest of all in this literary evolution is the fact that the same invention has been seized by the priests and conjurers of the conservative party for the purpose of preserving to their successors the ancient rituals and secret knowledge of the tribe, whole volumes of such occult literature in manuscript having been obtained by the author.(1897–8:112)

Given his fame *and* his association with the written medium, there is, in fact surprisingly little first-hand material on Sequoyah, which has meant that what we do have has been elaborated into, or supplemented by, legend. In the absence of very much sense of the man himself, he becomes whatever he can be made to stand for.

McKenney and Hall's chapter on him, in their *Indian Tribes of North America* (1842), includes most of the elements that are regularly recycled. They are at pains to praise him, but in ways which distinguish him from his race. His portrait, which they include, 'exhibits no trace of the ferocity of the savage; it wants alike the vigilant eye of the warrior and the apathy of the less intellectual of that race'. Face, expression and dress, they say, are 'decidedly Asiatic' and could be used to support claims for the Oriental origins of the Indians. Whether this association in their minds is because of the literacy of the East is not clear, but the further elements they choose to emphasise from his life also have the effect of isolating him, though this time by making him into a model American, a self-made man.[13]

Learning the skills of a silversmith, Sequoyah also notices that the whites had 'an art by means of which a name could be impressed upon a hard substance so as to be comprehended at a glance'. Wanting his own name on his products, he makes a die with a facsimile of his name. He also learns to draw, and their description of his progress from sketches 'as rude as those which the Indians draw upon their dressed skins' to 'very tolerable representations' is of a man who has 'spontaneously caught the spirit, and was rivalling the ingenuity of the civilised man (McKenney and Hall 1842:133–4). It was this ingenuity combined with 'that self-reliance which makes genius available' which allowed him to devise on his own a workable alphabet, after having refused to accept the generally held view of the Indians that the whites' ability was the result of sorcery. A veritable son of the Enlightenment, he 'considered it an art, and not a gift of the Great Spirit, and he believed he could invent a plan by which the red men could do the same thing (McKenney and Hall 1842: 137).

Such an invention as Sequoyah's, though, poses problems in many accounts, since strictly speaking it should not happen, given the peculiar limitations of Indian language and mentality. As a result there is a need to trace the steps by which it could have happened, in such a way as to leave intact the general view of Indians as natural. George E. Foster, for instance, seems to take up the account of Sequoyah's draftmanship in McKenney and Hall and elaborate it for his own purposes. In Sequoyah's dreams, he says, the 'songs of Nature ' often took 'the form of Cherokee words', and Foster's way of explaining this form is revealing about his reliance on the complex of assumptions about a language rooted in things which I outlined earlier:

> If he found in nature a tone, which he thought represented some word, he drew a picture of that which made the sound. In short, when he thought he had found a sound in nature that represented a tone elsewhere, he used a picture of this bird or beast, to convey this idea to others. (Foster 1885:97–8)

Sequoyah eventually realises this will not work, and moves to the use of arbitrary signs, of course, but Foster is less interested in this than in establishing the stages Sequoyah had to move *through*. Only then can he be given credit, as an exceptional individual.

The emphasis on Sequoyah's uniqueness is repeated by W.A. Phillips, who also feels called upon to account for it. Fastening upon a suggestion that his father had been an itinerant German pedlar, he claims that Sequoyah, though speaking no German, 'still carried, deep in his nature, an odd compound of Indian and German transcendentalism; essentially Indian in opinion and prejudice, but German in instinct and thought' (1870:544). Asiatic, Enlightenment man, or German transcendentalist, the one thing Sequoyah could not be was a Cherokee, and by the same token the *effects* of his invention could not be other than to make the Cherokee less Cherokee and more civilised. Whites and the more acculturated Cherokee were quick to see the advantages for Christianity, with the result that the first thing printed on the new press was part of Genesis, and there is plenty of evidence to show white and 'progressive' control of what was printed. Sequoyah's concerns, though, seem to have been quite different. He had a short answer, according to Foster, to someone who told him he must have been taught by the Great Spirit – 'I taught myself.' His first proper composition, according to John Howard Payne, who heard an account from the Cherokee Principal Chief, was not directed towards the making of Cherokees into Christians, but towards quite literally drawing lines *between* the two cultures. It was

> on the subject of the boundary line between his own country and Georgia and Tennessee. After that, he had a suit in the Indian Court at Chatouga. He wrote down a statement of his case. When he got there, he read his statement, instead of speaking; and all the people were amazed. (Bass:1932)[14]

Towards the end of his life he seems to have been concerned to make connections between the scattered elements of his people and to know more about other Indian languages, and Phillips describes him, in a nice phrase, as going West on 'a philological crusade such as the world never saw' (1870:547).

Of course there is a danger in just replacing these early Sequoyahs with one more to our particular taste. A rather bizarre example of this is an account which turns Sequoyah into a freedom-fighter. Traveller Bird's *Tell Them They*

Lie: the Sequoyah Myth, published in 1971 claims to be based on 'More than six hundred documents written by George Guess [Sequoyah] himself on thick ruled ledger books, scraps of paper...corn shuck paper etc.' and other documents that had been buried in caves. The book presents a totally different picture of Sequoyah. The famous portrait discussed by McKenney and Hall is actually of Thomas Maw. Sequoyah's name was neither Sequoyah nor George Guess (which he used as a joke: guess my name). Furthermore the actual syllabary preceded him, and was preserved on gold plates (fixed-value currency again). Far from being instrumental in 'civilising' the Cherokee he actively opposed white encroachments and used the syllabary as a conserver of tradition. The author, Traveller Bird, identifies himself only as a friend of the late Clyde Warrior, and 'a direct blood-relative of Sequoyah', and the book can certainly be seen as part of a polemical attempt to rescue Sequoyah from a white take-over. From our point of view, though, it is particularly interesting in its reversal and consequent highlighting of the symptomatic ways in which he is seen.

One curious aspect of Sequoyah's presentation in the available literature is the almost complete absence of any of *his* words, either written or spoken. Foreman quotes a contemporary report to the effect that he kept 'a journal of all the passing events which he considered worthy of record' (1938:37), and he was apparently writing a great deal on his last trip to the Cherokees in Mexico, but (unless we believe Traveller Bird's totally unsupported claims) none of this has survived, and we do not have his own story, as we do for Sam Blowsnake, for instance, who later used a Winnebago syllabary. Nor were any detailed accounts of his speeches preserved. Willard Walker refers to an account by Payne of trying to take down Sequoyah's words, with an interpreter at the ready, but being frustrated, ironically, by the power of his oratory:

> He talked and gesticulated very gracefully – his voice alternately swelling – and then sinking to a whisper.... Before long, poor I seemed entirely forgotten by the rest of the audience. First, one quarter of an hour, – then another, – and then another went over, and no translation came. (Foreman 1938:43-4, quoted in Walker 1984a:44)

Walker uses this episode to demonstrate the power of the spoken, even for the champion of the written within Cherokee culture, but the scene also brings out the irony of Sequoyah's portrayal or non-portrayal in writing. It is as if in inventing writing he effaces rather than expresses himself. His portrait has him displaying a page of his own writing, but it contains only a list of his characters, the *elements* of writing, signifying writing itself, the medium at the expense of any message. Interestingly, though, there is a more recent visual image of Sequoyah. Erwin Binder's sculpture of Sequoyah, according to Ron Kinsey (1979), concentrates on head, hands and book. The head is without the

turban, which Sequoyah wears in his famous portrait, since it would detract
from the purpose of giving 'a universal image of an American Indian'. The
hands, following Traveller Bird's version, have been mutilated, and the book
replacing the tablet represents the syllabary *in use*. So Sequoyah is rescued
from one imposed identity, only to be given another, as a 'universal' Indian in
the style of 1960s radicalism.

In reaching the point, with Sequoyah, of the writing Indian we have come
all the way across the ideological spectrum of natural/cultural across which
Indians have been stretched, and later chapters will examine the complex
ironies which attend 'speaking for yourself' in, or through the mediation of,
print. So far I have been trying to demonstrate the ways in which descriptions
and explanations of a wide range of Indian forms of expression can be seen to
have been shaped by assumptions about their primitive or retarded state, and
in doing so I have concentrated on what were seen as the formal properties of
the systems, and shown how attempts at drawing clear lines between savage
and civilised, natural and conventional, break down. In each case there is an
attempt to preserve for 'us' the province of writing, which involves a
characterising of 'them' as thinking, as well as expressing themselves,
differently. Michael Harbsmeier has argued that the creation of 'orality' as a
crucial defining factor in other cultures is itself a product of a sense of having a
general rather than restricted literacy in the observing culture. He draws a
distinction between Protestant and post-Reformation descriptions which
characterise the Indians by their lack of writing, and those by Jesuits, which
see the issue in more relative terms, in order to suggest that

> Only a closed world of universal literacy, a world, that is, which can think of
> itself as a literate world as opposed to other pre-literate ones – only such a
> world was able to discover and invent new worlds in terms of preliteracy and
> oracy. The transition from restricted to universal literacy in this sense thus has
> a symptom, as it were, the production and proliferation of texts describing
> other cultures and societies in terms of other modes of communication.
> (Harbsmeier 1989:203-4)

Examining texts which highlight the absence of writing in primitive cultures,
whether in tones of superiority (de Lery) or nostalgia (Lévi-Strauss),
Harbsmeier sees literacy being used as a 'mode of excommunication', a sign of
a society aware of what it has achieved, but 'conscious too of the price it has
had to pay for this achievement: the loss of the authenticity, presence and
indivisibility of the spoken word' (1989:203). Even without entirely accepting
Harbsmeier's large general claims for the role of Protestantism (though they
would be at least partly supported by the work of Ong and McLuhan), this
offers us an intriguing way of looking at the relation of writing to power.

Oblique support for Harbsmeier can be found in James Axtell's argument
that the Jesuits had much greater success in using the power of print in the
Eastern Woodlands because they exploited more successfully the association

of writing with shamanic powers. Far from writing automatically being associated with rationality and progress, and its attendant demystification of the magical, Axtell argues that for these particular cultures, since reading and writing were presented as primarily religious activities, books and written notes 'became invested with supernatural powers in their own right. Writing, therefore, did not banish magic from the native world, but enhanced and extended it' (Axtell 1987:306). The particular forms of enchantment offered by writing and the making of texts are the subject of later chapters, but first we must turn to the making of texts which present Indian speeches, in order to examine the extent to which the assumptions about nature and Indian language described here determine the presentation and understanding of them.

Notes

1. Most accounts concentrate on the life of the mind, congratulating Edwards on his ability to overcome his intellectual isolation. Even Kenneth Minkema's account of three generations of Edwardses skims over the lack of linguistic ability or interest on the part of Edwards senior, who had to have an Indian interpreter beside him in the pulpit. (Minkema 1988).
2. For Derrida's use of this idea see 'From Restricted to General Economy: a Hegelianism without Reserve', in Derrida (1978).
3. It is relevant here, with Derrida's deconstruction of the underlying metaphors of speech and writing in mind, to point out the way that Mallery's metaphor of value involves not just gold or some similar precious metal but the *reading* of the authenticating 'legend' written on it, which means that far from defining itself it is dependent on a system of signification external to it. It is also tempting to pursue the double use of the word *wampum* to describe a circulating medium (means of exchange and standard of value) and as a ceremonial item, with a mnemonic role, in terms of Derrida's parallel of the circulation of signs and the circulation of money, referred to earlier in relation to Mallery's idea of words as coins, and to ask whether this double role was originally one – that is, whether value/signification was originally inseparable from context. Clearly there is a distinction between the white and blue beads noticed, and taken over by the early settlers as repositories of economic value, and the wampum belts exchanged at meetings and treaties, but it is interesting how large the area of overlap is, and how difficult it is to separate the two functions in the situations where we find it described.
4. There are marked similarities here to the claims made for the Chinese ideogram by Europeans like Fenollosa, which then feed into tenets of Imagism and modernist poetry in general. This then provides a model for the translation of Indian poetry into haiku-like miniatures. The concern with concreteness continues to dominate some strands of American poetry, of course, and feeds into the ethnopoetics of Rothenberg and others, discussed briefly in Chapters 5 and 6.
5. For a clear brief account of these terms, and their origins in Pierce, see Steiner (1982).

6. See Takaki (1979) for an account of the development of the market economy and its effects on ways in which subordinate groups were used, and Horsmann (1981) for racist rationalisations by means of which Indians could be taken over by, but not taken within the dominant white society.

7. Jack Goody puts it clearly

> It is difficult to accept the absence of a linguistic element, even for gesture. For animals, gesture can be described as non-verbal communication. But for human beings, the coding and decoding of gesture must include a linguistic component, as in all processes of thinking or of conceptualisation.... How much more deeply is language embedded in the specifically human activity involved in graphic design, where the language appears as an intrinsic intermediary? As Leroi-Gourhan maintains, figurative art is 'inseparable from language'...; the whole development of graphic forms is linked to speech. (1987:8–9)

The inextricably conventional nature of visual representations has also been emphasised by Dennis Tedlock amongst others:

> In semiotic terms, the earliest visible signs are symbolic (or conventional) and indexical; if there are any icons here, they are diagrams rather than images. When images make their first appearance, in the late Paleolithic, they are highly schematic; instead of taking the form of self-explanatory scenes from life, they seem to require completion by means of verbal interpretation, just as symbolic and indexical signs do. (1985:121)

8. See Tyler (1987:35–49), who also takes up the idea of the rebus in relation to Derrida.

9. Mary Haas gives DuPonceau's original formulation of this idea, which she says is then repeated with variations throughout the nineteenth century

> A polysynthetic or syntactic construction of language is that in which the greatest number of ideas are comprised in the least number of words. This is done principally in two ways. (1) By a mode of compounding locutions which is not confined to joining two words together,... but by interweaving together the most significant sounds or syllables of each simple word, so as to form a compound that will awaken in the mind at once all the ideas singly expressed by the words from which they are taken. (2) By an analogous combination of the various parts of speech. (Haas: 1969:240)

10. Keith Basso's work, for instance, has shown the importance of *not* speaking, in his studies of language use among the Western Apache (1971), as well as the special significance of names and places (1983; 1988).

11. See, for instance, Stephen Horigan's (1988) tracing of nature/culture oppositions, which includes a brief account of the debate over ape and human language.

12. See Brotherston (1979), Goody (1987) and Tedlock (1983).

13. The most extreme version of this is F.A. Harper's *Sequoyah: Symbol of Free Men* (1952), which uses Sequoyah to demonstrate that 'only free men are creative'. Sequoyah 'created a form of capital.... Like any other item of capital in a free society the expenditure of much time and effort was required of some able and

willing person.' The book then becomes a treatise in favour of the 'right to one's own product' and other such anal-retentive natural rights.

14. It is interesting to note that the bulk of the surviving evidence of Indian writing in Massachusett, taught to them by John Eliot, is also on land transfers and disputes, rather than anything more spiritual. See Goddard and Bragdon (1988).

CHAPTER THREE

Indian Speech and Speeches

While I shall be concentrating in this chapter on the representation and textualisation of Indian speech and speeches in the eighteenth and nineteenth centuries, the actual pattern of textualisation begins much earlier. John Eliot, whose language work was referred to in the last chapter, published in 1685 *The Dying Speeches of Several Indians*, which he says were taken down 'in the language as they were spoken', and then translated by him. In spite of his deprecatory preface, in which he says that they are being printed 'not so much for Publishment as to save charge of writeing out of Copyes for those that did desiere them', they need to be seen in the context of a whole series of publications aimed at readers and potential financial supporters in England.[1]

Pious speeches by Indian converts were evidence, to use part of the title of another of his pieces, of 'the glorious progress of the Gospel' amongst the Indians in New England, and dying speeches had the distinct advantage that there was no danger of subsequent backsliding. Clearly, there were already conventions for such speeches within Christian writing, and they come into operation in Eliot's text, so that the Indians have little specificity of identity or of speech. Nehemiah, for instance, who was stabbed in an argument, and from whom 'a little was gathered up spoken by him' is reported as saying,

I see that word is true, 'hee that is well today, may be dead tomorrow...'. Now I desire patiently to take up my crosse and misery, I am but a man and must feel the crosse. Oh help me, help me.

'So he died' says Eliot, and this phrase re-echoes through these and other accounts, as the most significant point. In *The Day-Breaking if not the Sun-Rising of the Gospel with the Indians in New England* (1647) he incorporates a 'precious dying speech' of an unnamed Indian woman, and also highlights the death of Wampora, an important figure among the Indians, who 'embraced death' so piously that 'I thinke he did more good by his death, then he could have done by his life' (1647; 1834 edn:166). Within such overtly promotional documents as these the Indians certainly are most useful dying, but their words in general are always going to be used for white purposes, as Experience Mayhew, in a later example of the same genre, clearly implies when he says that he has sometimes translated and incorporated into his book 'such Passages [original emphasis] written by them in their own language as I think would be subservient to the End herein aimed at' (1727:xxiii).

Since there is clearly no conception in such documents of any value or legitimacy in Indian expression other than speaking in a Christian voice, it is redundant to talk of suppression or domination, but it is interesting to compare Eliot's accounts, which suggest that the Indians wrote down their various Christian statements, which he then translated, with the available materials actually written in Massachusett which have survived. Apart from Christian works translated by whites, most of what we have left from what Goddard and Bragdon describe as 'one of the earliest instances of widespread vernacular literacy' (1988:6) consists of distinctly secular accounts of land transfers, and even a complaint about white land-grabbing, which are more reminiscent of Sequoyah's first use of literacy discussed in the last chapter. In the course of this quite extensive textualisation of Indians as Christians, Eliot does become involved in the representation of a series of questions and answers, in which the Indians are presented as having an independent voice; I shall deal with this and other apparent dialogues and their implications for arguments about the power of a ruling discourse in Chapter 7. For now, though, I want merely to stress the way in which the words allowed to Indians in such promotional texts fix them in certain safe and comforting roles for a white readership.

While the death of Eliot's and Mayhew's Indians was comforting as a spectacle of Christian piety, later dying Indians offered comfort within a different frame of reference, that of inevitably doomed nobility. The focus, therefore, changes from ordinary Indians to leaders, and their language begins to exhibit the necessary rhetorical markers of nobility. A distinctive and persistent strand in the representation of Indians concentrates on their powers of oratory, which seem to have been regularly remarked upon from the earliest contacts. That this description exists side by side with the other characterisation of Indians as dumb or inarticulate should not surprise us, since it is only the linguistic manifestation of that complex of apparently contradictory ideas contained within the term 'Noble Savage', an area so exhaustively discussed as to prompt Hayden White to suggest that it 'may be one of the few historical topics about which there is nothing more to say' (1978:183). He then goes on, of course, to say quite a lot more, and of direct relevance to my argument in this chapter, by arguing that within the eighteenth century the Noble Savage theme can be seen to be used fetishistically, as the locus of a debate not about savages but about the role of nobility in an increasingly bourgeois society. It is used, he says, 'not to dignify the native, but rather to undermine the idea of nobility itself' (1978:191). When applied to North America this idea may give us some explanation for the *popularity* of surrender and protest speeches by Indians. In what became a well-used scenario Americans created a public space where could be acted out the renunciation of power by a nobility which was doomed by the very *fact* of its nobility.[2] The Indian in this scene, then, was doing double duty ideologically, in representing both the savage who had to give way to civilisation and a European aristocratic order which also needed to be dispensed with in the new bourgeois and democratic society. This may seem rather far-fetched, but it is important to stress the *public* nature of the Indians' reported rhetorical skills, and the status of those exercising them, as I hope to show.

As the term oratory implies, the occasion for the expression of this noble characteristic was one in which a particular Indian is addressing a group, and acting representatively, as a leader (this idea being employed ethnocentrically, of course, to include a whole range of Indian political and religious roles). The way Indians spoke in day-to-day situations is subject to a different set of ideological assumptions, but it is important to see that the two modes are interdependent, and that the nobility is in one way actually premised on the savagery. In terms of language, it is its very limitations which both chain it to the concrete and, put in a different context, allow it to be figural and poetic, as I shall demonstrate in relation to oratory. When functioning closest to the natural the Indians almost seem to lose language altogether, according to Rousseau, who confidently asserts that 'the American savages hardly speak at all except outside their homes. Each keeps silent in his hut, speaking to his family in signs' (quoted in Derrida 1976:253).

Actual accounts of Indians speaking rather than orating are rather thin, partly perhaps because of assumptions such as Rousseau's which would lead to untranslated speech being dismissed as grunts, just as later the Hottentots were confidently believed to have no language. Indians attempting to speak in English would be subject to the representations of inarticulateness described in the last chapter, but for the moment I want to concentrate solely on the ways in which the Indian, as orator or representative, is himself (and eloquence, like leadership, seems to be exclusively a male attribute in both white and Indian cultures) *represented* in texts produced for a white audience. To be more exact, the texts have been produced for, and shaped by, the cultural expectations of a white *readership*, but the Indian speech is presented in a dramatic context which has the effect of making it already overdetermined for the white reader. As a result the speakers are 'framed', so that *what* they are saying is actually less important than the fact and manner of their saying it. This, I would suggest, is one way of explaining the appetite for speeches whose *content* offered an often devastating criticism of white actions. Even as the Indians nobly and eloquently complained, that very nobility and eloquence was confirming the inevitability of their disappearance.

This presentation of Indians in a staged scene which re-enacts and confirms a particular white view of them is sometimes actually in a drama, as in Robert Rogers' *Ponteach: or The Savages of America* (1766), which was later used by Parkman for his portrayal of Pontiac. Although the play itself received a uniformly bad reception, Rogers had been encouraged to write it because of the interest in his initial portrayal of Pontiac in his *Concise Account of North America*; Pontiac had exhibited, according to Allan Nevins, Rogers' modern editor, 'a taciturn dignity'. (Rogers 1914:101) When Ponteach is confronted by swindling whites, he asserts his independence and nobility in iambic pentameters.

> The calumet I do not choose to smoke,
> Till I see further, and my other chiefs
> Have been consulted. Tell your king from me,
> That last or first a rogue will be detected,
> That I have warriors, am myself a king,
> And will be honor'd and obey'd as such.

At the end of the play his noble defiance and assertion of will is explicitly within the context of the renunciation of his land. The gods are seen to be endorsing the transfer of land from the natural aristocracy to their 'base' successors.[3]

> And thou proud Earth, made drunk with Royal Blood
> I am no more your Owner and your King
> But witness for me to your new base Lords,
> That my unconquered Mind defies them still;
> And though I fly, 'tis on the Wings of Hope
>
> Britons may boast, the Gods may have their Will
> *Ponteach* I am, and shall be *Ponteach* still.

The dramatic career of the noble Indian who dies out practically and politically, but survives in his words as a monument, an occasion for suitably comfortable melancholy reflections, is also well illustrated by John Augustus Stone's *Metamora, or the Last of the Wampanoags* (1829). In answer to his wife's question, 'is our nation dead?' he tells her

> The palefaces are all around us, and they tread in blood. The blaze of our
> burning wigwams flashes awfully in the darkness of their path. We are
> destroyed – not vanquished; we are no more, yet we are forever.

He dies leaving a curse on the white man, but the content of his words can be subsumed by the larger and grander narrative, which is reasserted by the stage directions, as Indian anger (and white unease) is subsumed in melancholy: 'Falls and dies: a tableau is formed. Drums and trumpet sound a retreat till curtain. Slow curtain' (Coyle and Damaser 1968:92-3). Thus, implicitly, the Indian can be contained within white society, made immortal by being translated, frozen, into an emotionally satisfying and non-threatening pose.

Clearly the ideological as well as the dramatic possibilities of the doomed Indian are huge, and have been exploited in a whole range of staged events, as well as actual dramas and films, ranging from presidential parades and expositions to Wild West shows. But my particular concern here is with the written versions of supposedly real (that is, actually delivered) speeches. These became available to a reading audience by the eighteenth century mainly through accounts of Indian treaties, for which, as Lawrence C. Wroth (1928) has pointed out, there was a good market. Later the speeches would appear in more general accounts of Indian tribes and leaders (see, for instance Drake 1832) and eventually in the twentieth century in special anthologies (Jones 1965; Vanderwerth 1971), or as sections in anthologies of Indian literature (e.g. Velie 1979). More recently still, as Rudolf Kaiser (1987) has shown with the case of Chief Seattle, particular speeches have reappeared in magazines as examples of Indian ecological awareness. What all of these have in common to a greater or lesser degree is the way that the publication of the speeches potentially makes them available to be read in ways that confirm a larger message, which the actual situation out of which they arose might have contradicted.

The early treaty accounts can perhaps be said to give most context, and most sense of a dialogue. They often give circumstantial detail, for instance about the giving of wampum belts at certain points in the speeches, not just as formalised gifts but as aids to the memory, reinforcing the idea that for the Indians these were carefully planned and structured occasions. These early accounts also give some information on the exact role and identity of the interpreters. Wroth, in making an interesting case for Indian treaties to be seen as some of the first real American literature, argues that we experience 'the quick stuff of an epic fermentation' (1928:325) in which all sorts of power struggles are taking place. The novelty and uniqueness of the form, he suggests, is because on these occasions the white representatives had to accept a conference procedure that was traditionally Indian:

> The conference, therefore, was not a debate: it consisted in the delivery of set speeches by either side in response to the proposals made by the other at the preceding session. Speaking only after deliberation in tribal council, and expressing the common opinion, the Indian had few ill-considered words to regret when the conference was ended. (1928:327)

Benjamin Franklin, who himself published a number of such treaties, compares Indian rules of debate favourably with the British House of Commons and gives instances of their skill, but he also points out that their very politeness prevents them from contradicting directly what is said to them. This allows them to avoid disputes, he says, 'but then it becomes difficult to know their minds or what impression you make upon them' (1784:104).

But there are also accounts to be found within letters and journals of conferences and confrontations where the Indians made their feelings *very* clear, as in David Avery's description, at the instigation of Eleazar Wheelock, of his meeting with the Oneidas to persuade them to set up Christian schools (McCallum 1932). He first gives an account of the standard polite speeches on both sides but then gives at length an account by an Oneida Indian Thomas, of an earlier and acrimonious meeting with an earlier missionary. This is interesting, since although it conforms to the standard patterns and is, of course, translated, it also presents Indians acting far from inscrutably. Thomas gives the formal exchanges, but explains that 'what seemed to lead & determine the council was what past in private between Mr Wheelock & Thomas before they met', when the missionary, Ralph Wheelock had spoken 'with an air of resentment & an elevated voice'. The Indians had then responded to his formal speech. He had spoken, they said,

exceedingly well! Very *sweet* words indeed'.... But brother do you think we are altogether ignorant of your methods of instruction? (Then takeing & shaking him by the shouder said) Why, brother, you are deceiveing yourself! We understand not only your speech, but your *manner* of teaching Indian. – Take care brother! – In the first place, correct yourself. Learn yourself to understand the word of God, before you undertake to teach and govern others. – You have spoke *exceeding* well, even to our *surprise*, that our children should become *wise in all things* by your instructions, & treated as *children* at your house, & not as *servants*! [emphasis in original]

He goes on to complain of the beating of Indian children at the school, and the meeting degenerates: 'Here they spake with high elevation of voice, & their answers back were loud shouts of contempt' (McCallum 1932:287–8).

The Indian response could be even more more pointed, as John Adlum's account of his visit to the Senecas in 1794 indicates.

When the interpreters had finished translating the first paragraph – The young Indians on the beams above, saluted me with an univers[al] roar, *vulgarly called farting*. I heard several of the elderly woemen exclaim Yaugh-ti-Yaughti which was as much as to say – shame, scandalous – I made a pause, ruminating within myself how I should act, and concluded to read another paragraph, and received another salute of the same kind. (Quoted in Abler 1989:204–5) [emphasis in original]

Odd glimpses as these go some way to qualify the impression given by the published accounts of unruffled formality and aristocratic dignity, and further suggest that, whatever the larger power relations, the Indians were quite capable of controlling these occasions. The picture that is emerging here, of Indians forcing the whites to play by their rules, is a misleading one, though, if it ignores the ability of the whites then to subvert, in a whole number of ways, the meaning the Indians gave to the event. The most obvious way was for the whites not to listen (see H.M. Stanley's later account of this tactic in Vanderwerth 1971:11-12). The more subtle and long-term way was to turn the whole event into a drama or tableau signifying the inevitable defeat of the Indian. Even in the early treaty accounts praised by Wroth, the very immediacy of the descriptions, with actions during and between the speeches given in the present tense, have the effect of presenting them almost as dramas, and he describes them in these terms. Once the noble orator comes to be seen as an actor in a larger historical drama a large part of the power of what he says comes to depend upon a melancholy sense of dramatic irony available to the reader or spectator and not to him. His words have been overwritten.

An anonymous writer in *The Knickerbocker* in 1836 describes this mixture of regret and sympathy: 'though we know it is the rightful, natural course of things, yet it is a hard heart which does not feel for their fate' (Clements 1986:9-10). Yet he also very acutely reveals the process by which this is turned into an aesthetic, rather than a moral, sensation, by its association with vanished grandeur. The orations, he says, are heightened in impressiveness 'by the melancholy accompaniment of approaching extermination', and will be 'as enduring as the swan-like music of Attic and Roman eloquence, which was the funeral song of the liberties of those republics' (Clements 1986: 11).

The comparison with classical oratory need not be for these aesthetic ends, of course, and one of the most influential references to Indian oratory approaches it from a slightly different angle. The speech of the Mingo Chief Logan was one of the most celebrated and frequently reprinted, but it is best known for its inclusion in Thomas Jefferson's *Notes on the State of Virginia* (1787). It was also, not surprisingly, made the centrepiece of a stage play. (See Seeber 1947:139). In Jefferson the speech appears not, as might be expected, in the section devoted to 'Aborigines', but as part of a lengthy rebuttal of Buffon's argument about the inferiority of American species. Jefferson challenges 'the whole orations of Demosthenes and Cicero, and of any more eminent orator, if Europe has furnished more eminent, to produce a single passage, superior to the speech of Logan, a Mingo chief' (Peterson 1975:99).

He then goes on to print the speech, and the supposed circumstances of its delivery, but it is curiously appropriate, in the terms of my argument, that when we look carefully at the details it becomes clear that what we have was never actually given as a speech, but was, at best, dictated to a white messenger via a translator, and given (spoken?) to Lord Dunmore. There have always been those, of course, who have questioned the authenticity of the whole speech, and Seeber (1947) has expertly assembled and sifted the conflicting evidence,[4] but my point has more to do with the ideological work which the written version, whatever its provenance, has been made to do.

To invoke classical oratory involved a claim for the power of eloquence. According to Cicero eloquence was the force capable of transforming humanity from barbarism to organised and civilised society (see Greenblatt: 1976:565). For Jefferson to find it in the New World was, therefore, for him a strategic move, another rebuttal of Buffon. His comparison of Logan with classical orators is not fleshed out sufficiently for us to know in what areas he saw Logan's superiority as lying, but it is quite typical that the details of the speech itself are less important than the general *impression* it made. Elsewhere, in fact, Jefferson describes being filled with 'awe and veneration' by the Cherokee Ostenaco and his 'sounding voice, distinct articulation, animated action and the solemn silence of his people', even though he 'did not understand a word he uttered' (quoted in Strickland 1977:375). The combination of simplicity and dignity is an ideal symbol of the New World as opposed to the Old, but by the nineteenth century what is implicitly in Jefferson a *continuity* between primitive and civilised in America, demonstrated by Indian eloquence, becomes an opposition, strengthened by the overlay of a broader Romantic opposition between nature and the restrictions of society and education. Amos Stoddard, for instance, writing in 1812, gives an interesting revision of Jefferson:

> Who at this day, except the untutored man of nature, can utter the language of Ossian and Homer? What man trammeled with the forms of modern art, can speak like Logan, mentioned in the notes on Virginia? The language of nature can alone arrest attention, persuade, convince and terrify; and such is the language of the Indians. (quoted in Sheehan 1969:350–1)

Logan is here used as a synecdoche for nature, though as Sheehan points out, as a half-breed and a heavy drinker he might better represent 'the unfortunate, culturally disintegrated Indian', and 'will not do as a noble savage' (1969:351). True eloquence, as opposed to the artifices of civilised speech, was seen as revealing to us the true Indian. According to the anonymous writer on 'Indian Eloquence' in *The Knickerbocker* in 1836, public oratory was an expression of the quintessential Indian normally concealed by his silent demeanour:

> The iron encasement of apparent apathy in which the savage had fortified himself, impenetrable at ordinary moments, is laid aside in the council-room. The genius of eloquence bursts the swathing bands of custom, and the Indian stands forth accessible, natural, and *legible* [my emphasis]. (Clements 1986:5)

As so often in writing about Indians, we find here the claim to be able to *recognise* what is essential and authentic, to be able, in an expression of colonialist superiority, to 'read them like a book'. Here it involves an interesting reversal of the normal view of private and public. What Indians say in private, or to each other, is seen as less expressive of their true selves than what they say in public to whites. The reassuring and self-serving nature of this idea for whites needs no elaboration, but the means by which this belief is sustained must be traced back to the identification of eloquence and poetic and figural language with primitive language – what the same author refers to as 'a poverty of language, which exacts rich and apposite metaphorical allusions' (1986:5). This is the same poverty which, as we have seen, supposedly allowed such facility with sign language, and it crops up regularly in conjunction with the idea of metaphor. Describing 'our barbarian brethren' in 1870 a contributor to *Harper's Monthly Magazine* gave the by then standard account: 'Their language being too limited to allow a wealth of diction, they made up in ideas, in the shape of metaphors furnished by all nature around them, what they lacked in words' (Sossing 1870:800).[5]

The *extent* of the identification of Indians with metaphor can be illustrated by two different newspaper accounts of the same Indian speaker. William Strickland, in an article on Cherokee rhetoric, quotes white responses to John Ridge on his speaking tour against 'Removal', but does not comment on the correlation in the accounts between Indianness and figurative language. The *Boston Patriot* describes Ridge's accent as

> peculiar, such as marks the Indian from the white man. His language was strongly figurative, though not strictly grammatical, but the more impressive, perhaps, on that very account, from its conformity to the Indian mode of expression. (Strickland 1977:381)

In New York, though, the correspondent for the *Commercial Advocate* saw Ridge as altogether more civilised and described his language as 'chaste and correct' and 'without the least observable tincture of foreign accent or Indian'. Having established him as civilised, even his rhetoric has to match, so that 'even his metaphors were rarely drawn from the forest', and going with this is the absence of gesture: 'he had little or none of that vehement action that characterises the orators of uncivilised tribes'. The accuracy of these accounts is not the issue here so much as the way that they involve a whole *package* of beliefs and perceptions, which can be further examined.

The perceived lack of abstractions, reflecting a lack of intellectual development on the part of the Indians, means that concepts must be built up from objects and their qualities or associations, thus preserving a vividness and natural power lost in civilised speech. This idea, of course, is widespread in Western thought in relation to the supposed qualities of the Chinese ideogram, and it takes on a particular literary interest through Ezra Pound's influential use of Fenollosa, but apart from Mallery's careful charting of the possibilities for abstraction within picture-writing, in which he effectively distinguishes between part-for-whole and substitutions on the basis of similarity, most accounts of Indian languages identify only an increase in emotional power rather than an increasing level of complexity and I would suggest that this is part of the ideological role of the idea of natural eloquence. In William Tracy's account of the speech by the Oneida chief known as Plattkopf, for instance, the whole thing is one extended analogy

> He looked upward, and pointed to the tree under which he stood, which, although still of great size and beauty was visibly marked with age and symptoms of decay. 'We were like this council-tree.... It drew its nourishment from the ground; it was not cramped and confined.... The white man came. We sold him a portion of our land. A root of the tree, which drew its sap from that land withered...'. He dwelt upon the figure, and continued his parallel between its decay and that of his nation, should it part with more of the land which was to nourish and strengthen its life and beauty. (Tracy 1871:545)

Within the space of a few pages Tracy several times refers to the analogy of the old tree, as in Sconondoa's description of himself, 'I am an old hemlock', and it is clear that he is himself involved in as much of a rhetorical exercise as those he quotes. Tracy invokes images of decay not, like the Indians here, to stiffen resistance to white demands, but to heighten the pathos, and here the occasion of the pathos is not even the passing of the Indian but, in an ultimate example of the aestheticisation of the Indians' condition, the passing away of the eloquence itself. Soon the 'remnants of the race' of the Iroquois who he sees as 'like the early Romans', will be 'lost in the blood of the white man'. As a result

> The themes which awaked their eloquence have passed away. They are now hardly children of the forest. The poetic elements with which their lives were surrounded have ceased to exist. Their language, singularly soft and beautiful in its tones and articulation, is daily becoming extinct, and soon it may be that all that shall be left of Indian eloquence will be its history. (Tracy 1871:545)

The falling cadence, the nostalgic and elegiac tones here depend upon a particular historical scenario of the disappearing Indian – so much so that the scenario has to be invoked even when the actual contents of the speeches might be saying something else, so that they can be inscribed within a larger white narrative.

An important element in this manoeuvre and one which links the aesthetic and the political, is the idea of the fragment or relic. The aesthetic power of the speeches is dependent on our being told that this is only a pale imitation, so that the frame, the context, is crucial in determining our response. Before we 'hear' Red Jacket, for instance, we are told

> Those who heard him speak, represent his expression, gesticulation and tones,

as wonderfully beautiful; and the translators, men of no poetic perceptions and
talents, always declared their inability to transfer the beauty of his sentences
into English. And yet, with all the difficulty of translation there are passages
which are wonderfully touching. (Tracy 1871:543)

The 'and yet' is misleading here, in that the difficulties and the partial nature
of what we get actually *contribute* to the aesthetic effect. Seeber refers to the
fashion 'to impute to Logan a power of eloquence and sentiment that quite
transcends the written record' (1947:140). If what is being expressed is
somehow transcendent, or quintessential, the actual medium becomes
secondary, as does even the content. All speeches become synecdochic,
remnants of a greater whole – what the anonymous writer for *Knickerbocker*,
quoted earlier, called 'the only relic of the literature of the aborigines'
(Clements 1986:4).

There is an interesting parallel here with the use made of the idea of the
poverty of Indian languages, in that it is precisely the limitations and absences
within primitive languages which allowed them to be poetic. Within this
aesthetic perspective the fragment or the ruin is always seen as more potent
and more evocative than the whole, and in later chapters I shall return to the
ramifications of this in translations of Indian songs and poetry, as well as the
more general issue of the idea of the inexpressible and the sublime in its
relation to translation and cultural relativity. The ability to fill in the gaps and
to complete the whole does not just have an aesthetic dimension. One of the
effects of seeing Indian speeches as fragments, as expressions of something
more than themselves, is to draw attention away from the actual details of the
speech's transmission and of its political implications and there is certainly an
irony in the use of the speaking and self-representing Indian to represent
something else entirely, and to act as a synecdoche for what is inexpressible
within white culture. The point of communication thus comes to represent its
opposite, by concentrating on the speech as *moment* rather than part of a
dialogue; by making it into tableau rather than process.

This same curious use of Indian oratory, whereby its specific Indian purpose
becomes less important, once it is published, than its metonymic role as
expression of the cultural and historical roles allotted to Indians by whites,
can be seen very clearly even when the published text is actually *authored* by
the Indian orator and the speech is made in English. The Mohegan Samson
Occom (1723–92) was perhaps the first Indian writer of any significance. After
his conversion to Christianity, and after gaining an education from Eleazar
Wheelock, he gained a considerable reputation as a preacher and toured
England giving sermons and drumming up donations for Wheelock's Indian
school. His subsequent disillusion with Wheelock, his suspicions that funds
he had acquired for Indian education were being used for whites, in what
eventually became Dartmouth College, and that he was being less well
provided for than his white equivalents are well documented in his letters to

Wheelock, which will be looked at later, but he is best known for his *Sermon at the Execution of Moses Paul*. This was first published in 1772 and ran to many editions, both in America and Britain. The bulk of the sermon follows the conventional pattern of exhorting the sinner to repent by holding up to him his wickedness, the imminent prospect of the torments of hell, and the possibilities of God's grace, but the actual circumstances of the sermon and its publication are worth looking at in some detail.

Moses Paul had earlier been converted to Christianity but had slipped into drinking while serving in the army and then in the navy. While drunk, he had pointlessly killed a respectable member of the community and his execution was therefore an opportunity to contemplate not just one Indian's downfall but to make him symbolise the particular weaknesses and susceptibilities of Indians. By having the sermon actually preached by a virtuous Indian (though one who also had shown his weakness for alcohol, as I shall show later), it was possible to stage a sort of moral tableau which encapsulated the moral capacities and disabilities of the Indians. My metaphor of the stage here is, I think appropriate, when we consider the very public nature of the affair and the degree of stage-management involved. Occom was invited to give the sermon in a letter supposedly from the condemned man but undoubtedly written for him, as Blodgett points out when he reprints it:

> Give me leave to further mention, that the same thing [that Occom should come and preach] is desired by many Gentlemen in Town, and also that if you should come, I have reason to think, not only that you will be obliged to put yourself to no expence while you are here, but that any expence you may be at in travilling will be made up to you by Gentlemen here. (Blodgett 1935:139-40)

Furthermore, even if the original purpose for publishing it was Occom's, the later editions *frame* his sermon and underline its representativeness by the intrusion of their own editorial authority. In the prefatory 'Advertisement' to the 1788 edition, for instance, the editor Rippon feels it necessary, after telling us that Occom is a 'native Indian', to say that what follows 'might, perhaps have been altered in a few places for the better, but it is presumed, that good judges will overlook the defects of it, and wonder they are so few'. At several points in the text, too, he interjects a footnote. When Occom, in trying to give some idea of the length of eternity uses a homely but striking image of a fly carrying away a particle of the earth every 10,000 years, and the time it would therefore take it to transport the whole earth, Rippon condescendingly tells us, 'Reader, do notice the Indian's Description of ETERNITY' (Occom 1788:13). This particular edition is also preceded by an unattributed 'Introduction' which offers us a fictional dialogue between Moses and Occom, setting up the scene for the sermon.

So far I have been emphasising the ways in which both Indian participants in this drama could be said to have been used for a wider purpose than their own.

To present Indian *Christian* virtue preaching to Indian vice in its most exemplary form of drunkenness and consequent ruin can allow the exercise of moral feelings without any troublesome questions about the white role in, for instance, the creation of Indian drunkenness. To leave it like this, though, would be to ignore the ways in which Occom himself was not just a pawn in a white game. While fully subscribing to the Christian values he had been taught, he had very strong views about his own worth in relation to some of his white colleagues, and a confidence in his preaching ability. His own preface to the published revised version of the sermon is modest, but it is also a very clear justification of his style. He has allowed his 'broken hints' to be published because most sermons are in

> a very high and lofty stile so that the common people understand but little of
> them. But I think they can't help understanding my talk: little children may
> understand me. And poor Negroes may plainly and fully understand my
> meaning; and it may be of service to them. Again, it may in a particular
> manner be of service to my poor kindred the Indians. Further, as it comes
> from an uncommon quarter it may induce people to read it because it is from
> an Indian.

In the sermon itself, after his general mediations on sin and salvation, Occom separates his audience into different groups, addressing first 'my poor unhappy brother Moses', then the 'reverend gentlemen and fathers in Israel' and finally 'the Indians, my brethren and kindred according to the flesh', and on first impression the fact that his criticisms are entirely directed towards the Indians, while the white reverend gentlemen are merely exhorted to keep on preaching and fulfilling God's will would suggest that he is entirely going along with the overall white stage-managing of the event. When we look, though, at the way in which he phrases his criticisms of the Indians' drunkenness it is possible to see an awareness of the curious 'overheard' nature of this pre-arranged conversation between Indians.

In speaking to Moses himself he points out that in some ways his sin is worse because he has had the chance to be saved, thus showing ingratitude both to God and to the whites who gave him this chance. He has been brought up

> under the bright sun-shine and plain, and loud sound of the gospel: and you
> have had a good education; and you can read and write well; and God has
> given you a good natural understanding: and therefore your sins are so much
> more aggravated. (1788:17)

Here he certainly seems to have taken over a white evaluation of education and its relation to personal worth, but a bit earlier Occom addresses Moses as 'bone of my bone, and flesh of my flesh' and tells him, 'You are an Indian, a despised creature; but you have despised yourself.' This may only contain a hint of a different view from the white one, but in its implication that if other people despise you then you have an obligation not to live up, or rather down, to their expectations it does link up with what I see as some rather complex linguistic strategies regularly used by Occom and others. Later, in addressing the Indians present he points out that drunkenness has made them despised, 'and it is all right and just, for we despise ourselves more; and if we do not regard ourselves who will regard us?' When he then goes on to describe the ruin that alcohol causes it is interesting how, although the whites are not mentioned by name, they are present by implication as those who rob the Indians and supply their alcohol, and it would have been difficult for those whites who were present not to be aware of this. Through drunkenness an Indian who has anything of value 'may lose it all, or may be robbed, or make a foolish bargain, and be cheated out of all he has'. Similarly those who supply the alcohol are only alluded to:

> And here I cannot but observe, we find in sacred writ, a woe denounced against men, who put their bottles to their neighbours mouth to make them drunk, that they may see their weakness: and no doubt there are such devilish men now in our day, as there were in the days of old. (1788: 23)

In order to read such passages, I am suggesting, we need to be aware of the extent to which Occom may be using the complex situation of Indians talking to each other, but being overheard and stage-managed by whites, and turning it, if only marginally, to his own purposes. To do this Occom first of all splits up his audience, addressing them in separate sections of the speech. But all of the groups are present in the audience hearing the parts not aimed at them, and Occom *uses* the fact that he is being overheard, and that therefore one section of his sermon inevitably spills into another. I am certainly not claiming an overall subversive purpose here, but when we link the possible ironies shown here with those found in his letters and the letters of some of Wheelock's other Indian pupils an impression emerges of self-expression both *within* the conventions of Christian piety they had been taught and also *beyond* them. In the next chapter I want to concentrate on some of the writings, private and public, of a number of Christian Indians, in particular Occom and William Apes to pursue further some of the methodological and critical problems raised in trying to talk about self-expression in such cases.

Notes

1. See Jennings (1976:228–53).
2. See Clive Bush's account of the political role of representation in an American national space, often imaged in theatrical terms (1977), and Norman O. Brown

(1966:109–25) for some characteristically suggestive passages on representation.
3. The rhetoric of the play can also be seen, though, in terms of revolutionary politics, as Laura Tanner and James Krasner (1989) have convincingly shown.
4. A modern example of the desire to ascribe special significance and authenticity to the speech can be found surprisingly in an article which claims to be using an ethnographic approach to the question of authenticity. Having made the interesting point that the famous question, 'Who is there left to mourn Logan?' need not be just white pathos but may well refer to the importance of the Iroquois ceremony of condolence at the tribal council, James O'Donnell then feels the need utterly to dehistoricise Logan, describing him as 'The Indian Everyman, who spoke to the existential plight of his people in 1774, even as Albert Camus and J.P. Sartre addressed the anomie of humanity in the 20th century' (1979:156).
5. It was also remarked upon by Schoolcraft, though he complained that 'the paucity of terms leads not only to the use of figures and metaphors but is the cause of circumlocution' (quoted in Bieder 1986:155). His reservations may have had something to do with his frustrations in learning Chippewa, which he found unexpectedly difficult and full of verbiage and repetition – though these in themselves would surely have made the language *easier* to learn.

CHAPTER FOUR

Christian Indians:
Samson Occom and William Apes

In moving from a published sermon to private letters we do, of course, have to be aware of the different conventions in operation, but the similarities are also very significant. In their letters to their mentor and his associates 'Wheelock's Indians' as they are significantly often referred to, are often presenting a public and extremely formalised face. This is partly the letter-writing convention of the time, but it is made more complex by the fact that Wheelock often copied their letters and sent them, corrected, to benefactors of the college. Furthermore it is clear that he sometimes actually wrote public apologies or confessions for them to sign, as in the case of Mary Secutor, for whom he had to write several:

> I May Secutor do with shamefacedness acknowledge that on the evening of the 8th Inst I was guilty of going to the tavern & tarrying there with much rude & vain company till a very unseasonable time of night where was dancing and other rude & unseemly conduct, & in particular drinking too much spirituous liquor whereby I was exposed to commit many gross sins, which offence is doubly aggravated in that it is a direct violation of a late promise I have publickly made before this school – all which wicked & sinful conduct of mine, I am fully sensable is much to the dishonour of God and very prejudicial to the design and reputation of this school. (McCallum 1932:237)

This can be seen as fairly straightforward ventriloquism, and interesting more for the light it throws on Wheelock and the connection he clearly made between institutional control and writing. (What else made him laboriously copy so many of his own and other people's letters?) Approached like this it can be contrasted with letters in which we seem able to detect a presence other than Wheelock's, or where the official and the vernacular voices seem to coexist, as in Sarah Simon's request to be allowed to go and see her sick mother;

for I donot think that she is long for this world I have no Reson to thing so.
for She is very weekly and always sick. my Parents is very near and Dear to
me: and being I do not desine to Ever to go home and live with hir again, I
Desire to beg that favour to go and see hir as ofen as the Doctor [Wheelock]
is willing I should for I dont want to ofand the Doctor in the least. but I feel
willing to do any thing Sir that you think is bast for me. Oh how I orto Blease
and adore that grat and kind God that put it in the hands of some of his
Pepple to take so much Care of the poor indions nee above all the rast.
(1932:229)

That the sudden lurch into a religious terminology here is not just a way of
keeping Wheelock happy is borne out by an anguished and moving letter from
Sarah Simon, beginning 'I have been this Some time back thinking upon
things of Religion; and I think thay do not look So plain to me as I have Seen
them.' Eventually she comes to her main worry;

and what I want to know is this am I uncurenable or not; the devil is jest
Redy Sometimes to make me think that because I have made a perfertion and
do not alwas keep upright. and it seems to meall the true Christian never
meats with Such a Struggle with Satan as I do and So that maks me fear that I
am no Christian becase the Devil is so bese with me more than he is with any
one Els. (1932:230)

Anyone familiar with Mark Twain's later use of exactly this mixture of the
vernacular and the official in *Huckleberry Finn* will perhaps find it difficult not
to see the religious terminology here as disconcerting and even false, but to
conflate our view with a contemporary one would be to make some dangerous
assumptions. When Twain has Huck wrestling with his conscience about
helping Jim to escape, the humour of the situation, as well as the profound
irony, lies in the fact that the language Huck uses is not his own, and yet he
believes it is an expression of his most fundamental feelings:

The more I studied about this, the more my conscience went to grinding me,
and the more wicked and low-down and ornery I got to feeling. And at last,
when it hit me all of a sudden that here was the plain hand of Providence
slapping me in the face and letting me know my wickedness was being watched
all the time from up there in heaven, whilst I was stealing a poor old woman's
nigger that hadn't done me no harm, and now was showing me there's One
that's always on the look-out and ain't agoing to allow no such miserable
doings to go only just so fur and no further, I most dropped in my tracks I
was so scared.

The crucial thing here is Twain's awareness of a reader who knows *more* than
Huck, and who can recognise the way that his education works against his
best interests and against his true feelings. (This in its turn tends to entail a

belief in an authentic self which is prior to education and language, of course, a belief that Twain himself was never again, and perhaps not even here, fully to entertain.) It could be argued that our historical situation has given us the hindsight to put us as readers of such letters as Sarah Simon's and a whole number of others in which Indian deficiencies are *assumed* and are built into the language of white Christianity ('My soul seems to be more and more upon the perishing Pagans in these Woods' – 1932:269) in the position of Twain's reader, and that we inevitably read with an awareness of ironies that are within the situation, but not within the mind of the author of the letter. This whole approach, though, which contrasts the ghosted confession of Mary Secutor at one extreme, with a spontaneous free expression at the other (with Huck Finn and most of the people I deal with here in the middle) needs to be set beside Foucault's comments on confession. Far from distinguishing between true and forced confession, he uses the structure of confession to question the whole idea of a free subjectivity and its expression.

> The confession is a ritual of discourse in which the speaking subject is also the subject of the statement; it is also a ritual that unfolds within a power relationship, for one does not confess without the presence (or virtual presence) of a partner who is not simply the interlocutor but the authority who requires the confession. (Foucault 1978:61)

The striking similarities brought out by this description, between confession and autobiography, will be returned to in a later discussion in Chapter 5 of the role of Indian autobiography as self-expression, but for now it is the complex relation between self-expression, freedom and power which need to be pursued via Foucault. Crucially, Foucault here uses the idea of confession to reject the automatic association of subjectivity with freedom. The most intimate, deep and authentic expression, the deepest truth, is in fact 'the effect of a power that constrains us' but instead of recognising this we believe that

> truth, lodged in our most secret nature, 'demands' only to surface; that if it fails to do so, this is because a constraint holds it in place, the violence of a power weighs it down, and it can be articulated only at the price of a kind of liberation. (Foucault 1978:60)

This idea that subjectivity may also be subjection, when applied to discourse should prevent us from an easy distinction between dominant and subversive modes, and Foucault insists that we must imagine rather a world of discourse as 'a multiplicity of discursive elements that can come into play in various strategies'. We need to make allowance for

the complex and unstable process whereby discourse can be both an
instrument and an effect of power, but also a hindrance and a stumbling block,
a point of resistance and a starting point for an opposing strategy. Discourse
transmits and produces power; it reinforces it, but also undermines and
exposes it, renders it fragile and makes it possible to thwart it. (1978:100-1)

Foucault is much stronger on demonstrating the effects of power than on
how it is to be undermined, and the example with which he follows this
passage seems to locate resistance in silence rather than discourse. Even if we
accept Foucault's argument that, as Peter Dews has paraphrased it, 'any
theory of sovereignty or self-determination must be abandoned, since the
'free subject' upon which such theories rely is in fact intrinsically
heteronomous, constituted by power' (1984:67), it is not easy to see what we
replace the old critical notion of subjectivity with. In particular what terms do
we use to talk about the effect of authorial presence in a text? Talk of hearing a
'voice' has been used in the past to try to fix and guarantee a meaning, through
the location of authorial intention, and has certainly become justifiably rather
suspect, but the use of such terms in Bakhtin at least suggests other
possibilities. As a way of avoiding what threaten to become the dead ends of
theories of closed epistemes and discourses, which are good at explaining how
we are locked into systems but offer no way out, the idea of dialogue and even
of presence has been seen as having special relevance to those groups denied
any specific identity within the dominant discourses, for whom the whole
proposition of a dominant discourse, without a corresponding idea of conflict
and change, can be seen as itself only the latest and most insidious intellectual
product of that dominance. As Arnold Krupat says, 'it is no accident that
those of us who work with hitherto marginalised materials show a certain
reluctance to give up the voice in favor of the text as recently defined'
(1989:20). Krupat, in fact, has specifically defended the use of 'voice'. He is, of
course, fully aware of the dangers of sounding like all those earlier whites who
claimed to be able to hear the authentic voice of the Indian, and who
consequently ignored all problems of textuality. He is as aware as anybody
that 'the writer is never present and that nonpresence cannot literally speak'
(1989:19). Nevertheless he wants to retain the metaphor of author as speaker
as 'a willed line of informed approach'. My own approach is similar, and tries
to buid in a recognition of the collaborative, and sometimes resisting, role of
reading in the creation of this voice, which in this case means being aware of
the impossibility of finally pinning down any historical figure's 'real' voice.[1]
    The difficulties of talking about self-expression and power can be seen
particularly clearly in the intermingling, in the early writings of Indians, of
their perceptions of their own inferiority and the injustices done to them. The
interconnection of these two issues was a historically determined matter,
given the unequal relation of whites and Indians. Indians were inadequate and
inferior to whites, if left in their natural state. If, therefore, they suffered

under the march of progress it was not anyone's fault, least of all the whites'. On the other hand, once they had had the chance of civilisation any backsliding was then a moral failing, and if there was a great deal of backsliding, then that seemed to reaffirm the idea of a natural frailty and inadequacy. (The later development in the nineteenth century of scientific racism, of course, confirmed this natural inadequacy, but did not necessarily remove the moral disapproval.) This is of course a white view, but how were Christian Indians to think of themselves and their actions? How were they to characterise themselves? We can only work for the moment with the evidence we have about how they represented themselves to *whites*, which is a partial matter at best, but if we look at the way they signed themselves in their letters to whites we find a predictably formalised series of self-abasements: 'Your Dutiful, Tho unworthy servant', 'thy unworthy and ungrateful Servant', 'Your undutiful Pupil', 'your affectionate though unworthy Pupil', 'your most noworthy and Ever Dutyfull Sarvent', 'your most unworthy and most obliged Humble Servant'. But when this humility is accompanied by a sense of grievance, as it quite often is in the case of Samson Occom, the same gesture of abasement can carry a sting in the tail. In a letter in which he complains of the poor funding of his next missionary expedition, 'but I have determined to go. tho no White Missionary would go in such Circumstances', and where his tone is what Blodgett describes as truculent, he ends:

> In a word I leave my poor Wife and Children at your feet and if they hunger, Starve and die let them Die there. Sir, I shall endeavour to follow your Directions in all things. This in utmost hast and with Sincere obedience, is from
>
>   Your Good for Nothing Indian Sarvant

Irony is notoriously difficult to pin down, of course, and for that reason profoundly subversive of any attempt at controlling the play of meanings in any discourse, and William de Loss Love, who wants to emphasise the dutiful Christian in his account of Occom, feels obliged to assure us of Occom's lack of irony on particular occasions. When Occom complains of having to make a journey without funds amongst the whites, and adds that 'if it were altogether among Indian Heathen we might do well enough' [i.e. they could rely on their generosity], Love tells us that it is 'a characteristic remark which he did not intend to be humorous' (1899:103). There can be no doubt, though, about Occom's tone in an exasperated and angry letter to a white neighbour Robert Clelland, who had been gossiping about Occom's drinking:

> You represent me to be the Vilest Creature in Mohegan. I own I am bad enough and too bad, Yet I am Heartily glad I am not that old Robert Clelland, his sins won't be charged to me and my Sins won't be charged to him, he must answere for his own works before his Maker and I must answere

for mine. You signify, as if it was in your Power to do me harm. You have
been trying all you Can and you may your worst, I am not concerned.

Here he throws back at Clelland his accusations, rather than try to justify
himself in Clelland's terms. They will both eventually be judged by the same
yardstick, and it will not be Clelland's. Refusing to 'spend my Time and
Paper' any longer, Occom's parting shot is a brilliant way of both giving
Clelland permission to 'represent' him *and* a way of totally rejecting it: 'I am,
Sir, Just what you Please, S. Occom.'

Occom's ability to 'represent' himself often involves this sort of
indirection, by which he moves himself in and out of the stereotype of the
poor Indian. In a long autobiographical account written soon after his return
in 1768 from England, where he had been fund-raising, and in order,
significantly, to counteract 'several Representations . . . made by Some
gentlemen in America Concerning me' he takes the opportunity not just to
refute their imputations that he had been converted specially for the English
trip but also to complain about his second-class treatment. He points out
that, unlike white missionaries, he did not need an interpreter (both Occom
and Fowler had learned to speak Oneida, which was not their native language,
according to Love – 1899:94) and was, as 'School master and Minister to the
Indians – their Ear, Eye & Hand, as well as Mouth'. In spite of this he was paid
less than the white missionaries, and he poses and then answers the question
why this should be. He tells a story of 'a Poor Indian Boy' who worked for an
English family who always found fault and beat him. When he was asked what
it was he was doing so wrong,

> he said he did not know, but he Supposed it was because he could not drive
> [plough] any better; but says he, I Drive as well as I know how; and at other
> Times he Beats me, because he is of a mind to beat me; but says he believes he
> Beats me for the most of the Time 'because I am an Indian. So Im *ready* to
> Say, they have used me thus, because I Can't Influence the Indians so well as
> other missionaries; but I can assure them I have endeavoured to teach them as
> well as I know how; – but I *must say*, 'I believe it is because I am a poor
> Indian'. I Can't help that God has made me So; I did not make my self so.
> (Peyer 1982a:18)

By putting himself in the same position as the poor Indian boy Occom is
mounting a criticism of the whites, for whom actual accomplishments are less
important than race, and he has by the end turned the phrase 'poor Indian'
from a term of self-derogation almost into an expression of solidarity. He is
fully aware of the danger of speaking so assertively, and even includes this to
add urgency to his argument ('I *must say*', and earlier, 'I speak like a fool, but I
am constrained'), and is aware that the most predictable response would be to
accuse him of not knowing his proper place. These criticisms were already
being made in relation to his experiences in England and in particular his

involvement with the Mason controversy, into which he had entered 'with an unbecoming spirit' (Blodgett 1935:103), and it is interesting to see how his awareness of Indian powerlessness, but *not* necessarily unworthiness, is couched in the same terms as his personal grievances:

> I am afraid the poor Indians will never stand a good chance with the English in their land controversies, because they are very poor, they have no money. Money is allmighty now-a-days, and the Indians have no learning, no wit, no cunning; the English have all. (quoted in Peyer 1982b:211)

Being the centre of attraction in England, Occom, according to Wheelock, 'Some times hath almost forgot what he was – it is a great mercy to be kept sitting at the feet of Jesus; I hope he will be kept so' (Blodgett 1935: 107). Certainly he was intensely and proudly aware of his key role in raising the funds to support the Indian school, and he became increasingly outraged by the emphasis on white students at the expense of Indians:

> I am very jealous that instead of your Semenary Becoming alma Mater, she will be too alba mater to Suckle the Tawnees. – I think your College has too much Worked by Grandeur for the Poor Indians, they'll never have much benefit of it. (Blodgett 1935:122-3)

It is worth commenting that this language of colour is also used by Wheelock, who refers to 'My black son Mr. Occum' (Love 1899:92). Occom complains that he went to England

> Hoping that it may be a lasting Benefet to my poor Tawnee Brethren, With this View I went a Volunteer – I was quite willing to become a Gazing Stocke, Yea Even a Laughing Stocke, in Strange Countries to Promote your Cause.

Here we find a hint of the humiliation as well as the celebrity involved in being exhibited as an Indian curiosity, which is not even recognised in the letters of his white companions, of course. To strengthen his case Occom also uses the device of having white people make his argument for him;

> The opinion of many white people about here is that you have been Scheeming altogether, and that it was a Pollicy to Send me over to England, for (Say they) now they dont Care anything about you –

Wheelock's response was, predictably, to reprove him for the sin of pride, but we can also perhaps see in his reference to good taste the way decorum, and all the arsenal of a Christian gentleman, can be used as a way of keeping social inferiors off balance and aware of their inferiority;

> Your letter has a very ill savor for a Christian or rather if I have any good

taste at all, it much savors of pride, arrogance & want of proper concern to
heal the bleeding wounds of our glorious Redeeemer. (Richardson 1933:358)

It is interesting to note that the same issue of pride arises with another Indian
missionary, David Fowler, who in defending himself from charges of being
proud and spendthrift complains he has been 'as faithful to you as if I had been
your Negro, yea I have almost killed myself in Labouring', and goes on to
assure Wheelock that he will be repaid so that

> it shall not be said all that Money and Pains which was spent for David Fowler
> an Indian was for nought. I can get Payment as well as white Man. O Dear me!
> I cant say no more. (McCallum 1932:103)

The uncertainty about status expressed here can be seen to be a pervasive
and often corrosive issue for educated Indians, whose language, right up at
least to Charles Eastman, reflects a conflict between the 'poor Indian' and the
Christian gentleman (see Chapter 5). It is interesting to notice in the letters of
some of the Indians Wheelock sent out 'into the field', complaints that sound
remarkably like those of later anthropologists thrown into a strange culture.
This is largely because they *were* alien cultures in some cases, since they were
sent to tribes whose language they could not speak. Hezekiah Calvin, for
instance, was sent to preach to the Mohawks, but asks to be sent to his own
people so that he need not be 'A dumb stump that has no tonnge to use, like as
when I was among the Mohawk Indians how tiresome was my life; could'nt
understand ym and no body to keep up a free discourse with' (McCallum
1932:58). On the other hand he seems to imply that he would have to *relearn*
his original language:

> And as for the thoughts of my going home, I greatly have a fond for that, that
> I might learn somwhat of my own Native Language that I might be the better
> fitted for the Design you have in view.

This very alienation from their fellow-Indians may have had more to do with
their poor success as missionaries than the backsliding which Wheelock tends
to assume. In many cases they may not have had a comfortable place to slide.
David Fowler's account of the Mohawks is full of the disgust and sense of
otherness which Stephen Greenblatt (1982:2) has argued implicitly or
otherwise accompanies so many ethnographic encounters:

> I am oblig'd to eat with Dogs, I say with Dogs because they are continually
> liking Water out of their Pales and Kettles; yea, I have often seen Dogs eating
> their Victuals when they set their Dishes down, they'll only make a little Noise
> to show their Displeasure to Dogs and take up the Dish. finish of what was
> left. My Cooks are nasty as Hogs; – their Hands are dirty as my Feet but they
> cleanse them by kneading Bread; their hands will be very clean after they have

kneaded three or four Loves of Bread. I am oblig'd to eat whatsoever they give me for fear they will be displeas'd with me; after this Month I shall try to clean some of them. for I must move along by Degrees. if they once get out with me it is all over with me. (McCallum 1932:94)

The experience here described has often been turned in ethnographic writing into a rite of passage for the doughty anthropologist, a threshold of ethnocentrism which he had to cross in order to be able to function, but within Indian writing it also fits into what is almost a genre of its own, the complaint, part aggressive, part conciliatory and submissive, to whites with power. This 'genre', as I will call it for the moment, can be found perhaps most persistently in speeches which, as I have shown, are vulnerable, in being textualised, also to being recontextualised, so as to lose their disturbing properties for the white reader. There are, though, examples of this mixture of complaint and accusation in public writing by Indians, and I now want to look in detail at some examples of this and the problems of interpretation they raise, in the work of William Apes.

It would be a mistake to assume that in moving to a work authored and published by an Indian we are necessarily moving further towards or away from an autonomous expression or an authentic voice. Anything that was published, at least until the point of widespread Indian literacy, was likely to reflect the tastes of a white audience, and conform to a large extent to what at least some of them thought it was appropriate for an Indian to write. Indian *writers* are mainly going to materialise, therefore, only when what they say meets a white need, as Christians or chroniclers of their own culture, for instance. In dealing with Occom I have tried to show how he actually exploits the ambiguities of his position as civilised Indian in his writing, even if he was less able to do so in his life, and I think it is possible to find the same strategies at work in some of the writing of William Apes, a Pequot Indian born at the end of the eighteenth century who became converted to Methodism and then was heavily involved in arguing for the rights of the Mashpee (or Marshpee) Indians of Cape Cod. It is the complex relation between on the one side the Christian civilised Indian, affirmer of white values, and on the other the Indian proud of his heritage and bitterly critical of white actions which is most interesting in his work. According to Peyer (1982b:44), as he became more politically active he either wrote less, or less has survived, but we do have enough to see the ways in which Apes was able to adopt and adapt white literary and polemical conventions.

Although I deal with autobiographies as a specific genre in the next chapter it is more appropriate to deal with Apes' autobiography, *A Son of the Forest* here, together with some of his other writings. It conforms to the overall pattern of the conversion narrative in which, after many lapses and tribulations, he is rescued from rum and degradation by Christianity, but in telling his story he has another agenda as well, a criticism of white attitudes,

carried out in a whole series of digressions. From one of these digressions
(which he himself marks as such by the regular use of 'but to return – ') we
realise that the full title of the book, *A Son of the Forest; the Experience of
William Apes, a Native of the Forest, Written by Himself*, which would seem to
fit into a standard white characterisation of Indians is also for him carefully
chosen to avoid the word Indian.

> I have often been led to inquire where the whites received this word, which
> they so often threw as an opprobrious epithet at the sons of the forest. I could
> not find it in the bible, and therefore concluded, that it was a word imported
> for the special purpose of degrading us. At other times I thought it was
> derived from the term in-gen-uity. But the proper term which ought to be
> applied to our nation to distinguish it from the rest of the human family is
> that of 'Natives' – and I humbly conceive that the natives of this country are
> the only people under heaven who have a just title to the name, inasmuch as
> we are the only people who retain the original complexion of our father Adam.
> (1831:21)

The argument about Adam is returned to elsewhere and seems to be
something of a hobby-horse of Apes', but what is notable here is the way he
has rejected a name from hostile outsiders (and one which calls Indians after
someone else, making them secondary, and second best), via a bit of word-play
which sees them positively (ingenuity) to a claim for their primacy, not just in
America but in God's creation. From the first page he is floating the issue of
descent, but far from defensively:

> My grand mother was, if I am not misinformed, the king's granddaughter, and
> a fair and beautiful woman. This statement is given not with a view of
> appearing great, in the estimation of others – what I would ask is *royal*
> blood – the blood of a king is no better than that of the subject – we are in fact
> but one family; we are all the descendants of one great progenitor – Adam.
> (1831:70)

Admittedly, as Arnold Krupat has put it in one of the very few critical
discussions of Apes, this pride in his origins 'derives from no indigenous,
Pequot sense of these matters' and in fact Krupat goes further and sees Apes
proclaiming 'a sense of self, if we may call it that, deriving entirely from
Christian culture' (1989:145). I would want to argue that it is precisely the
ruling out of bounds by Apes of a natural or unmediated Indianness as a
resource to fall back upon which is the most interesting thing in his writing,
but that this does not necessarily make him a white mouthpiece. Krupat
argues that 'the voice that sounds everywhere in Apes's text seems to mirror
very closely a voice to be heard commonly in the early nineteenth century, the
voice of what I have called salvationism' (1989:144).
I am concerned, on the other hand, to find those moments in which this

'voice' may be less or more than this, in order to question Krupat's assertion that it was Apes' wish 'to be the licensed speaker of a dominant voice that desires no supplementation by other voices' (1989:148). (In fact Krupat himself later allows for more complexity in Apes than this statement would imply.)

The forest is the scene for two interestingly contrasting episodes in the book which show the complexity of Apes' relation to his racial identity. Having been taken away at the age of 4 from his own family who were ill-treating him, Apes is brought up by a white family and acquires a dread of Indians as killers and scalpers. Out gathering berries, he comes across a group of white women whose complexion seems to him 'to say the least as *dark* as that of the natives' and runs home in panic. The irony here is not just at *his* expense, though, in that his naivety also points to the nonsensical nature of colour terms anyway. He further develops the irony by suggesting that perhaps his naive reaction was actually the right one. After outlining some of the white depredations he remarks that 'if the whites had told me how cruel they had been to the "poor Indian," I should have apprehended as much harm from them' (1831:23). As with Occom, that phrase 'poor Indian' is resonant with ironies, a white phrase turned against the whites, and the whole idea here of an Indian being in danger from whites when he ventures into the forest is both a historical truth and an ironic reversal of white fears, anticipating the startling opening scene of Thomas Sanchez' *Rabbit Boss* (1972), in which a Washo boy comes across white people (members of the ill-fated Donner party who tried to cross the Sierras into California) committing acts of cannibalism.

The second episode is a set piece using Romantic conventions of natural landscape to invoke a primal world, and one which is as completely imaginary to Apes, of course, as it is to any white, but Apes gives it a historical dimension. After describing a picturesque scene and admiring 'the wisdom of God in the order and beauty of creation' he tells us that

I then turned my eyes to the forest and it seemed alive with its sons and daughters. There appeared to be the utmost order and regularity in their encampment. Oh what a pity that this state of things should change. How much better would it be if the whites would act like a civilised people, and instead of giving my brethren of the woods, 'rum!' in exchange for their furs, give them food and clothing. (1831:70)

The attitude to change here is quite complex. The conventions from which this passage draws lend themselves to nostalgic regret, and an opposition between innocent but inevitably doomed simplicity and civilisation. Where Apes departs from the conventions, though, is in throwing into doubt the nature of the opposition and the inevitability of the change. For him it is not civilisation which destroys the primal order but whites *not* acting in a civilised way. We might want to see here a profound ambivalence on Apes' part, as a

Christian Indian committed to conversion and education, but what is clear
here and elsewhere in his writings is a refusal to accept white assumptions,
even while using the language in which they are encoded. His particular story,
in which he is 'saved' from the undoubted cruelties of his own Indian family,
would certainly seem to fit white preconceptions, but he is quick to prevent
this, with a characteristic interruption of the narrative:

> In view of this treatment, I presume that the reader will exclaim, 'what savages
> your grand parents were to treat unoffending, helpless children in this cruel
> manner.' But this cruel and unnatural conduct was the effect of some cause. I
> attribute it in a great measure to the whites, inasmuch as they introduced
> among my countrymen, that bane of comfort and happiness, ardent
> spirits – seduced them into a love of it, and when under its happy influence,
> wronged them out of their lawful possessions – that land, where reposed the
> ashes of their sires. (1831:2–3)

The crucial word here is, perhaps, 'unnatural', in that Apes is refusing to allow
whites to see Indians as separate from them. Instead he insists that the Indians
are now, because they have been so profoundly influenced by whites, almost
their own creations. This does not involve self-abasement for Apes, however,
since he uses it increasingly as a means of criticising white actions.

Parts of Apes' story are repeated in his next book, *The Experiences of Five
Christian Indians of the Pequod Tribe* printed in 1833, where as well as his own
he gives details of the conversion of his wife and several others. There is little
here to suggest any opposition to white values, other than attacks on the
hypocrisy of some Christians, and Apes even relates his encounter as visiting
missionary, with the 70-year-old Indian Anne Wampy and quotes her broken
English. After initial suspicion she is converted: 'I pray I look up to Jesus;
byme by me give up, then feel lightlike one feather; me want to die, me want to
fly – me want to go home. (Apes 1833:49) As well as having rather an echo of
Eliot's collection of dying speeches this certainly separates off Apes from his
subject here, and would give support to Krupat's point about Apes and his
desire to be the 'licensed speaker of a dominant voice', but an oddity about
this work is its pairing with a much more critical piece of writing. While the
two pieces are quite separate the overall title suggests a distinctly
complementary relation; *The Experiences of Five Christian Indians: Or the
Indian's Looking Glass for the White Man*. Peyer reprints the second piece
separately, and perhaps the 'Or' is an error, but it does underline the presence
of another side to Apes, which is both separate and joined to his Christianity.
The *Indian's Looking Glass* is a polemic against white racist attitudes, which
early on describes contemporary Indians in New England as 'the most mean
and abject, miserable race of beings in the world', and their communities 'a
complete place of prodigality and prostitution' (Peyer 1982a:44). As in Apes'
autobiography, he insists that there are *reasons*, and that it has taken a lot to

reduce ingenious and talented people to this condition. The reasons have to be sought in the white man, and in claiming to be holding up a looking-glass for the whites, Apes is performing a very complicated manoeuvre.

For a start there is an ambiguity about the title which allows us to visualise either an Indian looking at himself for the benefit of whites, or an Indian holding up a mirror so that the white man can see himself. This ambiguity is significant, given that as an educated Indian Apes could be said to have been created in the whites' own image. What he holds up to them, though, is not a flattering image of civilised humanity but the degenerate and demoralised Indians who are equally a creation of white civilisation. In this way the whites are forced to see in the mirror the results of their *own* acts, their own creations, rather than the 'other', the natural Indian. As another way of undermining the narcissistic self-regard of the whites, Apes attacks the ethnocentrism of white Christians, by an extended play on the idea of skin and colour. Having pointed out the hypocrisy of white racism, he tells us that he is 'merely placing before you the black inconsistency that you place before me – which is ten times blacker than any skin you will find in the universe'. Furthermore, if there is any disgrace in a non-white skin, it appears that God 'has disgraced himself a great deal – for he has made fifteen colored people to one white, and placed them here on this earth' (1833:46). To underline his point still further, he reminds his readers that Christ was a Jew, and that 'the Jews are a colored people' (1833:49). In invoking Christ like this, Apes is setting up a contrast between the fundamental principles the white Christians profess and their actual practice, and his rhetorical strategy is that of an earnest enquirer after knowledge: 'having heard so much precept, I should now wish to see the example. And I would ask who has a better right to look for these things than the naturalist himself' (1833:46). (The term 'naturalist' at the time seems to have implied both someone acting from the principles of nature *and* a researcher into that world, which fits very well with Apes' stance and allows him to operate from a position of some superiority.) In a scathing pun he eventually comes to the conclusion that Christian principles for the whites are merely 'skin-deep'.

Apes' next book, *Indian Nullification of the Unconstitutional Laws of Massachusetts relative to the Marshpee Tribe, or the Pretended Riot Explained* (1835) is a detailed defence of his involvement with the Marshpees of Cape Cod. Like the declarations of the Marshpee themselves (which he clearly had a hand in formulating), his defence is in the name and in the *language* of the American Constitution and the Declaration of Independence. Their declaration asserted 'That we, as a tribe, will rule ourselves, and have the right to do so; for all men are born free and equal, says the constitution of the country' (Apes 1835:21).

As usual in Apes, there is no appeal to a pure or natural Indianness, and this is particularly appropriate for the Marshpees whose status as 'genuine' Indians has been continually challenged, culminating in the much-publicised legal battle in the 1980s over whether the present residents of the area constituted a tribe, and could therefore claim ownership of the land (See Clifford 1988:277–346). Apes argues that the tribe has a right to the same democratic rights as whites, including the right to reject the imposition of unjust laws and taxes. Though they have been called paupers, he says,

> These are strange paupers who maintain themselves, and pay large sums to others into the bargain. Heigho! it is a fine thing to be an Indian. One might as well be a slave. (1835:44)

Here he is distinguishing Indians from slaves, and blacks are only mentioned by him as separate from Indians, but the issue of race and the mixture of races is in the background, even if, for good political reasons, he does not acknowledge it head on. The Marshpee were accused of not being a proper tribe because of the large amount of intermarriage with blacks and others – though blacks, of course were the main issue. (See McQuaid 1977:616–17). He does obliquely tackle this in an attack upon the prejudice of the white clergy:

> I greatly doubt that any missionary has ever thought of making the Indian or African his equal. As soon as we begin to talk about equal rights, the cry of amalgamation is set up, as if all men of colour could not enjoy their natural rights without any necessity for intermarriage. (Apes 1835:103)

He goes on to question whether intermarriage is so awful a prospect, and we may be reminded that his wife, whom he describes as of 'nearly the same color' as himself was probably a mulatto or mestizo, according to McQuaid (1977:612). This talk of 'men of colour' implies a widening of Apes' political terms of reference, and it is clear that he is particularly aware of the connections between his local dispute with Massachusetts and Jacksonian policy towards the Five Civilised Tribes and their dispute with the state of Georgia. 'If the good people of Massachusetts' he says, 'were as ready to do right as to have the Georgians do right' there would be no problem, but instead the Governor of the state has acted 'in humble imitation of that wise, learned and humane politician, Andrew Jackson, L.L.D.' (1835:95).

While a great deal of *Indian Nullification* is taken up with details of the Marshpee case, and rebuttals of particular charges made against Apes, there also emerges rather fitfully a critique of the prevailing political language in relation to Indians. Michael Rogin, in his provocative psychobiographical study of Jackson's relations with the Indians, points out that 'Americans uniformly employed familial language in speaking of Indians; most historians and political scientists have been systematically deaf to it' (1975:12). But Apes was far from deaf to it, and in the same scathing tone used for Jackson (quoted earlier) he also attacks the paternalistic pretences of the state. The Indians, he says, have to 'await the leisure of our father, the legislature', and 'our tender parent' seems to have no regard for 'his poor suffering babes in the woods' (Apes 1835:46). What later historians have identified as a characteristic Jacksonian approach is remorselessly taken apart in Apes' most powerful and sustained polemic, his *Eulogy on King Philip*. Given originally as lectures in 1836, and published the following year, this makes an interesting comparison with Occom's sermon to Moses Paul. Both men are Christian Indians, and both are aware of speaking to a white audience, but where Occom's criticism of whites is at best guarded, even disguised, as I have tried to argue, in Apes it is direct.

In choosing to praise King Philip, whose war against the white settlers in New England in the seventeenth century had ensured that he was seen as a murderous villain by their descendants, Apes is going on the offensive. His account of Philip is as a freedom-fighter, a man acting in defence of his people, with distinct contemporary relevance, and one of his ways of pointing up the relevance is his description of seventeenth-century events in the political rhetoric of his own day. In particular he returns to the attack on Indian Removal begun in *Indian Nullification*. He criticises a missionary who talks of clearing the ground for Christianity, and then solicits money to go and convert them,

> as if God could not convert them where they were; but must first drive them out. If God wants the red man converted, we should think he could do it as well in one place as in another. (Apes 1837:16)

This technique of invoking God to criticise those acting in his name is quite effective, as when he picks up Cotton Mather's reference to 'Philip of cursed memory'. He points out that Mather is claiming God's prerogative, and that 'if he wanted them cursed, he would have done it himself' (1837:14). Sometimes he slips into the Christians' own voice in giving their justifications of their actions, only then to reprove them in their own Christian terms. The Indians, he says ironically, for their 'kindness and resignation' towards the whites, 'were called savages, and made by God on purpose for them to destroy. We might say, God understood his work better than this.'

One of the crimes against the Indians which Apes stresses, and which allows him to connect up with contemporary reform feelings, is slavery. (It is interesting to note that Garrison's *Liberator* had weighed in on behalf of the Marshpees – McQuaid 1977:620-1.) Apes sees Philip's violence as a response to white violence and again uses Christianity as his club to beat the whites with: 'How they could go to work to enslave a free people, and call it religion, is beyond the power of my imagination, and outstrips the revelation of God's word' (1837:9).

As well as this religious language, though, he also returns very powerfully to the critique of paternalism, or the pretence of it by Jackson, in a parody of its language. First he gives a personal anecdote 'to amuse you a little', in which, having been invited by a Christian to dinner, he 'put my dinner behind the door; I thought this a queer compliment indeed'. This pretence of benevolence masking racism is then found elsewhere. Even the President, he says, thinks the Indians are not good enough to live with whites, and he moves into his voice:

> As if he had said to them... You see my red children, that our fathers carried on this scheme of getting your lands for our use, and we have now become rich and powerful; and we have a right to do with you just as we please; we claim to be your fathers. And we think we shall do you a great favor, my dear sons and daughters, to drive you out, to get you away, out of the reach of our civilised people who are cheating you.... So it is no use, you need not cry, you must go. (1837:46)

As well as an interesting anticipation of Michael Rogin's account of Jackson's language (1975:12) we could be said to have here a case of Indian rather than white ventriloquism, used to great polemic effect. I have tried to argue that Apes is most interesting for my purposes when, rather than claiming an 'authorised' Christian voice, he holds it up for inspection together with other available identities. In *Eulogy on King Philip* we have the full range of voices, since as well as the white Christian and political positions, Apes is also aligning himself with Philip, who achieved what he did as 'a son of Nature; with nature's talents alone', and to justify him 'is the aim of him who proudly tells you, the blood of a denominated savage runs in his veins' (1837:6). This solidarity continues to be asserted, so that after giving Philip's prophecy that whites would overrun the Indians, Apes, 'as a man of natural abilities', is led to pronounce him 'the greatest man that was ever in America; and so it will stand, until he is proved to the contrary, to the everlasting disgrace of the pilgrims' fathers'.

This is fighting talk, but it does not quite end the speech. Apes offers an olive branch of sorts by reading the Lord's Prayer in King Philip's language, and hoping for peace and righteousness for all, as 'the wish of a poor Indian', leaving us with that overdetermined phrase that has resounded through so much of this chapter.

Notes

1. A fascinating parallel to Foucault's ideas on confession can be found in Carlo Ginzburg's work on the Inquisition. He has recently made explicit the similarities between inquisitor and anthropologist and also questioned the pessimism of assuming the monologic nature of texts, and has invoked Bakhtin for support. See Ginzburg 1990:156–221.

CHAPTER FIVE

Autobiography and Authorship: Identity and Unity

In concentrating on the writings of Occom and Apes, two literate Christian Indians, I have so far been concerned with the relation of self-expression to literary, cultural and textual conventions, and the extent to which it is useful or possible to talk of finding a 'voice' or intention in such texts. These same issues, of self and its expression and/or creation in writing, now need to be examined in the broader context of Indian autobiography and Indian writing in general, and this will return us to the issues of orality and literacy broached in earlier chapters. I propose to look first at the range of texts covered by the term 'autobiography', and the critical problems raised, and this will lead to those texts which use, in different ways, autobiographical elements or techniques within fiction or poetry. The question of the unity of self and its relation to the text here reappears, not just as an interpretative issue (whether we can ascribe a voice or intention) but as a political and cultural one, in so far as it involves memory and Indian traditional values and forms of expression. A brief examination of the particular problems of using or adapting white literary forms to express or translate Indian traditional materials, an enterprise involving both white and Indian writers, should establish a basis for the discussion in later chapters of the usefulness of seeing many of the literary and ethnographic approaches to Indian materials in terms of a wider debate over modernism and postmodernism.

The concept of an individual life as an unfolding story which can be isolated, recalled and retold, made into a product for contemplation, is not one necessarily shared by other cultures, and in particular not by oral cultures. In dealing, then, with autobiographies apparently produced by members of Indian cultures we need to be aware that we are, in fact, dealing with *texts* produced by, and in, white literate America. The renewed critical emphasis on issues of textuality has involved an increased awareness that, as Paul Ricoeur has economically put it, 'with written discourse the author's intention and the meaning of the text cease to coincide' (1971:534). This sense of the 'othering' of the 'I', as it is uttered and 'outered' in a text, and the consequent problematic relation between this notion of text and the claims for certain sorts of authenticity contained within autobiography,[1] become particularly relevant with Indian autobiography, where the production of the text often operates to turn the speaking subject into an object, whether for study, entertainment or even the *frisson* of the exotic.

Autobiography has long had a special importance for underprivileged and under heard groups in America, partly because of its documentary and political potential for making public the conditions of many lives by its recounting of one typical life, partly because it seems to be the least elitist or specialised in form, but also because of the way the *writing* of an auto-biography can act out and confirm the development of an identity. Writing becomes thematised as the crucial means of *self*-expression.[2] But, of course, writing involves conventions which in varying degrees define the forms of expression, and even the self being expressed, and this is particularly relevant when one culture is expressing itself, or being expressed, in the literary and cultural forms – the texts – of another in a situation of political and cultural inequality. It would be a mistake, though, as David Brumble (1988) has so clearly demonstrated, to assume that white textual conventions are the only ones in operation. He has pointed to a whole range of Indian narrative conventions, such as coup tales, which different Indian autobiographers brought to the telling of their stories, which have been overlooked *as* conventions, out of ignorance of the context from which the particular life has been taken and textualised.

The Indian autobiographical material available ranges from memories recounted by an Indian in response to questions that have been translated transcribed, edited, rearranged and published with introduction and anthropological notes, to works written in English and published entirely under the control of their subject, but in developing an approach based on those texts which are most problematic in terms of intention, unity or authenticity I hope to be able to demonstrate its usefulness in dealing with more straightforwardly 'authored' works.

Indian autobiographies seem to present immediate problems of classifica-tion.[3] What are we to make of a work which announces itself as an autobiography 'by Clellon S. Ford', who is actually the editor? (Ford 1941). How are we to judge an autobiography like that of Crashing Thunder, in which the editor and translator seems to have supplemented or confused the subject's reminiscences with those of his brother? (Radin 1983). The convention being broken here is the normal expectation that, in an autobiography, the same person is the subject of the narrative and its narrator, even if not the physical transcriber of it. Langness and Frank attempt a clear distinction: 'To put it simply, autobiographies are reports by individuals about their own lives; what distinguishes them from biography is that the author and subject are one and the same person' (1981:89).

Within this convention, we are prepared for differences in outlook between the older narrator and the younger self – it is one of the peculiar pleasures of the form. Similarly, we are prepared for inaccuracies, even lies, since the guarantee of authenticity offered is not of historical accuracy or objectivity, but precisely of first-person subjectivity. Biography, in contrast, involves a second person, and Langness and Frank make this the central aspect of their definition:

> Compared to the solo voice of an autobiography, what we often hear in a biography is two voices singing different versions of the same melody. A biography is indeed a report by one person about the life of another, but the writer usually relies as much as possible on the subject's own expressive statements and deeds as the point of departure for interpretation. (1981:96)

Most Indian autobiographies, in fact, conform as much to this definition of biography as they do to the earlier one of autobiography, and the reason lies in the particular cultural situation in which they have been produced. Individuals in an oral culture have no context for the conception of autobiography which has been developed in literate cultures, and which depends on a set of interrelated common assumptions about the nature of self, its relation to history, its relationship of authorship to a text, and the concept of authenticity and authority which goes with this. The creation of an Indian autobiography has, therefore, required either the ability of a particular Indian to comply closely enough with the standards of written English and the conventions of literary marketing to be published or, much more commonly, the collaboration of several people – the subject, a white editor or anthropologist, and often another Indian acting as translator. The texts produced by this second set of conditions are inevitably multi-voiced, hybrid products in which we can hear in varying degrees the 'speaking' subject, but only through the ramifications and conventions of the written text. Editors and anthropologists have usually been at pains to play down their role, insisting on the authenticity of the original oral testimony, and their fidelity to its spirit, if not its letter, encouraging us to see the text as no more than a transparent medium through which to get at the original, and this claim can be seen as part of a larger strategy on the part of anthropologists to claim an objectivity by underplaying their own role in the creation of their findings. Later developments in anthropology (to be dealt with fully in Chapter 7) have increased the awareness of the dialogic and collaborative nature of all such research, and also the necessity for this fact to be acknowledged and built into the actual form of the final ethnographic text.[4] Only in this way, paradoxically, does the subject have a chance of not becoming totally object, since what we then become aware of is the interplay of two or more voices. If the white voice which is asking the questions and eliciting and guiding the story by means of them is suppressed in the final text, the effect is not, as often claimed, to allow the speaking subject to appear in his own right, but to give a false, because incomplete, account of the production of the text.

This is certainly the case with many celebrated Indian autobiographies, but rather than criticise them on grounds of historical or anthropological accuracy it is more productive, using the different perspectives of recent critical theory, to look at the whole range of such works as texts, rather than measuring them against some pre-existent reality. Arnold Krupat exemplifies this approach in his Foreword to the autobiography of Crashing Thunder in his insistence that 'it is of the nature of narrative always to be a textualization of the "facts" never the "facts" themselves' (Radin 1983:xiv). As a development of this, Krupat has suggested that the term 'Indian auto-biography' should apply specifically to those texts which exhibit 'bicultural composite composition' (1985:31). This entails seeing them not as a corrupted and inferior form, but as a new form which reflects precisely the cultural limitations and contradictions inherent in a situation where oral and literate cultures meet. Krupat distinguishes these texts from what he calls 'autobiographies-by-Indians', where the composition of the text has a single source, but it would be wrong, in distinguishing the two types, to assume that the second, apparently more pure form, is not equally implicated in cross-cultural complicities and contradictions. By establishing first in their clearest manifestations, the different voices in 'bicultural composite' texts, it should be possible to extend the analysis to single-source texts with the intention of showing the essential continuity of conflicting and collaborating voices, even when emanating from only one source.

Biographies of famous Indians have long been popular, but apart from a few accounts actually written in English by converted and civilised Indians, which follow the form of the providential narrative, like that of William Apes already discussed, and some fragments and memoirs, it is not until *The Life of Black Hawk* (1833) that we find an account which purports to be an Indian's own life history.[5] Given the absence of any context within Indian cultures for written autobiography,[6] any accounts we have must be seen as a response to a white initiative, whether at the personal level – being paid to answer questions – or at the cultural level, Indian realisation that a vehicle was not otherwise available for the publicising of certain views. Black Hawk's editor and interpreter both make introductory statements affirming that Black Hawk had expressed 'a great desire to have a history of his life written and published' (Jackson 1964:35), and that it was written to his dictation. In addition, Patterson, the editor, explicitly disclaims responsibility for the views exposed by Black Hawk, referring to himself only as 'amanuensis'. Here are many of the ingredients which are to recur in later autobiographies – the denial of any significant editorial role, the claim to be presenting the authentic Indian himself, but also, in the text itself, the unmistakable hand of editor or translator – producing something which conforms to the literary standards of the times. Black Hawk's introduction, for instance, is a letter to General Atkinson, his conqueror, and ends

May the Great Spirit shed light on your [gloomy hours] and that you may never experience the humility that the power of the American government has reduced me to, is the wish of him, who, in his native forests, was once as proud as yourself. (Jackson 1964:37)

This conventional flourish is Patterson's, even if the sentiments are Black Hawk's, and it has the effect of fitting Black Hawk into the mould of the defeated but noble redskin, which we have seen developed in the presentation of Indian speeches in Chapter 3. Forty-nine years later Patterson produced a different edition with new (and factually inaccurate) material; even after the first edition accusations of fraud had been made, but even if it were possible fully to establish Patterson's role this would not solve the problems which arise from the necessarily bicultural nature of this sort of text.

The widespread notoriety of some Indian leaders was based on, and helped to feed, the white fascination with inscrutable savagery, but mixed with this was always the alternative view of Indians as noble, heroic, even though inevitably doomed to destruction. The sensational reporting of Geronimo's desperate fight to maintain the independence of his small band of Apaches made him into a monster of cruelty, and not accidentally had the effect of exaggerating the heroism of his capture. When he published *Geronimo: His Own Story* in 1906, therefore, the editor, S.M. Barrett was at pains to put it in context (Barrett 1974). As prisoner-of-war (which he remained for almost twenty-three years), Geronimo agreed to tell Barrett his story, but only if he could tell it all, and in his own way. Official military objections to such panderings were finally overruled by the intervention of President Roosevelt himself, and Barrett reprints in the original edition the entire bureaucratic correspondence at great length, and apparently without any of the irony with which a modern reader has to see it. Barrett's apprehension about associating himself too closely with Geronimo's views results in a series of anxious footnotes dissociating himself from Geronimo's version of historical events and even, at one point, the insertion of a whole chapter to redress what he sees as the balance, listing Indian as well as white atrocities. These clearly labelled intrusions by Barrett would seem to imply that we have here Geronimo's own voice – sufficiently his own, at least, to make whites nervous. Certainly there are forceful and uncompromising sections, and there are times when it seems as if two views are struggling against each other to be heard, but both voices are speaking English, and it is Barrett's English. Can the following be Geronimo on religion, for instance? 'In our primitive worship only our relations to Usen and the members of our tribe were considered as appertaining to our religious responsibilities' (Barrett 1974:126).

In addition, the arrangement into chapters and topics, and the chronological order, is Barrett's. Geronimo's manner of storytelling was distinctive. According to Barrett, he would not talk when a stenographer was

present, nor wait for questions or corrections, and would only tell at any one
time what he wanted, but he would be prepared on a later occasion to

> listen to the reproduction (in Apache) of what he had been told, and at such
> times would answer all questions or add information wherever he could be
> convinced that it was necessary. He soon became so tired of book-making that
> he would have abandoned the task, but for the fact that he had agreed to tell
> the complete story. (1974:46)

The 'book-making', then, was a long way from his cultural expectations, and
the final product is, as John R. Leo puts it: 'an extraordinary mix; a text that
was never meant to be except by the 'writer' who is not its source' (1978:822).

While the titles of the chapters, and the division of the story into sections,
are clearly Barrett's doing, a textual convention, the book begins with several
chapters outlining the origins of the Apache through mythology and tribal
history, which has the effect of placing Geronimo's life firmly in a context that
is not that of his white reader. Similarly, it seems to be no part of Geronimo's
understanding of book-making, or even of narrative in general, to exercise
introspection.[7] He gives a record of events, and his main purpose seems to
have been to put the record straight rather than explore or even justify his
own character and feelings, which for him would not be separable from actions
and situations. In order to give even this version, though, he has had to go
against Apache practice, in that he talks of the dead. Geronimo is a
particularly striking example of the transformations forced upon Indians, and
the uses made of them, in the American popular imagination and media as
they moved from independent, alien and, therefore, profoundly threatening
figures during the nineteenth century to defeated, anachronistic survivors,
material for the exercise of suitable white emotions, whether the *frisson* of
horror or idealised nostalgia or pity. Indians became comprehended within
white linguistic and cultural categories – what Leo calls 'the encirclement of
signs' – and his article sets Geronimo's (or Barrett's) text usefully in this
context. He sees Geronimo as ultimately escaping this encirclement, as taking
on the system of values which imprisoned him, and using it for his own ends by
exploiting his notoriety in the rapidly growing media – selling original
photographs and riding in Roosevelt's inaugural parade, for instance. In this
way, *His Own Story* is Geronimo's way of subverting the system of values into
which he is being subsumed precisely by co-operating with it. It is, as Leo says,
'the story of Geronimo's refusal to be enclosed' (Leo 1978:834).

It is important, then, to place the upsurge of interest in Indian material
generally, both at popular and scholarly anthropological levels, in relation to
the actual decline in autonomy and independence of Western Indians.[8] As
they became subject peoples, they became, ironically, objects of white
attention, comprehended in all senses, and it is against the powerful popular

myth of the Vanishing Americans that these texts need to be seen. In them we have the close partnership of white and Indian, so often presented in American literature and popular culture, but contrary to the stereotype 'the white man is silent, while the Indian, no longer a mute or monosyllabic figure, speaks for himself' (Krupat 1985:47). Or seems to, because the text is not the voice, even if the white producers of the text are reluctant to admit it.

John Neihardt's decision to call his celebrated text *Black Elk Speaks*, illustrates this to perfection (Neihardt 1972). His intention is solely to provide a medium through which Black Elk can speak, and to this end he creates a style which successfully incorporates what we have come to expect a dignified old Indian to sound like, were he to write in English. This is a considerable step forward in literary skill from Barrett, but it need not have any connection with authenticity. As with Geronimo, we have a composite authorship, but whereas Barrett intrudes, and is at pains to dissociate himself from Geronimo, Neihardt puts himself and all his skills in the medium at the disposal of what Black Elk says – or what he would have said. Recent scholars have shown that some of the most celebrated and quoted passages are Neihardt's,[9] and, in fact, his own account of the creation of the text makes the composite authorship clear. Black Elk's words were translated by his son, taken down as stenographic notes by Neihardt's daughter, and then reworked and rearranged by Neihardt later. He referred to it later as 'a work of art with two collaborators, the chief one being Black Elk' (quoted in McCluskey 1972:238). He also later changed the title page from 'as told to' to 'as told through', which reflected more clearly what he saw as his achievement in recreating 'the mood and manner of the old man's narrative' (Neihardt 1972:xii), and so successful has he been, either in doing this or in conforming to and even helping to define our cultural expectations that the book has become a recognised classic and bestseller.

Black Elk, as a Lakota Sioux in the second half of the nineteenth century, lived through the destruction of his tribe's economic and political independence, and he gives vivid accounts of the battle at Little Big Horn, the rise of the Ghost Dance and the massacre at Wounded Knee, but he was also from an early age subject to visions, which marked him out within the tribe as possessing special spiritual powers. The book thus blends the historical and the spiritual to present a moving account of a world-view in which all aspects of existence are integrated into a whole, but which seems ultimately powerless to present the remorseless disintegrating forces of white civilisation. This gives Black Elk's account an epic sweep and grandeur untypical of autobiographies, in that the individual becomes almost incidental, even though fully realised and human, but as Paul A. Olson has shown, Neihardt, already working on an epic of the West, was particularly attuned to this:

He could communicate Black Elk's vision to others because he was himself a

writer for whom the juxtaposition of allegory and historical example which
teaches of religious forces and historic actions, was a possible mode. (Olson
1982:5)

Whether we are responding here to a Sioux vision and transcending our own
cultural limitations, or just responding to a predefined cultural category
which we recognise as 'primitive', is perhaps impossible to decide, but
knowledge of the marked shifts in popularity of different versions of
Indianness should encourage a distinct scepticism about our ability to
recognise or respond to something presented as transcending our own
cultural limits. The popularity of *Black Elk Speaks* in the 1960s has, therefore,
to be seen in the context of what the Indian came to represent in the period.
First published in 1932 and largely ignored, the book only became popular
after its paperback reissue in 1961, when the growing counter-cultural
predilection for the irrational, supernatural and primitive led to an increasing
interest in, and idealisation of, Indian culture. *Black Elk Speaks* seemed to
offer ecological awareness, mind-expanding visions and an indictment of
white American civilisation, and its success encouraged publication of many
other works of variable quality that presented Indians in this light.[10]

Black Elk subsequently worked with Joseph Epes Brown, and the
collaboration resulted in *The Sacred Pipe* (1953) an invaluable and detailed
account of Lakota religion, but it is important to remember that the Black Elk
known to us from these books is very different from the Nick Black Elk who,
as a mainstay of the local Catholic church, was remembered as someone who
'never talked about the old ways. All he talked about was the Bible and Christ'
(quoted in Kehoe 1989:66). But rather than seeing Neihardt as creating an
idealised image, it is just as plausible to see Black Elk himself as using the
creation of a book to enact a new self-creation, a revitalised, born-again
traditionalist. Even this last word is wrong, though, according to Alice Beck
Kehoe, for whom 'Black Elk's genius lay in organising Lakota religion
according to a Christian framework, emphasising characteristics amenable to
expression in symbols reminiscent of Christian symbols, yet keeping a Lakota
essence' (Kehoe 1989:69).

Kehoe is concerned to place Black Elk in a context of revitalisation
movements, which provides a useful contrast to the nostalgia of Neihardt as
well as an antidote to any tendency to see Black Elk as a pawn, an object of
someone else's textual production.

Neihardt's intention was to show the universality of Black Elk's message, to
demonstrate what Indians and whites had in common, and this has been a
common aim in literary treatments of Indians, but the development of
modern anthropological interest in Indian life histories was initially fuelled by
very different motives. Franz Boas' influential work in America had
transformed the anthropological method from a generalising and comparative
exercise to the collection of all sorts of material from one culture, with the

intention of showing its specific meaning within that culture, and life histories came to be seen as an ideal way of recording the minutiae of life from a native perspective. What was required was not the exceptional individual or the transcendent, supra-cultural experience, but the average and ordinary. Paul Radin's introduction of his subject as a 'representative, middle-aged individual of moderate ability' (Radin 1913:207) is typical of that of many other anthropologists, as is his claim in a later work to have a minimal role: 'everything in this manuscript comes directly from him and was told in the original and in the first person. It is needless for me to insist that I in no way influenced him' (Radin 1983:17). Radin's concern was for scientific objectivity, which led him to misrepresent or underestimate his actual editorial and translating role. From his first scholarly publication of 'Personal Reminiscences of a Winnebago Indian' (1913) complete with parallel Winnebago text, through to *Crashing Thunder*, published for a more popular readership in 1926, Radin had continually recorded and reworked several sets of material. Krupat in his Foreword to the last and fullest version demonstrates clearly the way Radin polished his translations, and apparently even combined materials from different life stories, but also cautions against discounting these texts as therefore more literary than scientific, since this would be to perpetuate that false distinction between the literary and scientific, whereby science escapes from the problems of textuality and language. Ethnographies, he insists, 'like histories and as well as fictional narratives, are texts and...no text can innocently represent the "order of things" independently of the order of language' (Radin 1983:xiii).

Radin's pioneering work with the Winnebago was characterised by a profound concern to capture what is distinctive about that culture and its members but, inevitably, he needs to express this distinctiveness in ways understandable within our conventions, since the alternative may simply be incomprehensibility. He talks interestingly about our expectations of autobiography in his preface to *Crashing Thunder*. Our conventions, he asserts:

> effectively bar any true revelation. No man who regards his thoughts,
> feelings and actions of sufficient importance for him to note them down in a
> diary or autobiography, ever admits to himself or to the world for whom he
> is writing, that his life has not been a unified whole or that it did not gradually
> lead to a proper and early heralded climax (1983:xxvi)

By contrast, Crashing Thunder's account lacks any retrospective unity, not subjugating the earlier point of view to the later, and this is particularly interesting because this particular narrative records a conversion experience. After several inconclusive attempts to have a vision as prescribed by traditional Winnebago religious practice, Crashing Thunder eventually experiences this by means of peyote, and becomes an adherent of the Native

American Church. The account's lack of retrospective patterning is, therefore, in very marked contrast to the convention of American providential autobiographies:

> When he describes his childhood he is a child, his youth a youth, the Medicine Dance a member of that fraternity, and finally, when he describes the new religion, it is as a staunch adherent. Everything in its proper place and time. (Radin 1983: xxxiv)

Radin is here praising precisely that lack of reflexiveness and self-awareness which would be seen as a deficiency in a conventional white autobiography, and in his introduction to a Navajo autobiography, *Son of Old Man Hat* in 1938, it is interesting to find Edward Sapir making similar claims:

> It is in no sense the study of a personality. It is a sequence of memories that need an extraordinarily well-defined personality to hold them together, yet nowhere is this unique contribution obtruded upon us. We are in constant rapport with an intelligence in which all experiences...are held like waving reeds in the sensitive transparency of a brook. Such concepts as 'ego' or 'frustration' seem heated and out of place when we try to feel with this intelligence. (Dyk 1938:viii)

If one impulse of anthropology is to demonstrate the self-sufficient differentness and viability of other ways of being and experiencing the world, a complementary one is, of course, to insist on the shared human characteristics which allow us to understand and respond to members of other cultures as full human beings; one regular feature of these anthropological autobiographies is the stress in prefaces and introductions on the personal bonds of friendship between editor and subject. Nancy Lurie, following in Radin's footsteps, elicited the life story of Mountain Wolf Woman, who was, in fact, Crashing Thunder's sister, and her introduction gives a warm and intimate picture of the old lady and her stay in Lurie's household.[11] Lurie's text is a typical multi-layered sandwich, where we are given a foreword, a preface, the text with extensive footnotes, then the first brief version of her life given by Mountain Wolf Woman, which she extended when she saw Lurie's disappointment – indicating the role of white expectations in the creation of such texts. After all this, there is commentary on both texts by Lurie. At several points Lurie refers to 'literary' and 'scholarly' criteria which decided the style of the English version. Unfortunately she never develops what she means by these terms, and when we look at all the layers of the 'sandwich', questions of authenticity become even more confusing. What role, for instance, does a letter from Mountain Wolf Woman, written in non-standard English, and reprinted in Lurie's introduction, play in the combination of voices? It has a very different sort of claim to authenticity from that of the rest of the text, which was spoken in Winnebago but is given to us in an English which is not like that of the letter. We are offered either her poor written English – which leaves us at a distance from her 'real' voice, though it is her own actual product – or a translation of her speaking Winnebago which uses all the (white) literary and scholarly resources available to recreate a sense of her real presence and speech, in all its resonances.

The same sandwich effect is often found even when the subject speaks good English, as is the case with the Hopi Indian, Don Talayesva. The editor, Leo Simmons, gives full information on his condensing and reorganising activities:

> The account is, therefore, a highly condensed record in the first person, and almost always in Don's own words or in words which he readily recognised in the manuscript. The report is not free narrative, but selected and condensed narration, interwoven with additional information obtained by repeated interviewing. It is greatly abbreviated and often re-organised. (Simmons 1942:7)

He also appends several chapters discussing the creation and analysis of this life history and a discussion of life histories in general, so that we have the opportunity to judge him and his approach, as well as Don Talayesva, and this is relevant to a notoriously sensitive issue raised in the book, the reluctance of Hopi and other Indians to reveal details of ceremonials to outsiders. The way anthropologists deal with this reluctance has thrown into sharp relief their assumptions about whether the Indians are subjects in their own right – and can make their own choices – or are objects of study, and can be coaxed, bullied, and deceived in the name of science. The latter has too often been the case,[12] and Simmons' account of overcoming Don's reluctance is notably devoid of any introspection on his part about the propriety of his actions. This absence of the personality of the editor, an anthropological convention designed to affirm scientific objectivity, is clearly revealed in all its limitations in Simmons' prose. He affects a passive style ('increasing interest was shown in Don's personal experience .... It was emphasised that .... It was explained in great detail that...' (1942:7), and his introductory statements take for granted the breathtaking and, in a colonialist situation, dangerous proposition that we are more objective in dealing with what is alien than what is familiar: 'The subject was selected from an alien society, and within a culture, greatly contrasted with our own, in order to insure objectivity and to emphasise the molding impact of culture upon personality' (1942:1).

In contrast with this desiccated style, but as a result of the initiatives by Simmons which it partly conceals, a vivid picture of Don Talayesva and his life emerges from his account. As Brumble points out, Simmons forces him towards an introspection and an interest in his own childhood which is foreign to him, with the ironical result that 'the harder Simmons worked to win from Talayesva material that was personal, material that would show how this individual really felt, the farther he moved his subject from being a typical Hopi' (1988:109).

Particularly clearly registered in the account are the conflicts and changes in one of the most traditional cultures caused by the intrusion of whites, of which this book itself is, of course, an instance. Talayesva's matter-of-fact narration of his dreams reveals both the fascination and the fears generated by his new white contacts. He dreams, for instance, of being arrested for 'writing false reports to Washington', but defends himself so well that he is sent back to school, at the age of 50, to become a judge. In the back room of the school a white woman helps him take a bath, with erotic embraces thrown in. Another dream provides a perfect image of the constrictions and threat represented by Christianity. At the instigation of missionaries, the Chief had been arrested for performing his ceremonial duties. Don discovers him 'imprisoned in a large box with his head sticking out a hole, and a man was standing over it with a big sharp knife, ready to chop it off' (Simmons 1942:378). Don rescues the chief by arguing the Hopi right to practise their own religion, thus acting the role of mediator in the dream which he took on in his life, and in the creation of his autobiography.

The process of culture change is also a major, but not so problematic, issue in *Guests Never Leave Hungry: the Autobiography of James Sewid a Kwakiutl Indian* (Spradley 1969). Once again, Sewid's own account is framed by ethnographic sketches, including a psychological test, and we are told that he was chosen as 'a non-Western individual who had successfully adapted to culture conflicts' (Spradley 1969:3). Certainly Sewid seems to exemplify successful bicultural adaptation – he is a highly successful and prosperous member of his community, who has gained his success by adapting to change. Kwakiutl society, though, has always institutionalised wealth and its public display, and has often been contrasted with other Indian cultures in its stress on rank, and what has been seen as an aggressive individualism, so that James Sewid does not perhaps have the same social or psychological barriers to overcome as Don Talayesva. There is, in fact, a touch of Ben Franklin (without the irony?) in the way Sewid reasons his way towards what will simultaneously be profitable for him and good for the society, and in the apparent absence of much self-doubt. He has an ability to move confidently from Indian to white, even signalling it for us: 'I'm speaking as an Indian now', he comments, when talking about child-rearing. A perfect instance is his action in persuading the whole community to adapt the traditional potlatch ceremony to his own ends. Potlatching, a ceremony and feast at which the ceremonial properties of high-ranking families were displayed, and wealth in various forms was ostentatiously given away and even destroyed as a means of gaining prestige, had earlier been banned by the white authorities, as offending against the Christian virtues of thrift and prudence, and had fallen into disuse. Sewid decided to reintroduce it, but as a way of raising money for the local hospital:

It just came to me that it would be a good idea to bring the potlatch custom
and the dancing out to the surface again and let the public see it because it had
been outlawed and lost. I had the idea that we wouldn't go and do it the way
they used to do it when they gave people articles to come and watch the
dancing. The way I figured it was going to be the other way around, like the
theaters, operas or a good stage program which was put on and the people had
to pay money to get in. (Spradley 1969:158–9)

Like Geronimo selling his photographs, Black Elk performing in Wild
West shows, or modern Indians catering for tourists, Sewid's response to
white culture is an ambiguous one, walking the line between being taken over
and taking over, and the autobiographies discussed have reflected this, often
not so much in the substance of the narratives as in their bicultural hybrid
form, where the different registers of language sometimes combine and
sometimes struggle for dominance. Even in the case of books clearly authored
by one person in the more conventional way this issue of conflicting language
does not disappear, as I have shown earlier with William Apes, since the two
cultures are then incorporated and may remain unreconciled, within the single
author and his text. Charles Eastman, who became a distinguished Indian
spokesman and public figure earlier in this century, was sufficiently 'civilised'
to write his own autobiography, and the two volumes, published in 1902 and
1916, provide an account of what we might call acculturation, but what
Eastman, in the terms available to him at the time, sees as the development
from savagery to civilisation.[13]

The big point of transition is the event with which the first book, *Indian
Boyhood* (1902) ends. Brought up as a traditional Sioux, believing that his
father had been killed by whites and fully expecting to avenge that death, the
young Ohiyesa, as he then was, is suddenly confronted with a man dressed in
white clothes who announces himself as his father. He had not been killed, but
has been converted to Christianity, and is determined that his son should
grow up in white ways. Eastman describes this in terms of death and rebirth: 'I
felt as if I were dead and travelling to the Spirit Land: for now all my old ideas
were to give place to new ones' (Eastman 1971:246). He says little more at this
point about what must have been a traumatic shock, and this is consistent
with the style and purpose of this first book, which is really an idyll, a picture
of Indian life seen through the experiences of a child, with unpleasant realities,
whether of tribal life or of increasing white encroachment, screened out.
Instead, to supplement the reminiscences, we are given myths and coup
stories, the whole account written in the conventional language used by
whites (and civilised Indians, apparently) to describe such things: 'As he
approached them in his almost irresistible speed, every savage heart thumped
louder in the Indian's dusky bosom' (1971:36).

From The Deep Woods to Civilisation, published fourteen years later in
1916, begins where the first volume ends, retelling the events of the pivotal

day when he regains a father, but a 'white' one, but we are immediately aware
of the tensions and contradictions which characterise that moment, and much
of the rest of Eastman's life: 'I could not doubt my new father, so mysteriously
come back to us, as it were, from the spirit land: yet there was a voice within
saying to me, "A false life! A treacherous life!" ' (Eastman 1977:7).

Eastman goes on to succeed in the white world, with a medical degree from
Boston and eminence as a government administrator, but he also becomes an
Indian spokesman, increasingly critical of white policies, and these conflicting
loyalties run through his book at all levels. At one level we are given a success
story, presented as a parallel movement from innocence to experience, and
from savagery to civilisation. We are told with pride of the eminent people he
has met, and his successes in white society in a manner reminiscent of Booker
T. Washington. We even see him collecting 'rare curios and ethnological
specimens for one of the most important collections in the country' by using
his knowledge of Indian customs to swindle their present owners out of them,
a method he complacently refers to as 'one of indirection' (1977:166).
Eastman seems here to play the exploitative white with no awareness of the
irony of his position, but elsewhere in the book, and running counter to the
primitive/civilised movement, is a growing realisation that white society does
not embody those values of Christianity for which he has been made to
renounce his past:

> When I let go of my simple instinctive native religion I hoped to gain
> something far loftier.... Alas! It is also more confusing.... When I reduce
> civilisation to its lowest terms it becomes a system of life based upon trade.
> (1977:194)

The contradictions are too pressing to be ignored, since they affect his entire
sense of himself, and his tortuous final paragraph only reflects, rather than
solves, them:

> I am an Indian: and while I have learned much from civilisation, for which I
> am grateful, I have never lost my Indian sense of right and justice. I am for
> development and progress along social and spiritual lines, rather than those of
> commerce, nationalism, or material efficiency. Nevertheless, so long as I live, I
> am an American. (1977:195)

It is as if here words and names have become like counters, so that he can
only vacillate from one spurious 'identity' to another, rather than think with
the terms available, and this is directly related to Eastman's and his educated
Indian contemporaries' problems at that historical point, in finding a means
of self-definition.[14] Eastman has taken over a terminology, revolving around
the opposition savage–civilised, which is just not usable to describe what has
happened to him, with the result that he can only simplify a complex process

into a series of crude oppositions. As a result, in the genteel English which he uses, Indians inevitably are presented as 'other'. Very occasionally the ironic possibilities are exploited, as in the description of college life, where 'I had most of my savage gentleness and native refinement knocked out of me', but more usually he follows the conventions, describing even his own feelings in atavistic terms: 'the sweet roving instinct of the wild took forcible hold upon me once more' (1977:174–5). The description of his return to the woods which follows is almost a set-piece, which moves from the past into the present tense, partly for immediacy but also suggesting a timeless present, outside history, thus conforming to the stereotyped oppositions into which Indians were forced.

The perfect place outside history, the idyll of childhood, is destroyed for Eastman, of course, in his books, by his father, the figure who might be expected to represent continuity with the past, in a sort of ironic reversal of Mr Compson in *The Sound and the Fury* who gives his son Quentin his watch, the symbol of family transmission and continuity, describing it as 'the mausoleum of all hope and desire'. Eastman's biographer describes him as retreating to his cabin in Canada in later life, and he brings out the impasse to which Eastman's Romantic and idealistic hopes of combining the best qualities of both races had brought him, as events and intellectual frameworks in which to see the relation of the races moved relentlessly on.

> He could no longer live the expectations of others in the white world; he could no longer return to the deep woods. He lived instead alone and on an island, his most symbolic act. (Wilson 1983:193)

This is the equivalent of the linguistic impasse over identity I described earlier as occurring at the end of *From the Deep Woods*, and the relation between writing and identity can be pursued further. To do this we need to look at the role of Eastman's wife, a powerful and determined woman who saw herself as friend and 'sister to the Sioux' but whose friendship, in accordance with the philanthropic views of the time, entailed an acceptance, even a hastening, of their disappearance in their traditional form. Elaine Goodale Eastman played an important role in editing and preparing Eastman's writings for publication, so it may well be that even here we have something approaching one of Krupat's 'bicultural composites'. In any case, according to Wilson, 'After the estrangement, Eastman was unable to publish any of his manuscripts because he had relied too heavily on his wife's editorial revisions, which he nevertheless despised' (1983:191).

It is tempting to see this situation as paradigmatic of a certain historical stage in Indian writing, in which the enabling means of expression, and of the creation of a self, are also deeply implicated in the destruction of any self rooted in a traditional past. Eastman was able to write about an Indian past only once it had been placed under erasure by situating it within a Romantic framework (even if he resisted his own erasure by complete assimilation, apparently to his wife's disappointment). For later writers this remains a key issue. How can the forms of white writing, not just autobiography but novels, poems and plays, be used to express and create Indian subjects (in all senses), and what role does the past play in this use? The way Eastman uses his father – to represent a rupture rather than a continuity but a rupture which is the creation of his new self, a scene repeated as the end of one book and the beginning of the next – can be used to point to a cluster of related concerns in American Indian writing, focusing on kinship, unity and the memory of the past. These concerns also involve formal and stylistic considerations, of course, which overlap with those of white writers wanting to translate or represent Indian traditional forms, and for whom modernist and post-modernist literary developments have been relevant. By seeing Indian writers in this context, and that of writing by other minorities, I hope to show not only its fundamentally conservative nature but also the problems of using that word cross-culturally.

The move from writers who are aware of themselves *as* writers, rather than as representative Indians, is not necessarily a move away from autobiography, and especially not for Indian writers, in whom a concern with memory and the past operates as a constitutive element in both writing and personal/cultural survival and growth. The most influential proponent of this approach has been N. Scott Momaday. Rather than accepting a concept of individual identity as a separating and enclosing of what is unique in a person, Momaday recreates out of his own memory and the Kiowa oral traditions which constitute a larger tribal history, a fuller sense of who he is. An Indian, he says, 'is an idea which a given man has of himself . . . And that idea, in order to be realised completely, has to be expressed' (1975:97).

Momaday's *The Way to Rainy Mountain* (1969) uses three strands of narrative – what the author calls 'the mythical, the historical and the immediate' – so that the retelling of the Kiowa tales of migration on to the great Plains is intertwined with personal reminiscences and commentary. A new awareness of place itself, of where he is now situated as well as of the past, is crucial to Momaday's new imagining of himself, and he sees this as equally true of others: 'We Americans need now more than ever before – and indeed more than we know – to imagine who and what we are with respect to the earth and sky' (Momaday 1975:101). The act of imagining is not, for Momaday, a way of escaping reality but of constituting it, and our own position in it, in a fullness we have been prevented from seeing because of reductive categories of self. In *The Names*, six years later, although the immediate focus is much more on family history he uses the same combination of tribal and personal memories, often by imagining himself into the position of an ancestor. History as sequence is not *denied* by this method, rather it is only by recognising sequence that any item in it is understood:

The first word gives origin to the second, the first and second to the third... and so on. You cannot begin with the second word and tell the story, for the telling of the story is a cumulative process, a chain of becoming, at last of being. (Momaday 1976:154)

Amongst the many family photographs in the book is one of Momaday's mother (whose actual Indian blood was fairly minimal) in Indian dress, and his account of her decision to see herself as Indian rather than as Southern belle emphasises the choice of self-creation by self-imagining:

That dim native heritage became a fascination for her, inasmuch, perhaps, as it enabled her to assume an attitude of defiance, an attitude which she assumed with particular style and satisfaction; it became her. She imagined who she was. This act of the imagination was, I believe, among the most important events of my mother's early life, as later the same essential act was to be the most important of my own. (1976:48)

It is important to stress the role of imagination here. Momaday is well aware of the fact that such choices of 'Indianness' move the issue of authenticity right away from blood and genealogy. The photograph of his mother shows a striking woman got up in the style of a Hollywood Indian maiden. The irony would seem to be then, that one imagines who one is, but only within the terms made available by the cultural situation and surroundings. There is no racial essence, or unified traditional sensibility which can be regained intact, and it is important to stress this awareness in Momaday, if only to counter some of his remarks about racial memory which suggest otherwise.[15] When Momaday says that 'an idea of one's ancestry and posterity is really an idea of the self' (1976:97), we should perhaps stress the word 'idea' as much as any of the others.

The question of whether Indian identity is measured by blood, expressed through kinship and genealogy, or through culture and place, remains a complex problem in Indian writing, reflecting the complexity of arguments over Indians' actual legal and cultural status in America, but in either case it is the problematic relation to the past and the role of that past in memory, personal or tribal, and in self-definition which continues as a major theme. One of Momaday's most important innovations was to take seriously the implications of the oral tradition for the form of a work based on it, and for the role of the storyteller, who becomes not anonymous but both a creative individual and part of a larger whole which precedes him. As David Brumble puts it, 'No Indian autobiographer before Momaday, I think, tried to imagine the literate equivalent of preliterate autobiography' (1988:178). Many of the same uses of continuity, community and kinship found in the works of Momaday discussed so far can also be found in Leslie Silko's *Storyteller* (Silko 1981), which also uses narratives and memories of the past and photographs to reconstitute and celebrate a cultural continuity. In many of the poems which make up its varied texts the 'I' blends in and out of characters, historical and mythical, from the past, so that the very *act* of storytelling becomes a demonstration and celebration of continuity and unity.

Nevertheless, the rupture to that continuity represented in Eastman's books by his father is a much more pervasive theme, even when only implicit, than the celebration of continuity, and it is surprising how often it is actually symbolised in Indian writing by an absent or failed father.[16] Sixty years after Eastman's book Gerald Vizenor, in an autobiographical essay, talks of coming to terms with *his* father. He was murdered when Vizenor was a child, and Vizenor as an adult investigates the case, to be told that his father was probably an alcoholic vagrant. 'Maybe your father was a wino then', he is told by the policeman, as a reason why the case was never followed up very thoroughly. 'Look kid, that was a long time ago, take it on the chin, you know what I mean?' (Vizenor 1976:82).

What, though, metaphorically, would constitute 'taking it on the chin'? Accepting the rupture and absence of guidelines from the past, and consequent alienation from a cultural heritage, which has certainly been Vizenor's way, or reconstructing some link by leaping over the generation that has compromised the continuity? This second option finds the most widespread literary expression, though in very varied forms. As Ray Young Bear puts it

You know we'd like to be there
standing beside our grandfathers
being ourselves
without the frailty
and insignificance of the worlds
we suffer and balance
on top of now. (Young Bear 1980:118)

To lose connections with this world is to lose identity, and the connections are ensured by kinship and community. As a character in Darcy McNickle's *Wind From an Enemy Sky* experiences it,

To be one among his people, to grow up in their respect, to be his
grandfather's kinsman – this was a power in itself, the power that flows
between people and makes them one. He could feel it now, a healing warmth
that flowed into his center from many-reaching body parts. (McNickle
1978:106)

These images of unity and centre can be developed, together with the view expressed by another character in the same novel that 'A man by himself was nothing but a shout in the wind' (1978:197), by looking briefly at a couple of works by James Welch and Leslie Silko, and then extending their characteristic approaches into a more general argument about Indian writing in relation to literary modernism.

Whereas McNickle's novels still have a sense of a tribal community of the recent past, which is breaking up, James Welch's first two novels deal with alienated young men living in contemporary America, whose attenuated sense of being Indian is expressed in terms of family relationships and their failure, rather than in more general racial and cultural terms.

Winter In the Blood (Welch 1974) begins with the return of the young (unnamed) protagonist to his home, and we are made immediately aware of the absence of the father. 'Coming home was not easy anymore.... Coming home to a mother and an old lady who was my grandmother. And the girl who was thought to be my wife.... None of them counted; not one meant anything to me' (1974:2). In a characteristic dual narrative movement, the plot moves forward, but only to disclose some information about the past, and at the same time we are gradually made party to the central figure's memories of the death of his father and brother. Guilt over the accidental death of his brother keeps him a 'servant to the memory of death', and his father remains an enigmatic figure: 'He never really stayed and he never left altogether. He was always in transit' (1974:21).

Increasingly, as the novel progresses, the key figure becomes Yellow Calf, an old man, blind and living alone who is, the central figure gradually realises, his grandfather. The recognition of this fact is crucial, because of the links it establishes with the past – links broken by the intervening generation. Yellow Calf represents an earlier world with its values rooted in the mythic and non-rational world. His whole way of life initially produces scepticism in his grandson, who suggests he is so old and silent he is more like a ghost: 'There's something wrong with you. No man should live alone.' To which the old man responds: 'Who's alone? The deer come...I can hear them. When they whistle I whistle back' (1974:66). This traditional image of spiritual harmony is reinforced by the description of the old man's remoteness from ordinary life.

> It was his eyes, narrow beneath the loose skin of his lids, deep behind his cheekbones, that made one realise the old man's distance was permanent. It was behind these misty white eyes that gave off no light that he lived, a world as clean as the rustling willows, the bark of a fox or the odor of musk during mating season. (1974:151)

The young central figure has earlier talked of his own 'distance' but it is a distance from himself, an inability to cope with and develop any full sense of identity. 'I was as distant from myself as a hawk from the moon' (p. 2). After a debauch in town, he feels only self-disgust: 'I wanted to lose myself, to ditch these clothes, to outrun this burning sun, to stand beneath the clouds and have my shadow erased, myself along with it' (p. 125). When he eventually patches together the story of Yellow Calf's secret liaison with his grandmother, making Yellow Calf his grandfather, he shares a piece of a common past in their shared laughter. 'And so we shared this secret in the presence of ghosts, in wind that called forth the muttering tepees, the blowing snow, the white air of the horses' nostrils' (p. 159).

The realisation does not constitute any truly redemptive knowledge. The novel does not end with any answers for the central figure or contemporary Indians in general, only the persistent need to reconstitute the links with a cultural and racial past in family terms. In this novel the problematic generation of the father is represented not only by the dead father, but by a step-father, Lame Bull, who amiably represents a concern for the present and for a prosperous life as a farmer. His response to the grandmother's death is characteristic: 'Oh, I know how it is – you're young, you take things seriously, you get older, you buy a bottle of good wine, you drink to those who are still living' (p. 135). At the funeral the young central figure, wearing his father's suit and tie, feels seedy next to Lame Bull, who is smartly dressed. The past cannot compete with the present, it seems, but as Lame Bull delivers a comically inept funeral oration it is the younger man who has saved his grandmother's tobacco pouch and, at the end of the novel, he throws it into the grave.

Winter in the Blood is, of course, more complex than this schema suggests, and there are other persistent themes and strands of imagery which develop this family situation, such as the anti-female impulses developed in the role of cows, which are seen as responsible for several disasters because of their stupidity – though this male orientation may also be related to the whole American Western novel tradition. *The Death of Jim Loney* (Welch 1980) published six years later, could be said to develop as much in the direction of a novel about individuals in small Western towns as in any Indian direction. It focuses even more relentlessly on an alienated young man and a problematic father. Jim Loney's inability to come to terms with his identity, and the isolation and anguish he suffers, is directly related to the breakdown of any family continuity. He has not known his mother, he was separated from his sister when they were both young, and his father fails to acknowledge him. With such a breakdown of continuity, it does not really matter whether his cultural heritage is Indian or white – it simply does not exist. 'He had no family and he wasn't Indian or white. He remembered the day he and Rhea had driven out to the Little Rockies. She had said he was lucky to have two sets of ancestors. In truth, he had none' (1980:102). Loney, not considering himself Indian, is always surprised to be considered one by other people:

He never felt Indian.... When Loney thought of Indians he thought of the reservation families all living under one roof, the old ones passing down the wisdom of their years, of their tribe's years, and the young ones soaking up their history, their places in their history, with a wisdom that went beyond age. (1980:102)

Significantly, Loney's wistful and idealised picture of Indian life centres on the transmission of culture by the family, not the substance of it, which is blanketed over in the term 'wisdom'.

The novel nowhere offers the sort of hope of re-establishing the continuity with a period or unified past hinted at in *Winter in the Blood*. There are no older figures to be located behind the father, and the father offers the son nothing that can help him. When, on the run from the police, he goes to his father for help, his father fails him:

> He had felt when he entered the trailer that there had to be an explanation to their existence and his father had given him nothing. In a way, Loney thought, this old man is innocent. He knows nothing, he cares nothing, and that makes him innocent. And Loney knew who the guilty party was. It was he who was guilty, and in a way that made his father's past sins seem childish, as though original sin were something akin to stealing candy bars. (1980:146)

The reversal of roles here is striking. The father has become the innocent, the child, and Loney has taken upon himself the burden of his own guilt and that of his father, and that burden is crushing. Not only are the sins of the fathers visited upon the children, but the guilt as well. There is no figure of forgiveness in this scenario, or figure of love from the past. All Loney gets from his father is a gun and money, and in a hopeless flight from the police, Loney half-deliberately gets himself killed.

If this novel's connection with the Indian past is deliberately vestigial, Welch's most recent novel, *Fools Crow* (1986), is a full-blooded (in all senses) account of traditional Blackfoot life in the nineteenth century being remorselessly destroyed by white encroachment. This raises different questions, in that as an historical novel it has to cope with all the usual problems of representing a very different culture and language. By not locating himself within the text in any privileged position as a Blackfoot Indian, Welch rather characteristically avoids any claims to authenticity, other than that of an imaginative and historically informed novelist, and the result is, in my view, a novel trying, not always successfully, to cope with all the problems of exoticism, romantic language, and idealised or simplified characters that the tradition entails. What is the effect, for instance, of translating Indian names? They surely did not have the same reverberations as they do now for us, so that we are constantly made uneasy by them. A deliberately alienating effect, or a failure of translation?

A different approach is taken in Leslie M. Silko's *Ceremony* (1977), which is an attempt at using traditional materials, formally as well as thematically. The basic narrative is interspersed with fragments of myth in the form of short poems, and the book begins with the suggestion that the whole modern narrative is clearly circumscribed by the traditional figures of myth:

Thought-woman, the spider
named things and
as she named them
they appeared

She is sitting in her room
thinking of a story now

I'm telling you the story
she is thinking. (Silko 1977:1)

In support of this idea, at the end of the novel Old Grandma professes to find
nothing new in the events around Laguna which have formed the narratives:
'It seems like I already heard these stories before ... only thing is, the names
sound different' (1977:273). Inside this timeless aspect, though, where the
more it changes the more it stays the same, the contemporary events of the
novel are mostly realistically presented, and the main point is to advocate and
exemplify the relevance and necessity of traditional concepts to modern life,
rather than just accepting the terms of the modern, or drowning in nostalgia
for a past that can never return as it was. To this end, as Betonie the main
medicine man figure says, ceremonies must change:

> At one time, the ceremonies as they had been performed were enough for the
> way the world was then. But after the white people came, elements in this
> world began to shift; and it became necessary to create new ceremonies....
> Things which don't shift and grow are dead things.... That's what the
> witchery is counting on; that we will cling to the ceremonies the way they
> were, and then their power will triumph, and the people will be no more.
> (1977:132-3)

The contemporary substance of the novel concerns the malaise of Tayo, a
returned soldier, who is without parents, his father being referred to fleetingly
only as 'that white man'. Tayo has been traumatised when he came to believe
that one of the Japanese soldiers he had killed was really his uncle. The delusion
triggers off the psychological collapse from which he recovers during the
novel. Discharged by the army, he is still ill, and his remaining family decide
that only a ceremony can cure him. His quest for health is paralleled in the
novel by a larger traditional quest theme, using cultural symbols of
drought – Waste Land imagery transposed to the American South West. The
illness, then, becomes a battle between forces of good and evil, expressed in
traditional terms of witchcraft, and the world Tayo inhabits becomes one
peopled with these forces. Silko is able to use Tayo's illness to good effect, by
creating a world where magic operates, and leaving it open whether this is the
way things are or merely part of Tayo's delusion. Tayo's own survival
becomes an aspect of the enduring struggle to create harmony and unity,

rather than chaos and evil, and he becomes able to understand his own sickness as related to greater forces of destruction. Silko utilises the presence, relatively near to the Laguna pueblo lands, of the original laboratories and testing sites for the atomic bombs which destroyed Japanese cities, and she develops the idea of this potential for destruction by relating it to the Japanese corpse that Tayo had mistaken for his uncle. The same force was destroying him, his uncle and the Japanese:

> There was no end to it; it knew no boundaries; and he had arrived at the point of convergence where the fate of all living things, and even the earth, had been laid. From the jungles of his dreaming he recognised why the Japanese voices had merged with Laguna voices.... He cried the relief he felt at finally seeing the pattern, the way all the stories fit together – the old stories, the war stories, their stories – to become the story that was still being told. He was not crazy.... He had only seen and heard the world as it always was. (1977:257–8)

Tayo's revulsion against the world he is expected to accept, then, is not crazy or aberrant, it is a healthy reaction. The world's values need to be changed, not his, and so his story need not end with defeat. The female figure who helps him together with Betonie, and who operates somewhere between the mythical and the realistic elements in the novel, tells him, in what could almost be a reproof to the pessimism of other Indian novelists, that his enemies

> want it to end here, the way all their stories end, encircling slowly to choke the life away.... They have their stories about us – Indian people who are only marking time and waiting for the end. And they would end this story right here, with you fighting to your death alone in these hills. (1977:243)

Unlike Jim Loney, who does die alone in the hills, Tayo is helped by Betonie and the forces, psychological or magical, with which he is able to put Tayo in touch. For Silko, recourse to tradition can heal the breach which destroys Loney. *The Death of Jim Loney* and *Ceremony* could be seen as representing alternative attitudes to modern Indian identity – the one pessimistic and emphasising rootlessness, the other optimistic and emphasising a continuity and tradition which can be salvaged and reprieved. Partly, of course, the difference can be accounted for by the particular location in each book. Many Indians in the South west have maintained their cultural continuity relatively unimpaired, whereas Plains Indians have suffered much more severely from cultural dislocation. Even allowing for this, the contrast between the two books is striking, extending to the form and style, as well as the stance on identity.

Silko's attempt to fuse myth with the realism of the novel form is an attempt to create or assert a continuum in which American Indian literature would run from oral narrative and ceremony straight through to novels written in English. In other words, she is insisting on the reconcilability of forms just as she is insisting on the reconcilability of traditional and modern concepts of identity. Equally important, she is extending the analysis from family and genealogy to economics and politics, even if the proposed relation in the book is shown only in its religious dimensions. But the conflation of the familial and the historical needs to be treated with caution. Richard King's penetrating study of this theme in southern writing (1980) shows how psychological categories are overlaid with historical resonances, but where, for instance, Faulkner's narrative forces an ultimate demythologisation of the past by confronting an event or issue and finding it to be compromised and ambiguous, distinctly *in* history, Indian fiction pushes back to a point which cannot be demythologised precisely because it is linked with *in illo tempore*, the time of myth rather than history, when men spoke to animals. It is the primal time, the 'distance' in which Yellow Calf lives in *Winter in the Blood*.

One of the distinctive features of the invocation of the past in a great deal of Indian writing is the rapid movement between a specific and local past, an actual relative or remembered story or event and a more absolute or transcendent claim. Simon Ortiz' short story 'Something's Going On', (1978) for instance, focuses on a son's sense of confusion when his father abruptly leaves home on the run from the police for killing a white man, and ends with his decision to find his father and help him. His father has lost a leg in World War Two, symbolising the deformations and limitations imposed upon Indians by whites. He has fashioned a crutch out of wood, and at the end of the story this is presented as a way of reuniting him with the process of reciprocity between man and nature:

> he touched the crutch which had become oak in the growing earth again.
> He began to cry then, softly and easily, with humility and recognition of his
> part among all things in the universe. (Ortiz 1978:42)

This invocation of unity is a recurrent theme in American Indian writing. Rather than seeing the world as made up of different realms of experience to which we apply different methods of understanding and evaluation (religious, scientific, and so on), there is a sense of a fundamental unity underlying the facets of experience, which is regularly characterised in traditional images of circles or living organisms. It could be argued that this idea of the local as centre, the idea that the centre and the circumference are one, could be a useful counter-position to the colonial assumptions of metropolis and centralisation on both economic and cultural levels, and I shall return to this, but in the existing body of American Indian writing, the idea of wholeness and unity are more usually an expression of a nostalgia without any political cutting edge – a nostalgia for a tribal unity, and for a simplicity which fits neatly into the patterns of literary Romanticism. This raises the problem of readership. It could be argued that by pigeon-holing most Indian literature in white categories like this I am ignoring the fact that, for instance, what may be read as derivative Romanticism within a white context may also have stronger and more complex reverberations within the relevant Indian cultures, where ideas of unity, or spirit, may carry a social and political dimension different from that in the larger society. Similarly, to suggest that Indian writers could express the complexity of their cultural and artistic situations more fully by utilising the full possibilities of Modernist juxtaposition and discontinuity or postmodern decentredness, could be seen as trying to co-opt them into what is a white literary mode, claiming to be a universal, or, at least, transcultural epistemological tool.

Certainly, for many Indian writers this sort of literary discontinuity is seen as a threat to their identity, just as secular and fragmented modern society is a threat to tribal cultures, and Duane Niatum expresses it very clearly:

> Although this may be the right view for the Anglo artist and individual, the Native American and tribal people everywhere would be committing suicide if they accepted this view themselves. For such an attitude undermines the very foundations of their tribal heritages. (Scholer 1984:27)

On the other hand, what if the sort of wholes or unities currently available have the effect of freezing Indian tribes historically, in acts of compulsive nostalgia, rather than ensuring the continuation of a living and changing tradition? Simon Ortiz is a good example of a writer educated in American literature and its forms who is intensely aware of his Indian heritage, and his description of a conversation with his father reveals an awareness of both positions:

> For example, when my father has said a word – in speech or in a song – and I ask him, 'what does that word break down to? I mean breaking it down to the syllables of sound or phrases of sound, what do each of these parts mean?' And he has looked at me with an exasperated – slightly pained – expression on his face, wondering what I mean. And he tells me, 'It doesn't break down into anything.'[17] (Scholer 1984:87)

As Kenneth Lincoln points out, Ortiz' response to the problems of fragmentation is to stress not only the underlying unity ('Underneath what looks like loose stone there is stone woven together'), but the way that the performance of speech and song in context reveals this: 'words complete their "sentence" when spoken, ritualised sequentially in song'. For Ortiz his own particular heritage is seen as an expression of something much greater – the basis for an implicit claim about an undifferentiated unity:[18] 'My father sings, and I listen. Song, at the very beginning was experience. There was no division between experience and expression' (in Rothenberg 1983:402). Derrida's painstaking deconstruction of phonocentrism, already referred to, has its parallel in De Man's work on the privileging of voice within Romantic poetry, so that it would certainly be easy to pigeon-hole Ortiz in this way, but it is also worth looking at the problems raised by Ortiz' use of 'the beginning' here, in relation to the widespread concern in modern American poetry in general for what George Quasha has called the 'primary'. It would be a mistake to dismiss this too quickly as a nostalgia for lost unities, a clinging to metaphysics, as Quasha has shown:

> The theme of 'return' to primary *logos* is characteristic of the recent efforts at restoring active language-consciousness, whether in Heidegger's or Barfield's meditative etymologizing or in the reoralizing tendency of contemporary poetry. It is not nostalgia, at least not in any simple sense, although there is often a mood of longing (*Sehnsucht/Pathos*) in the more Romantic thinkers (Heidegger, Barfield) and poets (Robert Duncan). The barely submerged longing is for the *primary*, the *direct*, that is also locatable somewhere between Whitehead's 'presentational immediacy' and Olson's 'one perception must immediately and directly lead to a further perception'.... The point is that, when Olson also says that the poem must be the 'issue of its composition, the poetic is now being understood as *emergent language – language specifically energized by its processual and eventual nature*, rather than by some set of qualities or formal conditions imposed according to an aesthetic. (in Rothenberg 1983:464)

Some Indian poets have certainly taken up Olson's approach for their own ends. Carol Lee Sanchez, for instance, seems to make explicit reference to him, in a poem which links the themes of creativity, breath and Indian identity:

> these roots go back somewhere
> related through syllable
> through time
> connect with a script not known.
> Some form that communicated
> alternative meanings
>
> still held in this construct
> in this time
>
> that master who began to define this form
> remarked on the search:
> the detective part of the work any
> creation comes from
> the *doing* will suffice
> the momentum of the forward push
> cause of the breath.
> (Scholer 1984:110–11)

The very idea of the local and the specific can be used, as it is in a great deal of modern American poetry, as a resource against a particular sort of universalising which is the cultural equivalent of colonialism. Leslie Silko has challenged this cultural arrogance, which she finds even in the white ethnopoets who attempt to attune themselves to Indian forms and views. In 'An Old-Time Indian Attack' (Silko 1979) she denounces: 'the assumption that the white man, through some innate cultural or racial superiority, has the ability to perceive and master the essential beliefs, values, and emotions of persons from Native American communities'. A few paragraphs later, though, she links this cultural arrogance with precisely those universalist and rationalist principles of the Enlightenment which would seem to work counter to assumptions of cultural superiority:

> If you examine the notion that the writer has the 'power' to inhabit any soul, any consciousness, you will find this idea restricted to the white man: the concept of a 'universal consciousness' did not occur until sometime in the eighteenth century. (1979:4)

The ramifications of this argument extend far into the whole debate over rationality and its relation to Western assumptions about science and progress, but here the issue is what resources can be marshalled against universalist assumptions which, given an imbalance of power, effectively mean domination and monoculture.

In one way, the stress on the extreme specificity of each tribe or group could certainly act against the stereotyping of an essential 'Indian' way of being, or even an easy assumption of universal similarities. This can be done through the stress on locality and place, which can draw on patterns of non-centralised and non-hierarchical perceptions which then operate as political, as well as aesthetic, counterforces. Michel de Certeau, for instance, as part of his concern for 'heterologies', discusses South American Indian political manifestoes in these terms, and sees the close connection of specific place and memory of a specific past as offering a definition of what is one's own (*propre*) and what can, therefore, be used as a base from which to oppose the prevailing hegemony of values, while avoiding any ideological common unitary position (1986:229). This would certainly seem to be an attractive formulation, offering, as it does, the prospect of a sort of pre-formed postmodern political and aesthetic sensibility. The role of literacy has often been seen as playing a crucial role in allowing (or enforcing) a move from this localism to more general and comparative views, and Maurice Bloch has traced the implications in the work of Goody and others. According to this view, says Bloch, 'In pre-literate societies, knowledge is buried in social relations. The value of what is said is not evaluated in terms of its truth but in terms of who says it' (1989:16).

As a result, it will not be possible to mount an argument or disagreement on grounds of reason or information separated off from the personal and situational. Only with the opportunities of recall and objectivity given by literacy can there be intellectual and political debate which is not personal, so that 'Literacy enables knowledge to be politically liberating' (Bloch 1989:16), and enables democracy. Postmodern suspicion of the universalising and homogenising role of the modern state, whether democratic or not, supported by one or another 'grand narrative', has led to a renewed interest in precisely the local and limited situation literacy is supposed to have rescued us from, and some of Lyotard's descriptions of the postmodern condition bear a strong resemblance to Stanley Diamond's image of the primitive. While Diamond's overall criticism of modern monoculture is generally in more Marxist than postmodern terms, his description of modes of thinking which are 'substantially concrete, existential and nominalistic, within a personalistic context' (quoted in Rothenberg 1981:133) has significant similarities to postmodern requirements, as does his stress on the ability to sustain, rather than repress, contradictions.

This may seem a strange combination of positions, but what it points to is the complexity of trying to pin down the political implications of the recourse to the local, let alone the primitive. De Certeau is careful to distinguish the use of specific place and cultural memory from 'the alibi of cultural identity (more or less grandiose and nostalgic) constructed by the science of ethnology' (1986:228), but in the case of North American Indians it is precisely the difficulty, perhaps impossibility, of making this distinction that dominates their political and literary statements. De Certeau implies that this sense of cultural identity is imposed from outside – by ethnology – but I would argue that even if this is so, the problem is now that available identities are not – certainly in North America – separable from this cultural one in any straightforward way. In particular, to write about Indian experience and be published in English is inevitably to be involved in an ambiguous area of cultural identity. The local and the specific which, to use de Certeau's terms, are made one's own (*propre*) through memory, and which are seen by him as a source of strength, are expressed in terms which are not *only* 'one's own', and therefore inevitably run the risk of becoming yet another second-hand cultural identity.

Another way of putting this is to say that modern Indian writers writing in English are not so very different from the white ethnopoets Silko criticises, in their relation to Indian cultures. Arnold Krupat has distinguished between Momaday and Silko as writers, seeing Silko as dialogically open to other voices, and allowing for the decentring properties of the oral storytelling tradition, and Momaday as more monologic, pulling all voices into 'the all-encompassing voice of lyric or epic, romantic or modernist, art-speech' (Krupat 1989:177). At the same time he is careful not to imply that these categories are exclusive, and indeed, I would want to argue that throughout her writing Silko is as involved in appeals to unity and presence as Momaday and, in terms of literary movements, corresponds more to T.S. Eliot than to the decentredness of postmodernism. These terms, though, are themselves problematic. In particular, we can see Modernism, as exemplified by Eliot, as a fundamentally recuperative and conservative attempt to restore lost unities, political as well as cultural, but it is equally possible to point to those other aspects of early modernism which exploited precisely the discontinuities and fragmentations that others found so threatening (see Murray 1989). Ethnography, as well as Indian writing, can be seen in terms of these two positions. James Clifford has argued persuasively that the initial moment of 'fragmentation and juxtaposition of cultural values' found in early surrealism and in the ethnography of the early years of this century, fails to be sustained as surrealism become literary and ethnography becomes something which contemplates a diversity of cultural orders, but no longer 'openly expects, allows, indeed desires, its own disorientation' (Clifford 1988:140). At one point, though, they shared in different ways a distinctively new orientation which allowed a genuine openness to other cultures:

> Unlike the exoticism of the nineteenth century, which departed from a more
> or less confident cultural order in search of a temporary frisson, a
> circumscribed experience of the bizarre, modern surrealism and ethnography
> began with a reality deeply in question. Others appeared now as serious human
> alternatives: modern cultural relativism became possible. (Clifford 1988:120)

This approach allows us to see early Modernist techniques as having a specific relevance and use in multicultural and cross-cultural forms. One of the useful elements is the blurring or actual destruction of categories of the literary, or of the culturally pure. As Clifford says: 'the ethnographic surrealist, unlike either the typical art critic or anthropologist of the period, delights in cultural impurities and disturbing syncretisms' (1988:131).

What is most surprising is that, with few exceptions, Vizenor being the main one, Indian writing is not as involved in these syncretisms as the work of some of the white poets attempting to translate or re-present Indian materials. Perhaps it is worth risking the charges of cultural imperialism or universalising to argue that the most useful opening up of cultural forms is still to be found in Jerome Rothenberg rather than any Indian writer, both in his anthologies and in his use in his own poetry of the most formally radical aspects of modernism. To be sure, there is in much ethnopoetics what Rothenberg calls 'the search for a primal ground' (1976:11), a fundamental concept of the human which would be comprehensive enough to include all those manifestations of 'the other' which we now exclude. In this broad context, translation is 'simply one of the key devices for that greater incorporation that it seems to me most of us are moving toward'. Incorporation, for Rothenberg, clearly is to be distinguished from an assimilation of other cultures into our pre-existing patterns, but even so it can seem to come uncomfortably close to the nostalgia for lost unities and presence, particularly when connected with claims for the speaking voice over the written text in terms of presence.

What crucially distinguishes ethnopoetics from these earlier romantic claims is, first of all, that the performance element is primarily a way of breaking away from the closed nature of the literary text rather than the speaking lyric voice being a claim of presence made within the conventions and confines of the literary text, as earlier. In questioning the closure of the literary text, it opens up formal possibilities of engagement with a huge mass of material formerly excluded from 'literature', and takes up the fundamental challenge offered to our society by potential contact with an unprecedented range of cultures. This new approach can then undermine the power of our own culture to use other cultures only to reaffirm our exclusionary sense of our superiority. Nathaniel Tarn, as both poet and anthropologist, has recognised the issues very clearly. In talking about the sense of discontinuity experienced in modern cultures, he argues that 'much of our major poetry has tried to deal with this in a conservative sense, the sense of these fragments I have shored against my ruin. It is perhaps for this reason that it seems to be form that mimes the cultural *sparagmos* [flying apart], whereas the content continues to proclaim a desire for the whole' (Tarn 1976:31). Rather than lament cultural discontinuity, then, we can see it offering reopenings through which we can become aware of the diversity that had been closed to us, and by rooting ourselves firmly in our historical and cultural situation can begin to recognise the specificity of other cultural moments not as totalities but as fragments, since it is from fragments that we have learned since modernism aesthetically to operate. The fundamental relation between these concerns and those of modern anthropology will be developed in my final chapter, but for now the connections can be suggested by Stephen Tyler's description of what he calls postmodern ethnography:

> A postmodern ethnography is a cooperatively evolved text consisting of fragments of discourse intended to evoke in the minds of both reader and writers an emergent fantasy of a possible world of commonsense reality, and thus to provoke an aesthetic integration that will have a therapeutic effect. It is in a word, poetry (Tyler 1987:202).

Notes

1. There has recently been an increased interest in the theoretical and political implications of autobiographical writing, the most developed expression of which is in the context of women's writing. See, for instance, Smith (1987) and Brodzki and Schenk (1988).
2. Frederick Douglass' account of how he achieved the status of a man, and its relation to literacy, is a particularly powerful instance, and one that has been much discussed recently. From a huge range of materials on autobiography and

marginalised groups, see Butterfield (1974), Stepto (1979), Davis and Gates (1985), Bataille and Sands (1984).

3. For full bibliographical details, and expert synopsis and commentary, see Brumble (1981). The fullest critical discussions are to be found in Krupat (1985; 1989), and Brumble (1988).

4. See, for instance, Clifford (1983b), Marcus and Cushman (1982) and Dwyer (1977).

5. See Jackson (1964) for a careful account of the publishing history and its implications. Also Krupat (1985:44-53).

6. There were, of course, pictogrammic and other methods of recording events, and Hertha D. Wong makes a case for seeing these as having an autobiographical role. (1989).

7. See Carter Revard's (1980) comparison of Geronimo with a fellow Apache, Jason Betzinez, who was educated and wrote his own story, and Krupat (1985:55-74).

8. The early captivity narratives offer an ironic reversal of the situation addressed by the texts in this chapter, in that they describe a white being captured by Indians, being enclosed within Indian culture, whereas Indian autobiographies can be said typically to describe or enact the enclosing of the Indian within white cultural forms, even if not within white society.

9. See especially DeMallie (1984). Also, McCluskey (1972), Olson (1982) and Castro (1983).

10. See, for instance, Erdoes and Lame Deer (1972), Mails (1979), and for a low-point of countercultural mystification, influenced by Castaneda as well as Black Elk, Doug Boyd's *Rolling Thunder* (1974).

11. For the particular dimensions of Indian *women*'s autobiography, see Bataille and Sands (1984). Lurie (1966) discusses the role of earlier women anthropologists and what they collected, as does Helen Carr.

12. See Brumble (1983), and the subsequent discussion with Karl Kroeber in Swann (1983).

13. Brumble points out the prevalence of Social Darwinist and corresponding racist assumptions about the Vanishing American during Eastman's formative years at Dartmouth, giving him an evolutionary view of Indian–white relations that can sound bewildering, and even callous, to our ears. It could be said that Occom's forebodings about Dartmouth as 'alba mater' were coming true, but in a more complex way than he anticipated. See also Wilson (1983).

14. See especially Hazel Hertzberg's (1972) account of the search for an identity amongst a number of Eastman's contemporaries.

15. Brumble (1988:173-4) gives a careful but sympathetic reading of Momaday's views.

16. From *Cogewea: The Half-Blood*, where the heroine's parents are written out of the story in the first paragraph, up to the present, the problematic or absent father occurs with surprising frequency. In John Joseph Mathew's *Sundown* (1934) the father commits suicide, realising too late that he has aided in the destruction of traditional life by co-operating with the whites. In Darcy McNickle's *The Surrounded* (1936) the young protagonist is alienated from his white father, and relates to his Indian mother, who is returning increasingly to her Indian roots, and McNickle's *Wind From An Enemy Sky* (1978) focuses on the relationship between Bull and his grandson, with the middle generation absent, dismissed in a few phrases. Probably the best-known Indian novel, Momaday's *House Made of Dawn*

(1968) begins with the return of the central figure, Abel, drunk and demoralised, to his grandfather, and we are told within the first few pages that he does not know who his father was. Perhaps the most nightmarish and graphic image of the breakdown of kinship at the expense of the young is in Hanay Geiogamah's short play *Body Indian* (1980), where a young man crippled by the loss of a leg, and rapidly becoming alcoholic, is robbed by his elderly kinsmen of the money for his rehabilitation. At the end of the play they unfasten his false leg while he is unconscious, and sell it to buy more booze! While the concentration has been on fathers and sons there are, of course, equivalent concerns in the presentation of Indian women. Michael Dorris traces the relation of three generations of mothers and daughters in *A Yellow Raft In Blue Water* (1987) and Louise Erdrich's concern for the ambiguous legacy of Indianness is powerfully addressed in generational and familial terms, notably in *Love Medicine* (1985), where the father, unlike the failed figures of so many novels, actually himself represents a positive blending of past and present which can help his son.

17. This idea of a sentence which cannot be broken into parts has interesting similarities with the early views of Indian languages as polysynthetic or incorporative described in Chapter 2, and with Jonathan Edwards' description of Mohegan, in which he points out the interrelatedness of terms, on the analogy of kinship and ownership (Edwards 1787:9–11).

18. This characteristic shift from the familial to the metaphysical could be seen as leap-frogging the more specific and real issues of communication that arise between children educated in the white world and parents who are not. An interesting contrast can be found in Richard Rodriguez' *Hunger of Memory* (1981). The child of Spanish-speaking Mexican immigrants in California, Rodriguez learns English and gains success in the academic world, but his book is a powerful and moving exploration of what is lost as well as gained. Returning home he experiences dislocation and distance.

> I could not cast off the culture I had assumed. Living with my parents for the summer I remained an academic – a kind of anthropologist in the family kitchen, searching for evidence of our 'cultural ties' as we ate dinner together. (1981:160)

What distinguishes Rodriguez from Indian writers, though, and what made his book politically controversial, is that he sees this loss as an inevitable part of the acquisition of a sense of a public self, which is gained by mastery of *language*. His account expresses the pain of separation from roots, but refuses what he sees as the illusory comforts offered by being a representative of his people, by speaking for them:

> I did not give voice to my parents by writing about their lives. I distinguish myself from them by writing about the life we once shared. Even when I quote them accurately I profoundly distort my parents' words. (1981:186)

Rodriguez sees the public nature of language and especially of writing, as paradoxically the instrument of self-discovery, and he relates this directly to his own act of autobiography, which in Bakhtinian terms dialogises his own voice: 'The reader's voice silently trails every word I put down. I re-read my words, and again it is the reader's voice I hear in my mind, sounding my prose' (1981:187). In both his awareness of the dialogising nature of 'going public' and his scepticism about regaining or representing intimacies and unities of family or race Rodriguez offers an intriguing challenge and contrast to the more optimistic claims of many Indian writers.

CHAPTER SIX

Grizzly Woman and her Interpreters

Indian myths were originally recorded, if at all, as curiosities, but by the nineteenth century, as part of a larger Romantic interest, they were beginning to be presented as a sort of primitive literature. Any attempt to deal with or present Native American myths as literature immediately begs a whole number of questions about the translatability not only of the myths themselves but of the assumptions and beliefs that underlie them. Earlier mythographers may have been able to invoke a universal idea of what was poetic, and to argue that this shone through or transcended the differences between cultural forms, allowing them to ignore both the context and the forms in which they encountered myths. More recently, though, concern for the specificity of cultures and uneasiness about generalising from Western assumptions have ensured that myths are seen within an ethnographic context.

Ethnographic information, however, serves to throw light not just on the meaning and *content* of the myth, but increasingly on the conditions and significance of its telling. The oral dimensions of myth, then, and the inadequacy of our own conceptions of literature to cope with them, have been given increasing attention. The irony is that such a scrupulous concern not to erase cultural difference by recourse to easy overarching concepts like literature can have the effect of closing myths off and making them *only* objects of ethnographic study. The challenge of translating without effacing all the various elements in such a way that the final product is accessible not just as ethnography has produced fascinating work by Hymes, Tedlock, Rothenberg, Mattina and many others. My purpose in this chapter is, by concentrating on one body of myths which has attracted the attention of some major scholars over many years, to examine the ways in which the creation of the texts themselves, to say nothing of their accompanying interpretations, have depended on assumptions about larger wholes or totalities, like myth, literature or culture. It is the incompleteness and instability of these assumed totalities, as well as their necessity, which I am particularly interested to explore.

To use the word 'myth' as I have done here already invokes a sort of totality, which closes it off from other forms of narrative, or even other ways of thinking. Myth has generally been seen in Western societies as the area of the irrational, a way of thinking superseded by rational and scientific thought. As such, it can either be a privileged enclave (it does not have to be true in scientific terms to be meaningful) or, almost indistinguishable from this, dismissively marginalised (it does not have to be true because its claims are irrelevant). There are clear similarities here to the position of both literary and religious discourse, and the treatment and presentation of myth often tends to operate uneasily between treating it as one or the other. What I am more concerned with here, though, are those approaches to Native American myths in which the main concern is not to translate them into universal categories of the spiritual or aesthetic, but to see them as part of a cultural totality. The collection and examination of myths then becomes a way of constituting that totality for the scholar, and knowledge of that total cultural system at the same time enables the understanding of the myth.

An important assumption here has been that myths are a communal product, and that they therefore can be used representatively, which has led to a persistent stress on what is common to different versions, rather than what is peculiar to each one. The stress on the communal rather than the individual, on system rather than single instance, was, of course, one of the distinctive breakthroughs in the development of anthropology and sociology. Unfortunately, while it allowed Western 'developed' people to see the power of culture rather than the individual, and therefore potentially to see what they had in common with tribal cultures, the same methodology applied to tribal cultures, in stressing their total integration and unity and ignoring or suppressing the cultural 'impurities' and acculturations, marked those cultures off and reinforced the standard view of them as wholly 'other'. Thus we have the conjunction of a developing methodology which required the articulation and reconstruction of a closed system, with a larger cultural imperative to salvage and preserve apparently vanishing cultures, not in their actuality, which would have raised large and difficult political questions, but in a symbolic form as collection of knowledge and/or artefacts.[1]

What interests me particularly is the process by which the whole as culture, or culture as a whole, has to be assumed before the creation of the collection can take place, and the way this cultural whole is simultaneously created by that collection. One of the main thrusts of recent critiques of ethnography has been the demonstration of the ways in which the creation of ethnographic texts has entailed assumptions such as these about cultural wholes, and I shall return to this issue in the concluding chapter, but for now I want to concentrate on similar processes in the collection and presentation of myths.

Myths are offered to us in texts implicitly or explicitly as belonging to one or another system in which they have meaning. This may be the social system of the tribe, the specific social context of its performance, the linguistic forms of the text, or even world religions, or a universal system of archetypes. Dependent on which system is involved are a number of significant decisions about what is translated and how it is to be done, but my main concern here is the way that any system of meanings which is invoked in order to substantiate or fix the meanings of a particular myth tends to link into other systems, which then make that particular translation or interpretation inadequate. This has the effect of making any claims for interpretative fullness or transparency of translation – which are perhaps two aspects of the same totalising dream – founder, not because of the transcendent mystery of art or myth, or the primitive mind but because of both the inherent instability of wholes and systems and the particular instabilities and complexities of the cross-cultural relations that are involved in this particular enterprise of presenting North American Indian myths in English. As Arnold Krupat has expressed it,

> we must read the texts we have, from Henry Schoolcraft to the present moment, as in need of unfixing, a process by which we acknowledge that any meanings which appear to be present are never fully present. (Swann and Krupat 1987b:124)

All the anthropologists I have chosen to deal with have, in their various ways, a common concern with the relation of meaning to system and structure and a sustained interest in the mythology of the north-west coast of the United States and Canada. Franz Boas' work in this area spanned almost the whole of a long working life, and involved the close co-operation of native informants. Foremost among these was George Hunt, and his and Boas' joint work still provides a huge resource for scholars, as well as exemplifying a method which has been profoundly influential. Melville Jacobs was a student of Boas, and in many ways both he and Dell Hymes, in their stress on a linguistic basis for understanding a culture, are continuing the Boas tradition.[2] Lévi-Strauss has written eloquently about his long-standing passion for north-west coast art, and some of his most celebrated work is on the myths and art of this area, utilising Boas' earlier work.[3] My aim in examining these interlocking materials and approaches is not so much to try to make them supplement each other and therefore build up a more adequate view of the myths they discuss, since this would be to beg the questions I am trying to open up about interpretation, but to show the way that the systems in which they see meaning being generated are inevitably incomplete and imply another system.

Boas' fundamental concerns for cultures as wholes, in which all the elements are interlocking, meant that the way to find the meaning of an event, custom or myth was to understand the articulated system of ideas in that culture, rather than using comparisons with other cultures or finding its origins within that culture or elsewhere. Boas' method relied primarily upon a linguistic knowledge and therefore an extensive use of native informants, who were used to compile what became one of the characteristic products of Boas and his followers, the dictated text. Published simply as *Kwakiutl Texts* (Boas and Hunt 1905) or *Bella Bella Texts* (1928), these volumes in their very titles proclaim their concern to capture the language. The subject matter was not irrelevant, of course, and what was sought was representative cultural information about religion, mythology or daily life, but what was most important was that the recording of it be as authentic and untampered with as possible. In one way the collecting of texts acted as a way of not coming to conclusions, an endless deferral of the generalising or synthesising which would constitute an ethnography. To this extent these texts reflect the assumptions of 'salvage' anthropology, in its conviction that the culture is fast disappearing, but they also reflect a concern to find a way of turning a temporal process, a flux, into a form that can be fixed and then returned to at leisure and studied. It is a way of *creating* the objects of study, as much as recording them. In this way, the collecting of texts is like the collecting of objects for museums, and Boas' active role in shaping the philosophy of ethnographic collecting and presentation offers interesting parallels (see Cole, 1985, and Dominguez, 1986 and, for a more general discussion, Price, 1989).

Just as the original ownership of an ethnographic object was usually obscured once it appeared in a collection, so the process by which a speech situation became a text usually involved the loss of the speaker's name and background, and of peculiarities of performance. This was partly because Boas wanted *representative* language practice (he often complained about the impure forms he had to collect), but also because the very process of recording it on paper determined what was significant. This excluded what could not be transcribed and what was prejudged as insignificant, such as repetitions, false starts and asides. In addition, this concern for the common and representative meant that, in the collecting of data, Boas gave less attention both to the esoteric aspects of religious life and to specialised artistic production. He specifically warns against concentrating on

> the highest form of thought only, which is held by the priest, the chief, the leader. Interesting and attractive though this field of research may be, it is supplementary only to the study of the thoughts, emotional life, and ethical standards of the common people, whose interests centre in other fields of thought, and of whom the select class forms only a special type.[4]

This anti-hierarchical approach is part of that more general attempt at circumventing the dangers of ethnocentrism which also included a strong reliance on native informants. Boas' reliance over many years on George Hunt, and the leeway he gave in collecting artefacts and texts on a wide, apparently random, range of subjects, has led Irving Goldman to claim that 'the results are as close to authenticity as field work can get', and that 'in the special sense that the Kwakiutl texts were not organised by Boas in conformity with traditional anthropologist schedules, they may be regarded as "raw data" ' (1980:335). To accept this view, though, would be to ignore George Hunt's awareness of what Boas wanted, and the extent to which, therefore, Hunt was acting as ethnographer rather than informant, and it is worth concentrating briefly on the relation of the two men to each other, and to their respective cultures.

Brought up amongst the Kwakiutl, with Kwakwala, their language, as his first language, but able to speak English (he was the son of a Scottish father and a Tlingit mother), Hunt was an ideal informant for Boas. Boas taught him phonological inscriptions, and over a period of some forty years he sent Boas many thousands of pages of handwritten material as well as helping him during his visits.[5] He also collected artefacts for Boas, and in his way of talking about them in his letters there is, on occasions, a fascinating ambiguity. Where, for instance, he talks of finding a 'fine specimen', we have to wonder which criteria he is using, and when he talks with pleasure of getting a 'wonderful' secret story out of his own wife and her family which 'will show you and me what I did not know before', it is presumably a different feeling from that experienced by the narrators whom he sometimes describes as 'pleased' by their own stories. Marjorie M. Halpin, writing on William Beynon, another informant for Boas this time amongst the Tsimshian, argues that he is really, like Hunt here, playing the part of ethnographer rather than informant, and at the end of her article she raises a question equally relevant to Hunt: 'I keep wondering why Beynon did it for all those years. He certainly was not well paid, nor did he achieve what I would consider adequate recognition for his work' (in Liberty 1978:152). Her implicit answer is that it was genuine ethnographic curiosity, which has the advantage of making figures like Hunt and Beynon less passive instruments, and more initiators, but the material available on Hunt's role is suggestive rather than conclusive.

Throughout their correspondence, Boas is clearly both directing the overall shape of Hunt's activities and dependent on his knowledge and his initiatives. During a field trip he writes back to his wife describing an ideal field situation, 'I feel like a spider in a web to which everything is flying. I tell Hunt what I want and he brings the people to me' (in Helm 1966:195), and a letter to his brother uses similar imagery: 'I did not lose any time, because I had George Hunt with me. He would always find my victims, whom I then pumped dry' (Rohner 1969:287). The metaphors here are interesting, in that they make Boas both active and passive. Things come *to* him, and he is drawing from his hosts (as a parasite, as well as a guest does), and this accurately reflects the ambiguities in his role of recorder. When he is away from the north-west, which is most of the time, Boas is confident in Hunt's ability to know what he wants, and to collect it, but this is the confidence of a man in ultimate control, who has a trained subordinate, rather than a willingness to allow a random collection, as Goldman tends to suggest.

One of the strongest impressions gained from a reading of Boas' correspondence, though, is of the isolation of Hunt from Boas' professional circle. His letters to Boas crop up periodically amongst the formal and businesslike day-to-day letters, and in their openness and their direct and personal tone, and particularly in their use of non-standard English, all of which combined can come over as naivety or simplicity, they underline the inequality of the relation between the two men, and just how different this professional relation was from all of the others included in Boas' professional correspondence. This is also because Hunt is often in the position of supplicant, requiring something from Boas, whereas we could argue that the reality of the situation was, in fact, the reverse, as Boas sometimes exasperatedly lets slip in his letters to other people: 'He knows exactly how I depend on him' (Rohner 1969:183), and on another occasion, when it looked as if someone else might engage Hunt, he describes himself as 'trembling with fear' (Rohner 1969:183). A key instance of Hunt's position is a heartfelt letter of complaint, in which he explains that his whole position in his community is being undermined by his work for Boas. In its half-angry, half-abject tone, it takes its place along with those of Wheelock's Indians in Chapter 4, in a huge range of letters and speeches by Indians reflecting the position of ultimate powerlessness, even of those on whom whites most relied, and the radical inequality in the white–Indian relationship. The tone of Boas' letter in response is friendly and sympathetic enough ('My dear George'), but it is significant that his reply is printed by Stocking without Hunt's original letter, which is described as 'a moving complaint – the more moving for its mis-spellings and fractured grammar'. The erasure of Hunt here is entirely typical. Boas' overall stance can best be described as impersonal and businesslike, and makes a sharp (and dare we say, sometimes refreshingly honest) contrast with later more self-questioning ethnographers. Commentators have varied in their evaluation of his dealings with the people he used and studied. Some have viewed him as impatient and manipulative, and support could certainly be found in the abrupt transition in a letter to his wife, as he and Hunt arrive at Alert Bay and bad news is waiting for Hunt:

> One of his children, an eight-year-old boy, was very ill, and possibly already dead at the time the news reached him...I am very sorry for him, but I could not help him. If the people had written more clearly earlier, I would have sent him home, of course. It is always annoying to work with Hunt, because I cannot make him understand certain things. (Rohner 1969:243-4)

Is the annoyance here because of a disagreement between them? Does Hunt

feel aggrieved that he was not sent home, or has Boas moved on to the subject
of his ethnographic work? Admittedly, this dates from early in their long
association, and is perhaps anyway misleading. A letter two months earlier
mentions that 'I walk now with George every evening for two hours', but there
is absolutely no indication of what they talked about. What evidence Rohner
has produced, including interviews with those amongst the Kwakiutl who
remember Boas and Hunt (Rohner 1966:218), suggests that Boas was a highly
respected figure, and it is perhaps more useful to look at Boas in terms of the
values of his own time. In particular, given his scientific approach (science
understood at that time to be based on scrupulous objectivity and the finding
of general laws), both his own and his informants' subjective feelings were of
distinctly secondary importance and could not be built into the research itself,
and it is quite conceivable that this stance, combined with his own dignity,
courtesy and a certain business sense, commended itself at least as well to the
Indians he encountered as the more diffident and self-analysing style of later
anthropologists.

There is nowhere in Boas, as in so many later anthropologists, any claim for
the fieldwork experience itself as a formative or redemptive event. Rather, it
was a necessary task, and if he could establish reliable sources of information
without doing it himself, through Hunt or through his students, all the better.
The gathering of material came before any introspection or self-examination,
but also before any large-scale speculations or system building. Some
commentators have suggested that it was precisely his failure to stay for any
extended period in the field which may account for the fragmentary and
inconsistent nature of his view of the Kwakiutl (See Rohner 1969:xxix).
Instead, he piled up more and more material. From the point of view of my
overall approach in this chapter, the assumptions here are interesting – first,
that more experience would find a whole or an informing structure, secondly
that it was there. What we have instead in Boas is *text* without, now, much
possibility of checking it against anything other than another text, and in this
way, Boas' texts both in their scope and their inconsistencies, push us further
from a coherent structure, even as they seem to offer the material for
constructing or finding one.

Boas' reminiscences of how one of his Indian informants who had been
brought to New York responded to the city, have been indirectly preserved
by Roman Jakobson:

In conversation Boas loved to depict the indifference of this man from
Vancouver Island toward Manhattan skyscrapers ('we build homes next to one
another, and you stack them on top of each other'), toward the Aquarium ('we
throw such fish back in the lake') or toward the motion pictures which seemed
tedious and senseless. On the other hand, the stranger stood for hours
spellbound in the Times Square freak shows with their giants and dwarfs,
bearded ladies and fan-tailed girls, or in the Automats where drinks and

sandwiches appear miraculously, and where he felt transferred into the universe of Kwakiutl fairy-tales. In the same way, his whimsical tangling of the Indian vernacular and English presented Boas with invaluable clues to the particularities of Kwakiutl grammatical concepts. (1959:142–3)

Crucial here is the way that Boas, while obviously aware of the humour created by incongruity of systems (and presumably of the two-way nature of the joke, in that it made him question *his* categories and assumptions about what was normal), is ultimately more interested in the inferences that can be drawn to find the rules which the incongruities reveal. This has to be seen in the context of Boas' insistence that, as Jakobson describes it, 'meaning can and must be stated in terms of linguistic discriminations, just as, on the other hand, linguistic discriminations are always made with regard to their semantic value'. Grammar, then, for Boas, could not be separated from semantics. He would not accept a non-semantic theory of grammatical structure, and any defeatist allusion to the imaginary obscurity of the notion of meaning seemed, to Boas, itself obscure and meaningless (see Jakobson 1959:143). The 'whimsical tangling' of the Kwakiutl visitor, then, is interesting not in its surreal or incongruous opening up of new possibilities of sense/nonsense, but in its revelation of the rules of Kwakwala. When two separate wholes mingle or collide, it is only of interest in revealing the rules governing each whole. Outside the whole, where the rules break down, is nonsense.

Later I shall be returning to Boas' visitor, and the use made of him by Lévi-Strauss in a more self-conscious structuralism, but for now it is enough to register Boas' concern for system as generator of meaning. Melville Jacobs, amongst others, has seen this as an essentially structuralist view of language (1959a:126; see also Stocking 1974:8), but has distinguished this from his work on myth, which is much less developed theoretically. Jacobs sees Boas as retaining a diffusionist view, whereby the meaning is located by tracing it back to an earlier version. This method, which had earlier been combined with a universalist emphasis, would be equivalent to a view of meaning based on etymology rather than synchronic usage. Boas' main assumption, of course, in accord with his concern for the integrity and interrelatedness of cultures, was that myths were related to recognisable features of their society, but whether a myth or folk-tale was a straightforward reflection ('it must reflect the habits and conflicts of life of the society in which the narrator lives')[6] or needed to be treated as an oblique or partial expression of pressures or contradictions in or between particular groups, was not something he gave much attention to, any more than he did, for most of his life, to the variations in individual performance. Variations in myths were interesting in so far as they pointed to what did *not* vary, or to the construction of a new regularity, just as the Kwakiutl visitor's 'tangling' revealed rules in language. In his assumption, in collating texts, that, as Jacobs has described it, 'his informant was a mouthpiece for a socio-cultural heritage' (1959a:126), Boas had no difficulty in turning an oral storytelling performance by a specific man or woman into an unauthored 'Kwakiutl text', because that was what it most *essentially* was.

It is time, now, to look at part of such a text, a version of a myth dealing with Dzonoqua, in which we can see many of Boas' practices exemplified:

> (One of the) villages of the fist Dza'wadrenox' was at Wuxe'datsle. The name of their clan was Wio'quma'e, and the name of their chief was K'a'de; and K'a'de had a princess [a girl], and her name was She-who-will-be-made-a-Princess.
>
> When She-who-will-be-made-a-Princess became mature, they made a small house for her after four days, and she went at once to observe the taboos. She only sat (there). She had no hat, and she had no straps on her body. She only had (a string) around her neck, to which was tied the bone (tube) for drinking water and the copper scratcher.
>
> She sat all the time in the house, her knees pressed against her breast, and she clasped her knees the whole [length of the] day. She arose (however) early in the morning before the ravens awoke, and she also went four times into the water every four days. She staid in her small house for sixteen days.
>
> Then she entered her father's house, and (part of) her eyebrows were pulled out. At that time her face changed to (look like) the face of a woman. Then she went into the water again four times every sixth day. (Boas and Hunt 1905:86–7)

This is the opening of a story which goes on to describe how She-who-will-be-made-a-Princess, in spite of warnings about the Dzonoqua, walked in the woods, met a 'stout woman', who gives her clothes made from mountain-goat wool and a variety of other adornments in exchange for having her eyebrows cut like the young girl. The girl brings her back and tells her father that this is Dzonoqua. Her father's warrior uses a stone chisel to kill Dzonoqua under the pretence of cutting her eyebrows, and her body is then burned. The girl leads her people to the Dzonoqua's home, where they find a mask which they name Nightmare – Bringer-Nest-Mask and various other objects.

> Then he called his tribe. It was the summer season, not the winter-dance season. Then he gave away the dressed skins which he had taken from the house of the Dzo'noq'wa. Then She-who-will-be-made-a-Princess received the name She-who-will-be-sought-after, and K'a'de had the name of Dzo'noq'wa Chief, for he had obtained by murder the Nightmare-Bringer-Nest-Mask and the clothes and dressed skins, and the clothes of the maturing girl, and for this reason the clan Wio'quma'e has a great name. It means 'the very first ones'. This is the end (1905:92)

The title of the volume from which this is taken stresses its documentary and linguistic purposes. In this volume the English text is parallel, but in other similar collections it is not unusual to see the English meaning along the bottom of the page like a sort of extended footnote. If we think for a moment

of the intended reader of such a volume which was published and sold, and
which can be found in all the larger libraries, we find a strange situation. The
number of people who could then read and understand Kwakiutl must have
been absolutely miniscule – whites did not know the language, and native
speakers could not read it, and would have no interest in reading it anyway. So
we have a text in which half the page is there *not* to be read. One of the
functions is to act as the 'other' of the English, and in addition, it acts as
repository of evidence, a sort of silent corroboration. In later years such texts
have fulfilled a larger function, not only for later scholars but for native
peoples themselves, whose oral traditions may have been broken or
disappeared and who can now read the text fully, and who now constitute the
bilingual readership for whom the text is ideal, but this is not the one for
whom it was originally intended.

In texts like this, then, the salvage and collecting intentions really
determine the form of the text. Boas did publish translations in more
accessible form, both in German and in English, and refers in his letters to
plans to popularise some of his material, but he came to feel that these were
only justifiable when a reliable original text was not available.[7] Because of this
concern, then, no attempt is made to locate the context of recitation, nor
usually the presentational peculiarities, although interestingly, in this
particular story, the manner of speaking of the Dzonoqua is noted. In the
English version it appears as

> Then the stout woman spoke, and said, 'Oho mihistrehess! lehet mehe nowhow
> ahask youhou whahat dihid theyhey doho toho youhour eyheyebrowshows
> toho mahake youhour eyheyebrowshows loohook soho prehettyhy?' Thus said
> the stout woman to She-who-will-be-made-a-Princess. (1905:88).

A footnote tells us that 'following the initial consonant and vowel of each
syllable, an 'h' is inserted, followed by the repeated vowel of the syllable'. The
Dzonoqua speaks throughout in this manner, but a few sentences only are
given here in this peculiar style. The effect or purpose of this in performance is
not pursued. The Dzonoqua speaks like this, he says, not the teller of the tale,
who is invisible, or rather inaudible, here as elsewhere.

To find out from Boas what this myth means, we would look to those places
where he discusses Dzonoqua's ritual role. In *The Social Organisation and
Secret Societies of Kwakiutl Indians* he describes

> the Tsonoqoa, a wild woman who resides in the woods. She is represented as
> having enormous breasts and as carrying a bucket, into which she puts children
> whom she steals in order to eat them. Her eyes are hollow and shine with a
> wild luster. She is asleep most of the time, her mouth is pushed forward, as she
> is, when awake, constantly uttering her cry 'u,hu,u,y'. (1895b:372)

Here he gives another myth involving Dzonoqua, presented only in English, and with a different purpose, as his prefatory remark indicates: 'The following tradition describes this spirit quite fully.' The narrative which follows describes a boy from the clan Wisentsa meeting a giantess who is chewing gum which is as red as blood. She carries him and the other children off in the bucket she carries on her back. Meanwhile, the mother of one of the boys finds a little boy in her house who had originated from the mucus from her nose. He grows up in four days, and goes in search of the Dzonoqua and the missing children. At the Dzonoqua's house he finds the children and a woman rooted to the floor, who warns him that Dzonoqua is returning. The boy tricks Dzonoqua into putting her head between two stones, and smashes her head, but the rooted woman warns that she will only properly be killed by shooting an arrow into a knot-hole in a certain hemlock where she will go when she comes back to life. This he does, washes the children's eyes with urine, and returns to heaven. There are a number of elements here which recur in similar myths, such as the rooted woman, and the bucket in which Dzonoqua carries off the children, but recognising recurrent features can push us away from the specific myth towards a larger pattern and, even then, recognition of a pattern is not the same as a working out of the meaning of the myth within that culture. Given the provisional and dispersed nature of much of Boas' material, we really have to go to later scholars for help in linking Dzonoqua with relevant Kwakiutl cultural patterns,[8] since without them we are forced to look for points of contact with other stories, either within our own culture (leading to an ethnocentric reading), or with as many other cultures as we can (leading to the problems encountered in the universalist myth-collecting based on similarities of content which preceded Boas).

An ethnocentric or universalist reader might focus on the plot (the confrontation of the young girl, or boy, and the ogress) or on the characters (whether we can explain or identify with the young girl or the ogress),[9] or the happy ending (the rescue and the gaining of wealth), but beyond this the details remain recalcitrant and meaningless. The issue of pubescence is evident enough, but the ethnographic information that pubescent girls wore goat's-hair clothing, described as having come from Dzonoqua, moves the pubescence theme from psychological feelings and motivation to social behaviour. This is especially so when we become aware of the fact that, as She-who-will-be-sought-after, that is as potential bride, the girl will be at the centre of a social network of gift and name exchange, which pervades north-west coast cultures. In particular, they are heavily oriented towards lineage and property, and the display of clan possessions on certain public occasions is an important indicator and creator of prestige. From this perspective, then, the most important part of the myth is the end, where the Wioquamae clan's claim to the ownership of the Dzonoqua mask is validated by the giving away of skins taken from her house, and implies a system of gift-giving related to prestige of which the potlatch is the most famous, if still disputed, example.[10]

The myth then becomes a charter myth, in that it accounts for, and justifies, the ownership of certain names and ritual objects, in particular here the mask, and the stress on the mask also alerts us, the ethnographically informed readers, to the importance of transformation in this culture. Masks are not merely a disguise, nor a conventional imitation, but a way of becoming the mythical creature or of taking on, as clan or family representative, the powers guaranteed in the shorter myth. (It could, perhaps, be argued that to the extent that the creation of the ethnographic text validates the objectivity of the anthropologist and his power to wear the impersonal mask of scientist, they too can be seen as charter myths.)

This complex shifting of identity between man, animal and mythical creature, represented most graphically in the transformation masks which are made to reveal one face beneath another and also, according to Walens, in the persistent theme of consuming, whereby one thing is transformed into something else, once grasped, makes it difficult to put characterisation or psychological motivation, or any aesthetic category dependent on them, high on the agenda in reading those myths. Their meaning tends to become entirely defined by their function, and they are defined by that cultural whole which they are themselves collected so as eventually to constitute, in the endlessly deferred ethnographic total description. Boas' own work both in its urge to include and collect and in its deferral of that condition, can therefore be seen as characteristic of a certain set of anthropological assumptions in which the fragmentary and provisional nature of the actual materials, and of the relation to a changing culture, is played down, is seen as a temporary transition between the cultural whole which preceded the work (the actual Kwakiutl life-style which was disappearing), and the scientific whole which will be re-formed at some point in the future (knowledge). Johannes Fabian's analysis of the anthropological denial of a shared time, of 'coevalness' (1983:37–69) is perfectly demonstrated here, in the way that the discourse of anthropology elides the actual temporality of its own involvement by evoking two other 'times' which are actually reduced to spatial wholes in the way that they can be captured or held. If you can hold a whole you make a hole in time, and turn it into space. A curious illustration of the mutual incompatibility of these two spheres, and even of the displacement of the former by the latter, is given in Boas' description late in his life of a ceremony he witnesses, in which many of the necessary bowls are absent because, as he informs his children, 'they are in the museums in New York and Berlin. Only the speech is still the same.' Presumably, the bowls were acquired by Boas himself. Characteristically, whatever Boas felt about the ironies of this, or whether he felt anything, he keeps to himself.[11]

Boas' main collecting efforts, though, were of materials to be turned into 'texts' in the original language, and this same concern can be seen, and with even more urgent justification, in collections of north-west coast texts by one of Boas' pupils and followers, Melville Jacobs. Jacobs' recordings of

Clackamas Chinook tales on which I intend to concentrate were literally the
last chance before knowledge of the stories in the original language died out
with the old people who had it. What we have, then, from Jacobs, is a bilingual
record of Mrs Victoria Howard's stories (with audio recording of some of the
material, too), but these stories come to us as remnants of a no longer existing
culture, and he is aware of his inability to provide the sort of sociocultural
background necessary to any final understanding. There is a certain irony,
then, in Jacob's position. By the time anthropology has developed a
sociolinguistics which could place the linguistic materials it collected, that
background was becoming unavailable, and Jacobs sees earlier ethnography as
a missed opportunity. Boas and his early followers, he says,

> did not record the wrong things in the field. Because they did not pursue
> theory, they failed to collect many necessary things. Their dedication to
> linguistics and diffusionist method, and their lack of concern with devising
> fresh scientific procedures, prevented them from comprehending that a socio-
> cultural background must be analysed in conjunction with a close analysis of
> texts. (1959a:137)

Jacobs' own presentation of texts is based, as with Boas, on a full
academically oriented bilingual version (though horizontally split so that the
Clackamas Chinook runs along the *bottom* of the page, and could be seen as in
a secondary or supportive position to the English text). Jacobs then published
two books designed for non-linguists, in which he attempted to relate the texts
to, on the one side, their cultural background and, on the other, to the general
category of literature. By taking just one of a set of related stories about
Grizzly Woman and looking at Jacobs' treatment of it, it should be possible
to follow up in detail some of the problems generated by this dual focus on
cultural background and literary work.

In one of a number of stories which deal with Grizzly Woman, we are first
introduced to a young man, Gitskux, who lives with his elder brother and the
brother's wife. Grizzly Woman arrives on the scene, and presents herself as a
second wife for the brother. The children of the first wife avoid Grizzly
Woman, who takes their pet raccoon. The first wife secretly kills the raccoon.
Gitskux brings a raccoon back and gives it directly to the children. Grizzly
Woman kills the raccoon, the two wives fight and Grizzly Woman kills the
first wife and puts on her skin. Gitskux, forewarned of this by the first wife,
returns and trails Grizzly Woman by feeding her until she is comatose. He
returns the skin to his first wife, who returns to life. They burn Grizzly
Woman.

Grizzly Woman returns, the wives fight, Grizzly Woman's rage swells and
she eats up all the people. She vomits up the first wife's head, which floats
downriver and is retrieved by Gitskux and his brother. Gitskux is captured by
Grizzly Woman, but the older brother escapes with his wife's head. He finds a

house with a woman who becomes a good wife, and produces two boys. She tells the older brother that Gitskux is being kept as an anus-wiper by Grizzly Woman, and tells him how to find him. The older brother finds Gitskux and gives him flints to put on his head. He then cuts and kills Grizzly Woman when she next sits on him. They burn her, but leave her bones, and return to the good wife, who cleans Gitskux and his hair grows.

The good wife warns that because they failed to grind Grizzly Woman's bones she will return and kill her and take her skin. This eventually happens, and the children recognise and fear the new mother. The brothers return, and Gitskux removes the skin while she sleeps. They burn her, and the good wife, returned to life, grinds her bones and blows them away. When the children are grown, the main figures separate. The good wife becomes a water-being, and Gitskux goes into the mountains.

Some of the elements here are repeated in other stories involving Grizzly Woman. In one story, for instance, she arrives in a village and becomes the headman's wife, systematically kills all the other women, and is eventually killed herself. Another tale involves sisters, the elder of which is Grizzly Woman, who kills her sister. In retribution, her own children are killed, and she goes berserk (literally, in that she takes on the characteristic of a bear), and attacks everyone. Driven out of the village, she paints her face with menstrual blood and continues to rampage. In yet another version, a daughter of Grizzly Woman kills her, only to find the same characteristics appearing in herself. When she is in the menstrual hut, the children see her becoming a Grizzly, claws and all. She eventually eats everyone in the village.

Intensely aware, as he was, that the text itself was only a fragment of a culture, and that what had surrounded the fragment had already partly disappeared, Jacobs attempted to make that fragment meaningful, on the one hand by reconstructing from it, and placing it within, an ethnographic whole which was Chinook culture, and on the other hand by emphasising the text's literary and imaginative qualities which would tend to place it in a more general transcultural category called literature. Two different wholes, then, are involved, and this double intention causes problems, of which Jacobs is uneasily aware. As folklorist, Jacobs would like to be able to reconstitute aspects of the society itself and, where possible, substantiate his reading of the myth by reference to other material from the same culture, but in the case of Chinook this is almost impossible. He has worked out what he considers the right method of collecting too late for this particular culture, but he outlines what he sees as the ideal procedure. Henceforth, he says – though it is perhaps arguably a lament for lost opportunities in the past –

first priority in field method should go to ascertaining from informants their associations and feelings about each unit and type of literary content and style. Speculations of kinds which characterised parts of the analysis should be minimised or replaced, wherever possible, by specific responses from native informants. (Jacobs 1959b:271)

What is particularly interesting about this move towards a sort of native reader-response approach is the way that it moves towards the second sort of whole, the literary, in that one of Jacobs' main justifications for this method is not just the reconstitution of the whole culture as something to be known by science, but the fact that Jacobs' detailed 'write-ups', as he calls them, 'will permit far greater appreciation and enjoyment of exotic literatures than folk-lorists ever made possible for readers of their publications, or even for other folk-lorists'. Would our enjoyment be increased by knowledge of the literary devices of another culture which would allow us to integrate them with our own literary codes and make them less exotic, or would knowledge of the specific ways of the culture help them to make sense in their own way, so that we recognise and understand, without losing their exoticism? The difference may seem unimportant, but Jacobs' uncertainty about the relation between the literary and the sociological runs through his discussion of Victoria Howard's narratives. Nowhere is this seen more clearly than in his psychological speculations about the stories, the psychological being an area which can be invoked to show literary universality and specific social patterns of behaviour. While explicitly rejecting the archetypal approach to myth, Jacobs does use psychological terms as a way of generalising the events in the stories, which can have, at times, the effect of actualising the events and treating them as if they were characters in realist novels, and at other times, of using them as case studies, examples of extreme social deviance. He diagnoses Grizzly Woman, for instance, as 'a paranoid homicidal psychotic', and elsewhere she 'may be characterised, in psycho-analytic terms, as an oral and anal sadist'. Referring to aspects of her revealed in other myths, he tells us that 'a woman of that kind is also a narcissistic genital compulsive' (Jacobs 1960:221). A woman? Perhaps, but she is a bear, too, and a supernatural or myth-age creature, which points to the limits of psychological realism as an approach. When he tries to generalise this psychological element out into the society as a whole, Jacobs falls back into a very straightforward correspondence between society and story. Pointing out the patriarchal residence patterns, which would support Oedipal patterns, he finds a hostility to women in general and older women in particular, and sees this expressed in the figure of Kicimani or Grizzly Woman, who 'represented not a known person or type, but the culture's judgements and sentiments about certain kinds of women'. Elsewhere he assures us that 'actually, Clackamas were saying in this myth that women get more Grizzly-like as they get older' (1959b:160).

At other times he acknowledges the inadequacy of the terms of psychological realism, and invokes the literary demands of the story. Even here, he still wants to reintegrate psychology by referring to the particular role of women in this society, and a specific example demonstrates the various manoeuvres he engages in. When Gitskux and his brother leave the good wife alone, even after she has warned them of Grizzly Woman's imminent arrival, Jacobs sees a problem of credibility:

I do not know what an informant might have said in response to a query as to why the mother stresses a quick return of the man so as to minimise the children's terror. The informant did comment frequently that Myth Age people 'were very foolish' and 'they did not have good sense'. In Mrs Howard's mind, their lack of judgement was evidenced by a departure to hunt upon the very day when they ought to remain at home in order to prevent murder, especially when they knew that a slaying will occur during their absence. It seems to me that literary demands necessitated a single device: the raconteur removes the hunters from the village in order to allow the plot to proceed with the killing and the flaying. The device exposes the inexorability of fate. Since Grizzly is bound to return, the wife will certainly be killed and her children will be orphaned.... Maybe the plot treatment at this point and the device of absenting the men exhibit the relatively weak social position of a mother and wife who, with fatalistic resignation, knowing there is little she can do, does nothing to persuade the men to stay at home on a day fraught with doom... Clackamas may have been so sensitive about their food supply that they assumed that a precultural hunter must go away to his labours every day. (1960:223-4)

It is worth nothing, here, that Mrs Howard's remarks, which are used by Jacobs as corroboration of his argument, could equally be seen as a way of *not* speculating about psychology or motivation, as can her disavowal of a man who perpetrated appalling acts – 'he was just mean like that'. One of Jacobs' problems is that having invoked the demands of plot, or of the literary, his terminology is heavily dependent on Western concepts, particularly those of tragedy. Here he talks of the 'inexorability of fate', and elsewhere of the merely 'theatrical devices', the story as a whole as a 'woman's drama', and a 'drama of adult men and women whose lives are bedevilled by a bad woman', and (sounding more like Eugene O'Neill all the time) – 'a tragic drama of family relationships'. As in classical tragedy, the social effect was presumably communal and cathartic, and what Jacobs calls 'the myth screen' worked 'to relieve everyone's inner awareness that such destructive sentiments and consequences occurred in the very best families and establishments' (1960:229).

As well as these uneasy attempts at placing the myths within Western conventions, Jacobs does also, of course, try to develop an inventory of literary devices specific to the oral narratives of this culture, involving stylised epilogues, repetitions and formalised patterns of speech or action, and one could argue that it is only the absence of sufficient data of this sort that forces him back to Western categories like tragedy, which he uses as if they were universal.[12] One could also, though, question once again the dual purpose of this sort of classifying and categorising. Even if it overtly claims to increase our understanding of native literary forms, it is also part of a long-standing scientific concern to order and clarify as the means of knowing. Jacobs is concerned with making these myths accessible to general readers because, he argues, of their literary merit, but recognition of that merit depends on as full an awareness as possible of the cultural context in which it operated. In contrast, then, to the lyric and Imagist mode of earlier attempts in English at presenting myth as literature, which used a minimalist effect to create an effect of universality – emphasising the fragment, but implying a common whole – Jacobs' method needs to present oral literature 'not in word or sentence translations, but in interpreted and annotated presentations'. This accounts for his attempt 'to reconstruct for each story as much as I could of what I deduced was happening before, during, and after the narrator's recital. I have tried to "hear" the audience and the community, as well as the raconteur' (1959b:2–3).

Surprisingly, one set of factors which he does not recognise as significant for the appreciation of the literary are specifically linguistic features. This is partly because of the limited sample of his materials, so that linguistic deviations from a norm for literary effect cannot be located, and partly perhaps, because of the limited use of recorded audio performances for analysis. As a result, apart from noting a few phonological and morphological features, none of which he sees as distinctive for literature, he ignores this side of the stories and his presentation of them is in 'straight' prose. This is where the work of Dell Hymes offers an important development of Jacobs' approach, while at the same time continuing to raise more questions about the relation of parts to whole.

In recent years Hymes has developed a mode of presentation of myths in translation which reflects the patterns he finds in them and which, he argues, constitutes them as literature:

> If these instances of the first literature of North America are to be understood as literature, rather than relegated to the status of documents merely, there is no choice but to give them the garb of literature visually as well as analytically.... It is necessary to see the recurrences, repetitions, contrasts and alterations in the original wording, and if at all possible, to see the original wording in an attractive, efficient and effective format. (Hymes 1983:139).

It is crucial for Hymes' enterprise that these patterns and recurrences are linguistically, as well as thematically, signalled in the original version and, unlike Jacobs, he claims it is possible to find linguistic variations and deviations which have literary significance in pointing us toward a literary structure. This is true even when we only have written versions – in fact he has performed some of his most interesting demonstrations on what are now languages that exist only in print. The exact relation between linguistic, thematic and narrative organisation in Hymes is worth pursuing, at least because of the issues it raises about what is translatable.

In an early and influential analysis of another tale of a murderous woman (or what is taken to be a woman), Hymes claims to locate a crucial organising principle revealed by a contrast of linguistic registers, involving different expressions for urinating.[13] This linguistic feature alerts us to the real focus of the story, which is not on the young girl who hears the 'wife' or on the 'wife' herself, as Jacobs, the original recorder of the story suggested, but on Seal, the sister, who insists on maintaining propriety in speech, at the expense of denying the reality before her. This shift in focus is justified for Hymes by the fact that the story can then be seen to share a common structure with other myths of the culture, and we see here a characteristic Hymes procedure. A linguistic feature alerts him to a patterning, but the patterning is *more* than linguistic, it is narrative and ultimately cultural. In his essay 'How To Talk Like A Bear in Takelma' (Hymes 1979) he picks up two linguistic devices – the prefix 'S' for Coyote's speech, and 'X' for Grizzly Bear's speech. This had already been noted by Edward Sapir, but by analysing several texts Hymes shows a variation in their use: 'the contrast between presence and absence of expressive prefix reflects choice in use' (1979:104). It is this stress on expressive prefixes which turns out to be crucial in another essay on a Grizzly Woman story in which Hymes isolates, in the *naming* of Grizzly Woman, an alternative in prefix. He finds a movement between 'wa' and 'a', and zero as prefixes for Kitsimani, Grizzly Woman's Name, and shows that this variation is related to passive and active roles filled by her at different points in the story. Broadly speaking, when she is a wife, or dead, or in some way not dangerous, she takes the prefix 'wa'. As Hymes points out, this cannot be represented in English translation, or naming practices, but it has serious implications for our reading of the story. For instance, Jacobs' psychologising becomes even more dubious. If she is a differently named being, why should we expect consistency of character? Similarly, it emphasises the question of women's roles, and Hymes does use this to stress the fact that this is a woman's story. Also, though, it raises questions about translation and the presentation of any translation, in that the linguistic element itself, and in particular 'the recurrent initial elements', come to represent for him 'the regulatory principle itself' (Hymes 1977:438). It is not that they are the whole key to meaning and organisation, but that they combine with rhetorical and thematic element in ways that reveal a structure unavailable to us if we were to try to model the stories on our own cultural and linguistic forms. We need to locate 'the form–meaning covariation specific to the ethnolinguistic tradition of the texts, a covariation between an underlying narrative analysis of experience, as it were, and various overt linguistic markers and recurrences' (Hymes 1980a:66).

The reference to narrative here is important, both for Hymes' analysis and for his choice of how to present the story in English, as for him narrative patterning is culture-specific and cannot be adequately represented in the uniform prose format that we tend to use for narrative: 'All American Indian narratives, I believe, will prove to be organised in terms of lines and verses, and sets of verses. Where syntactic patterns are present, they will play a role, often a major role'. (1980b:8) The fundamental connotation, however, will not be linguistic, but 'a conception of narrative action. That conception, which can be called a rhetorical conception, will have it that sequences of action will satisfy one or another of two basic types of formal pattern'.[14] These formal patterns, built up of units of two and four or three and five comes increasingly to determine Hymes' presentation, in which he blocks out narrative units of varying sizes (verses, stanzas, scenes, acts, are the terms he uses, drawing with deliberate eclecticism from different Western literary conventions). This dual insistence on narrative and verse refuses the division between what is appropriate to poetry – now usually thought of as lyric, especially in the tradition of Indian materials – and what to prose, reinstating the possibilities of verbal organisation which had been lost by the assumption that narrative meant prose, with all aesthetic elements stripped away. Whether in the end we agree with, or can recognise Hymes' divisions, it is certainly true that we read his versions differently and with our attention directed more as if there is an authorial and patterning intention than in most prose versions.[15] Nevertheless, the form on the page is constructed out of a written text, and is concerned to bring out underlying structure rather than actual oral performance in a particular case, unlike the work of Dennis Tedlock. The distinction is an important one, in spite of the superficial similarities in appearance of their English versions, since Tedlock is concerned to try to carry over on paper the actual intonations, stresses and pauses of Zuni performance – what Anthony Mattina has called 'English translations with Zuni *intonations* – English texts with a Zuni accent' (1987:132-3), rather than the underlying meaning and organisation of a narrative whose existence precedes the particular performance. Hymes' concerns are always fundamentally formal, and he explicitly acknowledges his debt to Russian Formalists and early structuralists (1977:448). His concern for recurrences are not, as with Tedlock, primarily rhetorical, but as aids to the discovery of formal laws: 'concentration of naming and choice of prefix do indeed provide foregrounding in texts and do express underlying conceptions of identity' (1981a:157-8). It is because of this sociolinguistic belief in the inextricability of linguistic and social structures that Hymes is sceptical of claims made by Tedlock for the necessity of the oral performance itself, in so far as it would stress only the sound rather than other linguistic features. At the same time, Hymes is suspicious of what he calls the structuralist 'leap to universals' of Lévi-Strauss and in fact sees a remedy in a return to 'a Boasian stance' (Hymes 1977:448), which would insist on the specificity of linguistic practices within cultures. There is no doubt, though, that Hymes' approach is a structuralist one, and that therefore his work does involve an implicit claim to have discovered more fundamental links of organisation and, inevitably, meaning, which means that the narrative of his own work is that of a discovery. His characteristic method is to present his findings within a narrative which moves from a problem to the pleasure of a discovery which solves it. This means that translation is towards the end of discovery, and an escape from our own categories by means of a recreation and recognition of other categories, another system. Anthony Mattina sees Hymes and Tedlock as having the same aim, 'to record myths so as to maximise interpretive transparency' (1987:133), but the ideal of transparency here is also an ideal of totality – a totality of understanding, in which we can seal off the work of art, and see it whole, or we can circumscribe and totalise the other culture in which it operates. But in fact any reading of Hymes inevitably leads us out beyond the organisation he finds, as do his own amplifications and commentaries on his texts. Krupat puts the problem most clearly:

> Mythographers must choose and limit and specify in order to write their texts at all. This is, however, the very reason why those who read and study those texts must unfix them as a necessity of the impossibility of transferring the qualities of oral performance to writing: of the impossibility of any 'writing' standing alone and fully present. (Swann and Krupat 1987:124–5)

What we have so far, then, are the myths from anonymous Kwakiutl individuals, collected by Boas and produced as texts, part of a collecting towards a deferred understanding of a cultural whole; Victoria Howard's myths recorded by Jacobs with the same intention, but already with a knowledge of the practical impossibility of a Boasian totality because of absence of data, and therefore a preparedness to try to complete the fragments both sociolinguistically and cross-culturally; and Dell Hymes' Formalist concern with the actual organisational principles of the text itself, but with a keen sociolinguistic, rather than narrowly aesthetic, awareness. Hymes' rejection of structuralist universalism should not blind us, though, either to his own structuralism or to the interpretive power of Lévi-Strauss' method when applied to precisely the myths on which Hymes works, and it is through Lévi-Strauss that we can connect up most clearly Grizzly Woman and the Kwakiutl Dzonoqua.

Hymes himself actually makes the connection with Dzonoqua when he points out that the name Kitsimani is to be found in opposition to another Chinookan name, here given as Atunaqua, but he does not develop the connection beyond the realm of the linguistic (1983:130). There is a problem from a strictly Boasian position, or indeed from any functional or structuralist position, in accepting cross-cultural similarities at face value. If in two cultures we have a similar figure or theme, it would be dangerous to assume either that they have a self-evident meaning or common origins (the mistake made by universalist myth collectors like Frazer), or that they mean the same thing or are fulfilling the same function in each culture. The Boasian concern to find meaning within a cultural frame makes it difficult for us to know how to relate Grizzly Woman and Dzonoqua, but Lévi-Strauss offers one way of doing this and relating them to other broader aspects of north-west coast cultures. Rather than looking for the meaning of the Dzonoqua myths in language – that is, something specific to the culture where it is located – Lévi-

Strauss characteristically looks elsewhere. In *The Way of the Masks* (Lévi-Strauss 1982) he links up the physical characteristics of the Dzonoqua, as expressed in masks and carvings as well as in myths, with two sorts of masks, the Xwexwe of the Kwakiutl and the Swaihwe of their neighbours the Salish. These masks show a marked similarity of design (obtruding cyclinder eyes, gaping mouth and enormous tongue), but have opposing connotations and functions in this society. The Dzonoqua is opposed in many physical respects to these masks, and is also amongst the Kwakiutl opposed in function and significance to the Xwexwe mask. To explain this, Lévi-Strauss demonstrates the connection 'between the character of Dzonoqua and accumulated or distributed wealth' (1982:88), and in a number of instances, as in the myth described earlier, with pubescent girls. The connection between the two is marriage, and the distribution of wealth at the associated potlatch, and Lévi-Strauss sees two aspects of the ogress Dzonoqua being revealed:

> First of all she is a kidnapper, but she is also the holder and dispenser of the means for giving the potlatch, among the most prized items of which are the coppers. An articulated mask in three parts, when pulled apart through manipulation of the strings, reveals a copper background, which thus seems to stand for the ogress' very essence. But upon reaching nubility (that is, marriageable age), the young girl becomes comparable to Dzonokwa, and this on two counts. She offers the coppers to her future husband, and she steals from him, in advance, the children to be born from this union ... looked upon from a certain perspective, the opposition between the two roles filled by the ogress underlines her unsociable character; but from a different perspective, the young girl would seem to fill a social role and an economic function that give her the appearance of a *tamed* Dzonokwa. (1982:89–91)

Marriage, then, as a flow of wealth needs to be regulated and so does a woman's power. Dzonoqua appears in winter ceremonies as a sleepy, almost drugged figure, and it is as if, when tamed and socialised, she offers wealth – hence, Lévi-Strauss's reference to young girls as 'tamed Dzonokwas', who facilitate the movement of wealth and, of course, produce children, whereas Dzonoqua eats or steals children. The regulation of wealth and social relations in general, then, is dependent on the right sort of marriage, and in *The Naked Man* (Lévi-Strauss 1981), the fourth and concluding volume of his massive *Introduction to a Science of Mythologies*, Lévi-Strauss relates stories of Grizzly Woman or Kitsimani to this theme via a related set of stories involving the figure of the lewd grandmother, who insists on having sexual intercourse with a bear or other animal or, after it has been killed and butchered, the relevant part of him. This is an example, in Lévi-Strauss' scheme, of extreme exogamy, a marriage too far outside the group, and stands in inverse relation to the ever-present threat of extreme endogamy, incest. Intertwine these themes with those of the distribution of wealth and the recurrent imagery of hunger consumption and transformation, and we are able to understand some of the more puzzling exchanges between characters, as Lévi-Strauss is able to show:

> The fact that the myths constantly play on the ambiguity of the concept of consumption/consummation understood sometimes in the literal and alimentary sense and sometimes in the figurative, sexual sense, emerges very clearly from the admonishment addressed by the hero to his grandmother in a Salish version... after catching her in culpable congress with the only piece of meat she had agreed to carry: 'This is something to eat, not something to marry!' to which the old woman replies, 'I had to do it, since you won't sleep with me'. Whereupon the hero retorts: 'Grandmother, I'm hungry'. (1981:169)

What Lévi-Strauss finds is that Grizzly Woman stories can be placed as one of the variants which operate as preludes to the story of Birdnester, which he has painstakingly followed throughout the Americas. In the prelude 'a mother, who, amongst other things has an ambiguous relationship with her children, appears first of all as a menstruating woman, changes into a cannibalistic wild beast, and finally perishes'. Within these variants he finds 'a system involving four terms, each of which is definable by the semantic function of the chief character: an incestuous sister, a chaste sister, a lewd grandmother, and a mother who turns into an ogress during menstruation' (1981:169). What we have here is Lévi-Strauss' characteristic technique of seeming to move further and further away from a particular item in order to explain it. By placing the contest with the ogress within a larger myth which involves a later visit of the hero to heaven, and an encounter with Sun's daughter, Lévi-Strauss is able to contrast 'two female protagonists: first, the ogress, a chthonian creature or one that has an affinity with the subterranean world; then, the Sun's daughter, a celestial creature whose home and ancestry all place her on the side of daylight' (1982:79). Elsewhere he contrasts Dzonoqua with another giver of wealth, Quomogua, whose wealth comes from the sea, in order to locate by contrast the meaning of the wealth she gives. This method of only establishing meaning by referring to the elements which are absent is equally applicable to myths and masks: 'Like a myth, a mask denies as much as it affirms. It is not made solely of what it says or thinks it is saying, but of what it excludes' (Lévi-Strauss 1982:144). One casualty of this approach is any localised intention or function for the myth. In the case of Grizzly Woman, for instance, both Jacobs and Hymes stress the fact that it is a woman's story, but it is hard to see how this fact can be incorporated in Lévi-Strauss' approach so as to be given any importance, given his premiss that myths are an expression of a whole and undifferentiated society.

This sense in Lévi-Strauss of a whole system, and how it can be reconstructed from fragments, can be further developed by returning to Boas and his Kwakiutl visitor in New York. What Jakobson refers to as the 'whimsical tangling' of languages which gave Boas glimpses of the rules governing the two languages, and the bizarre conjunctions of New York in which the visitor 'felt transformed into the universe of Kwakiutl fairy-tales' (quoted in Clifford 1988:239) are picked up by Lévi-Strauss in describing his own experience of New York. He writes powerfully, even rhapsodically, of the surreal juxtapositions of New York, and in particular of the experience of the North West Coast room of the Museum of Natural History, organised by Boas, and he has described the efforts made by him and artist friends such as Max Ernst to collect north-west coast art in New York and acquire it for France.[16] It is perhaps not unfair to suggest, as James Clifford does, that New York is the most extended fieldwork that Lévi-Strauss ever undertook, in the sense that the conjunctions and incongruities of New York itself are recognised by him both in the art of the surrealists with whom he is associating at the time and in the art of British Columbia, which he was discovering not in British Columbia but in strange conjunctions in the shops and museums of New York. This art, he says, possesses 'the almost monstrous faculty to perceive as similar what all other men have conceived of as different' (quoted in Jonaitis 1981:14), and it is precisely this awareness of similarity within difference which is to run through all of Lévi-Strauss' later work.

In an essay comparing his own work with that of the painter Max Ernst, he underlines this point:

> Like his paintings and collages, my work on mythology has been elaborated by means of samples from without – the myths themselves. I have cut them out like so many pictures in the old books where I found them, and then arranged them on the pages as they arranged themselves in my mind, but in no conscious or deliberate fashion. The structuralist method, as we know, operates by presenting and systematically working out binary oppositions between elements supplied by observation.... The method is easily recognised in Max Ernst's definition of 1934 where he extols 'the bringing together of two or more elements apparently opposite in nature, on a level whose nature is the opposite of theirs'. This is a double play of opposition and correlation, on the one hand, between a complex figure and the background that shows it off, or on the other, between the constituent elements of the figure itself. (Lévi-Strauss 1985:243–4)

Note here the characteristic playing down of the creative act, that is, the selection and ordering involved by an individual, which is related to Lévi-Strauss' lack of interest in whether the order he finds/reveals/creates is his own or the original culture's. Earlier in the same essay he refers approvingly to Ernst's description of his own work as merely 'lucky finds that have not been falsified' (1985:243), but the confidence which allows the creative self to be abandoned like this is not a rejection of order or form, but the invocation of a more fundamental sense of coherence and unity. As James Clifford argues:

> Surrealist art and structural anthropology were both concerned with the

spirit's 'deep' shared springs of creativity. The common aim was to transcend... the local orders of culture and history. Surrealism's subject was an international and elemental humanity 'anthropological' in scope. The object was Man, something it shared with an emerging structuralism. But a conventional division of labour was solidifying. With the project of probing and extending humanity's creative esprit, the two methods diverged, one playing art to the other's science. (1988:243-4)

Lévi-Strauss may have gone in the direction of science, but the surreal elements in his work are still to be found in the dense intertextuality and playfulness of his writing – as, for instance, in his naming one of the chapters in *The Naked Man*, 'Soluble Fishes', a direct allusion to an André Breton text. Certainly, his concern for north-west coast art, and in particular masks, continued, and it is in his *Way of the Masks* and *The Naked Man* that we can find not only the further development of the Dzonoqua/Grizzly Woman theme which I have used, but a way of focusing on what claims Lévi-Strauss is finally making.

His claim that masks are not what they are, but what they transform, points us to one of the overall stratagems in his work, and can be used as counterpoint to a view of his work, admittedly propounded by himself, as moving towards a unified end. This second view is furthered by Lévi-Strauss' extended musical analogy, and a Western one at that (harmony, counterpoint, resolution), whereas the idea of masks in endless transformations, which have no actual fixed point or resting place and are themselves by definition an absence, a nothing in themselves, a covering, but not of anything which, if revealed, would explain them – this points away from coherence or a totalisable project. This is, of course, close to the theme of Derrida's celebrated critique of Lévi-Strauss and the idea of structure,[17] but I am arguing here that the model of the masks rather than of musical form may give us a better idea of what actually happens in the extended project of the *Introduction to a Science of Mythology*, of which *The Naked Man* is the fourth volume. Viewed in this way, it can be seen to be, like a number of Modernist works of art, more post-structuralist than structuralist in its actual working methods, whatever it may actually claim for itself. If we look, for instance, at the way Lévi-Strauss, at the end of the fourth volume, defends himself against charges of ignoring philology and, therefore, the specificity of each version, we find his usual claim for a common structure, but put in a way which points towards a more post-structuralist idea of what Derrida would call citation:

If as is shown by the comparative analysis of different versions of the same myth produced by one or several communities, *conter* (to tell a story) is always *conte redire* (to retell a story) which can also be written *contredire* (to contradict) it is immediately understandable why it was not absolutely essential... to study the myths in the originals instead of in a translation... properly speaking there is never any original; any myth is by its very nature a

> translation and derives from another myth... that some listener tries to
> plagiarize by translating it in his fashion into his personal or tribal language,
> sometimes to appropriate it and sometimes to define it, and therefore
> invariably distorting it. (Lévi-Strauss 1981:644-5)

Here, we have the characteristic movement (some would call it sleight of hand) from the idea of fidelity to 'original' material, in the sense of a particular local significance to the idea of an 'original' in the sense of an originary myth. By discussing the second, Lévi-Strauss claims to have dismissed the need for the first.

It is, of course, an article of Lévi-Strauss' structuralist faith that the right method will reveal a structure underlying these versions, which will function *in place of* the original, in the sense that it is the end of the quest, but I would argue that the actual experience of reading the whole of the *Introduction To A Science of Mythology* is one of deferral and incompleteness much more than of reaching completion. This can constitute one way to criticise his project in his own terms and to return a verdict of not proven, pointing to the manipulation and selectivity of evidence, but more fundamentally it can be a way of arguing that precisely because of Lévi-Strauss' actual method, we are made aware of the instability of any separate system. Philology, he accepts, would 'give more scope and depth to the interpretation', but he insists that it would not

> essentially affect the semantic content. The gain will be rather on the literary
> and poetic side: it will make it easier to appreciate the aesthetic properties of
> the text, whose message – given the fact that translation allows the myth to be
> understood as myth – will hardly be modified. (Lévi-Strauss 1981:645)

Here, at the end of his huge undertaking Lévi-Strauss is echoing his earlier distinction between the untranslatable poem and the absolutely translatable myth. In fact, it is not just that translation does not harm the myth, but that it reveals it *as* myth. In its transformations we see the form.

In a curious sense, then, both Lévi-Strauss and Hymes are wanting to cancel out translation itself as an intrusive element or, to put it another way, they are trying to neutralise their own language. For Lévi-Strauss, it is irrelevant to myth 'as myth'. For Hymes, it must be made as transparent as possible to reveal the patterns within the original, and to do this our own language acquires a sort of instrumentality and uniformity. In this way, they are in a long tradition of translations in which the linguistic diversity of English is not a resource to be used. This is partly the problem of knowing how to use an appropriate range of voices and registers of language, of course, but it is also related to assumptions about organic and unified cultures. It is noticeable, for instance, that most translations of Indian materials avoid neologisms or any risk-taking with the points of conjunction of languages,[18] and that Lévi-Strauss' interest in surrealism is at the level of conjunctions of ideas, rather than languages. In other words, the mixing of cultures and cultural levels within cultures is very restricted in the language of translations, in what seems to be a recuperative manoeuvre against the 'dissemination' as Derrida would put it, of meanings, so that we always know which system we are meaning, and finding meaning, within. The problem is not necessarily solved, of course, merely by trying to match vernacular levels or by verbal experimentation, especially if the overall end is a 'total translation' which may still imply two separate spheres to be joined, or by the use of 'Red English', especially if it seems to reinforce a white stereotype of the semi-articulate Indian.

Perhaps Lévi-Strauss' massive unifying project is only the most extreme example of a consistent impulse connected with the collecting and translating of myths, which is that of reconstituting and rediscovering a lost totality. James Clifford has connected this with the impulse to collect artefacts as well as myths, and pinpointed Lévi-Strauss' experience of New York as an archetypal expression of modernity: 'The chronotope of New York supports a global allegory of fragmentation and ruin. The modern anthropologist, lamenting the passing of human diversity, collects and values its survivals, its enduring works of art' (1988:24).

For Lévi-Strauss, as Clifford points out, some of the most important of these survivals were to be found in the scholarly works of earlier anthropologists like Boas, whose salvage ethnography meant that the authentic culture to be redeemed was to be found in these books, rather than in the surviving remnants of the cultures. It follows, then, that if that lost whole is to be reconstituted, kept pure, it must be protected from intrusions and impurities, not only from white culture but from what Indian cultures have now become. Lévi-Strauss' conclusion to *The Way of the Masks* powerfully demonstrates both the belief in this totality and the distance from it, not only of whites but of present-day Indians, when he describes his findings as 'scattered threads' for the reconstruction of a backdrop of a stage on which 'the actors of a play for which we do not have the script have left their footprints' (1982:228). They are, of course, though, *our* footprints, because the final – or original – totality to be involved is always implicitly man, a common humanity. Only by recreating the other as whole can we become so ourselves. In Robert Frost's words, only by going

> Back out of all this now too much for us
> Back in a time made simple by the loss
> Of detail

can be found what will make us 'whole again beyond confusion' (Frost 1972:156–7).

Notes

1. See Clifford (1988:230–8) on collecting, and its relation to classificatory and taxonomical versus collagist approaches to other cultures.
2. A good brief account of the argument for a full linguistic understanding rather than an impressionistic approach was given on behalf of the Boas tradition by Robert H. Lowie, against Margaret Mead in 'Native Languages as Ethnographic Texts' (1940). To talk of a linguistic basis for research is, of course, different from talking about the linguistic *model* in anthropology associated with structuralism. The figures under discussion in this chapter could be said to demonstrate the differences and the continuities between these two uses of linguistics. See Kaplan and Manners (1972:163–88) for a brief critique of the linguistic model in relation to the idea of culture.
3. As well as the materials used in this chapter, see Lévi-Strauss' extensively discussed reading of the myth of Asdiwal (1978). For a discussion of his treatment of this myth see Leach (1967).
4. Franz Boas, 'The Ethnological Significance of Esoteric Doctrines', quoted in MacDonald (1981:226). MacDonald sees the effect of this as being a neglect of the role of shamanism on the north-west coast. See also Jonaitis (1981). Towards the end of his life Boas did give more attention to collecting variations in oral performance – see Rohner (1969:290) and Helm (1966:198). Boas has also been criticised from the opposite position in relation to his work on the Kwakiutl, for failing to live up to his own prescriptions, and ignoring the lower-class Kwakiutl, thereby forming a picture of a *limited* group, but presenting it as typical or common. (See Verne Ray's review of Melville Herskovits, 'Franz Boas: the Science of Man in the Making' (1955).
5. See Rohner (1966), and his introduction to *The Ethnography of Franz Boas* (1969). For a more sceptical view of Boas, see Spier (1963).
6. Jacobs (1959a:130). See also Boas (1930b).
7. See his early *Indianische Sagen* (Boas 1895a), and his reference to the possibility of 'a nice little article for *Scribner* or *Century*' in Rohner (1969:79).
8. See particularly Goldman (1975) and Walens (1981).
9. The figure of the wild woman with pendulous breasts seems to be remarkably widespread. Cf. Hayden White's description of the Wild Woman of medieval legend: 'She was supposed to be surpassingly ugly, covered with hair except for her gross pendant breasts, which she threw over her shoulders when she ran' (1978:167).
10. From a huge range of discussion of potlatch, largely based on Boas' inconclusive writings, see particularly Goldman (1975), Drucker and Heizer (1967) and Codere (1950).
11. Rohner (1969:297). He goes on: 'It is strange how those people cling to the form, though the content is almost gone. But this still makes them very happy.' In a rather less sanguine description in a letter a week earlier to his sister, Boas talks of the 'shabby impression' the lack of original artefacts and furniture makes (Rohner 1969:295).
12. He explicitly justifies this 'stress on Chinook literature as a kind of theatre' by pointing to the 'terse summarisations of action', absence of psychological

interpretation and 'the actual "dramatic renditions" of the narrators' (Jacobs 1959b:7).

13. Dell Hymes (1977). See also Jarold Ramsay (1977). Frank Kermode uses Hymes' analysis as part of a discussion of the uses and limitations of structural analysis. Interestingly, he completely ignores the linguistic stress which is what makes Hymes' approach distinctive, preferring to concentrate on broad issues of structure – only then to decide that structuralism is not flexible enough to deal with large-scale works of literature (1969:891).

14. Hymes (1980b:8-9). This passage is also discussed by Anthony Mattina in his helpful and incisive 'North American Indian Mythography: Editing Texts for the Printed Page'. See also for a very clear account of the issues, Hegeman (1989).

15. There are, of course, exceptions, and Howard Norman's work (1976 and 1982) would be a good example.

16. See Elizabeth Cowling (1978). Lévi-Strauss' own account is to be found in Lévi-Strauss (1982:9-10).

17. Jacques Derrida, 'Structure, Sign and Play in the Human Sciences', reprinted in Derrida (1978).

18. Rothenberg's own work of 'total translation' and his anthologising of similar work by others is the obvious exception here. See also James Clifford's discussion of Aimé Césaire (1988:75-81).

CHAPTER SEVEN

Dialogues and Dialogics

In earlier chapters I have tried to show the degree of ideological investment in the idea of the authenticity both of Indian expression itself and of the forms in which it appears in written texts describing or representing it. Implied along with the idea of authenticity of expression and representation, of course, is a speech situation in which communication difficulties can be overcome or transcended, so that the recipient of the speech is also authenticated, and the situation becomes a version of what James Clifford has called the 'fable of rapport' (1988:40). Alternatively, the recipient may be completely effaced, except as objective observer and recorder. The complementarity of these two terms, of authenticity and objectivity, in white textualisations of Indian speech and in language use in general has, I hope, been clearly enough demonstrated, but the idea of dialogue, which is increasingly being presented as an alternative that is both politically and methodologically superior, needs careful analysis. My approach will be to look first at a series of texts which claim to be, or to represent, dialogues and then in the light of the issues these raise to look in detail at some of the claims made in recent theoretical discussion of dialogue, and its relation to the question of a reflexive anthropology.

The long-established use of the dialogue form as a device for the propounding of an argument, stretching back to Plato, has, of course, always involved an agenda set in advance, in which the participants played clearly defined roles, leading to the emergence of the correct view. The truth is never in doubt, and the other positions are put up only as straw men, but the well-established conventions of the form make it irrelevant for us to object that, for instance, the actual identities or characters of the figures in dialogue are subordinated to the development of the argument, or to criticise the suppression or misrepresentation of the true nature and views of one of the participants. The situation becomes more complex, though, when different and more realist claims are made for the dialogue. Some fascinating and ambiguous instances of this can be found in the writings of John Eliot, which offer surprising parallels with later techniques. As well as publishing his *Indian Dialogues* in 1671 (Bowden and Ronda 1980), Eliot throughout his writings gives instances of the question and answer sessions conducted at his meetings with Indians he was trying to convert, so we have quite a diverse range of materials, which differ in the extent to which they are explicitly used as idealised models or presented as actual conversations. His earlier accounts include lists of Indian questions and answers presented, like the dying speeches discussed in Chapter 3, as evidence for the 'Day-Breaking' or the 'Glorious Progress' of Christianity in New England for a white audience and even the *Dialogues*, supposedly written with Indian preachers in mind and presenting Indians speaking with each other and not with whites, are written in English. (Eliot says that he thinks it desirable that his Indian preachers learn English, though he may eventually produce an Indian version.) The *Dialogues*, though, differ from the speeches in being quite explicit about their status as a sort of training manual and model for new Indian preachers. They are, he says,

> partly historical, of some things that were done and said, and partly instructive, to show what might or should have been said, or that may be (by the Lord's assistance) hereafter done and said upon the like occasion. (Bowden and Ronda 1980:61)

The *Indian Dialogues* are presented in a stylised dramatic form, with at least some of the protagonists being named after actual Indians known to Eliot, such as Waban, one of his earliest converts. These characters pursue their daily life amongst other Indians, who sometimes join in the conversation approvingly, but in the manner of their speech there is little to distinguish them from whites or from each other. Where the distinction is really made is between Christian and pagan, as one of the Christian Indians, Piumbukhou, is at pains to explain to his kinsman. Refusing an invitation to 'great dancing, and sacrifice, and play' where he could again meet his friends and family, he explains in terms hardly likely to endear him to those he seeks to convert, that he cannot serve two masters, and must keep his distance.

> I desire that I were able to pull you all out of that deep pit and filthy puddle; which to perform, I should utterly be disabled, if I should go in myself, and so be defiled with the same filth, which I persuade them to forsake and cast away. (1980:64)

Clearly it was no part of Eliot's plan for his Indian missionaries that they should build bridges or negotiate between the cultures, reflecting that more general Puritan absolutism which leads the editors of Eliot's dialogues to describe the Puritans as 'religiously and culturally aggressive, against all forms of behaviour they considered ungodly' (Bowden and Ronda 1980:240). What one Christian Indian calls 'the narrow way of heavenly joys' is to be achieved at the *expense* of Indian culture, not in any sort of accommodation with it. Accordingly, Eliot's erasure of any positive differences in his pagan characters, in that they are characterised by their *lack*, rather than by their possession of *different* beliefs from the Christians, reflects the process whereby they must be turned into nothing, mere blanks, before they can become Christians. Peneovot, for instance is so filled by Waban with 'a sense of my own vileness, that I see matter of endless confession. And I see so much nothingness in myself that I see endless matter of petition and supplication' (1980:107).

This language of self-abasement is of course widespread in religious writing of the time and it would be quite wrong to suggest that it was developed in order to destroy Indian morale. Nevertheless the situation presented in these dialogues, in which the Indian, as alien and potentially dangerous, disappears, leaving behind in his place only a speech which is both elevating and reassuring does bear a strong resemblance to the dying speeches and the speeches of surrender and acceptance looked at in Chapter 3. This can be seen perhaps most clearly in Eliot's treatment of the figure of Metacom, or King Philip, or, as he is called in the dialogues, Philip Keitasscot. Here we have a figure whose subsequent actions were far from reassuring to the whites, and who is later treated by William Apes, as we have seen, as a hero. For Eliot, though, he is a sachem anxious to hold on to his authority, and his eventual submission to God's power offers another reassuring scene. When Philip accepts that 'though I am a sachem here on earth, I shall be but a subject in the day of judgement' he is giving way to the authority of God, and indirectly to his ministers, on religious matters even if he needs further reassurance on worldly authority. To his objections that he will lose his followers and status, the Christians reply that as long as he is a Christian he can continue to rule, since equality and democracy operate in the realm of religion only: 'Church order doth not abolish civil order, but establish it. Religion teacheth and commandeth reverence and obedience to civil rulers (1980:128). This is one of the few times in the dialogues when there is any sense of the political bargaining and negotiating which was the actual context in which religious and cultural conversion was taking place, and it could be argued that in line with Eliot's other writings, the effect of the textualisation of the Indians is to elevate Indian–white relations from the distinctly murky area of political and economic coercion to a purer realm of transparent communications and willing converts.

The fact, though, that all of Eliot's accounts of his dealings with Indians have to be seen, in different degrees, as part of a sustained promotional campaign to gain support from England, in which both Eliot and the Indians were to be textualised and made emblematic, does not mean that everything within the writings can only be seen as direct products of Eliot's propagandist intentions. In particular, Eliot gives us, almost incidentally sometimes, and out of context, lists of questions asked by the Indians. Questions from both sides were important to his missionary approach, as he makes clear in describing the posing of various questions, 'to see what they would say to them, that so we may skrue by variety of means something or other of God into them' (Eliot 1647:4). The Indian responses to these leading questions are paraphrased by Eliot, and it is clear that eventually he manages to establish a formal pattern of 'correct' response when he describes some of the Indians as 'catechised', but in his listing of some of the Indian questions in *The Glorious Progress* (1649) there is much more variety, and since these questions are merely listed, rather than given a context, the effect for modern readers can be almost surreal, as in 'Why must we be like salt?', or 'Why did Christ compare the Kingdom of Heaven to a net?' Many of the questions, though, can best be compared with those of an anthropologist, in that they are attempts at understanding an alien way of thinking, as in 'Doth the Devill dwell in us as we dwell in a house?'

James Ronda, in arguing that the Indians made incisive criticisms of Christians and their missionary work, picks out some of these questions and puts them in the context of revitalisation movements in order to question the assumption that Indian societies just collapsed. In particular, as he points out, there is evidence actually within the Christian records of sceptical and persistent questions which are not answered (or answerable?), like 'Why did God make Hell before Adam sinned?' (Ronda 1977:71). Such questions are presented by Eliot, of course, not as a challenge, or a rejection of Christianity, but rather as evidence of a thirst for God's word. 'Let me give you,' he says, 'a taste of their knowledge by their Questions' (1649:84). By knowledge, of course, Eliot means Christian knowledge, which has the effect of screening out any other considerations raised by the questions. Rather than interrogating Christianity, they are used as evidence for pre-existing beliefs about Indians, but the fact that Eliot can contain and over-read any subversive implications, whereas we might read these questions differently, as Ronda has done, raises important questions about the extent to which definitions of what is repressive and what is subversive are related to the historically situated reader rather than being inherent in any particular material or situation.

Stephen Greenblatt, in discussing Thomas Harriot's *Briefe and True Reporte* of Virginia and its inclusion of criticisms of English beliefs, generalises the question in a very useful way.

But why, we must ask ourselves, should power record other voices, permit subversive enquiries, register at its very center the transgression that will ultimately violate it? The answer may be in part that power, even in a colonial situation, is not perfectly monolithic and hence may encounter and record in one of its functions material that can threaten another of its functions. (Greenblatt 1981:50)

While Eliot then, is textualising these questions for one purpose, overwriting them, and imposing his overall meaning on them, he cannot completely control or predict their meanings or uses in other spheres. In the same way, Greenblatt suggests, the collecting of materials in order to constitute Indian culture as a knowable entity which can then be 'brought into the light for study, discipline, correction, transformation' can have effects which are simultaneously destabilising and consolidating.

> The momentary sense of instability or plenitude – the existence of other voices – is produced by the power that ultimately denies the possibility of plenitude, just as the subversive hypothesis about European religion is tested and confirmed only by the imposition of that religion. (1981:51)

Greenblatt can stand here as an important reminder of the difficulties involved in trying to identify oppositional elements within textual products of a culture without also seeing the ways in which they can be used to confirm the power they seem to us to undermine, and I have used Eliot and his turning of difficult questions into evidence of Christian knowledge as an example. Yet in the same article Greenblatt queries the means by which we identify the subversive in such texts in the first place, and suggests that 'we locate as "subversive" in the past precisely those things that are *not* subversive to ourselves, that pose no threat to the order by which we live' (1981:52). In other words if dominance and subversion are not fixed, but relational, qualities in societies of the past, the same applies to our own culture and our perceptions of it, and the implication is that we can never be sure where power and its subversion are located. Carolyn Porter has argued very forcefully against the implications of what she sees in Greenblatt as the essentialising of power in this way.

> Once power is absolutized as a transhistorical force which relentlessly produces and recontains subversion, any resistance or opposition to such power always already presents itself as a form of subversion: as a resistance from *within* power's domain. Consequently, those cultural spaces of possible resistance which were marginalised by a focus on the dominant discourse have functionally been erased altogether. (Porter 1988:767)

She objects particularly to the way the discursive field is narrowed to one set of discourses, 'those that form the site of a dominant ideology' and then treated as if this could stand for the limits of discourse altogether. She insists that there are *other* social groups, non-literate but not without language, which can operate as 'cultural spaces of possible resistance',[1] and she therefore sees Greenblatt's equating of Algonkian and English lower orders as having the effect of limiting the discursive field actually at work in English life:

> I would insist that neither of these cultures is without agency of some sort,

but it is, after all, easier in some ways to 'other' a people whose language you need not even bother translating, unless you are John Eliot and are willing to textualise it first, than one whose polyglot vernacular can be deployed to foster a threatening ideological position. (1988:774)

While Porter's objections to a sort of discursive defeatism seem to me extremely valuable, her distinction between Indians and English speakers returns us to the issues of translation and textualisation I have been pursuing, and my argument has been that the textualisation of Indians, the bringing of speaking Indians into the discursive field, offers particularly complex instances of the issues raised by Greenblatt and Porter.

One of the major difficulties in finding a way out of the absolute hold of discourse is how to find a way of constituting any knowledge of Porter's 'cultural spaces of possible resistance' which does not entail their textualisation and consequent slotting into discursive formations. This can be demonstrated by looking at rather an oddity, John Smith's *A Dialogue Between an Englishman and an Indian* (1789). This brief text, like Eliot's *Dialogues*, is written by a white man, and the Indian's voice can therefore be said to be a white creation. Intended to be performed in a lighthearted context at Dartmouth College, it has the Indian besting the Englishman in argument, and exposing his prejudices, but in language which fits very well with the educational aims of Eleazar Wheelock, already dealt with in detail in Chapter 4. The Indian asks,

> Do you discover the temper of a christian, when you wish destruction to whole nations? Have you one spark of that generous benevolence to mankind, which stamps a dignity on the human soul, when you regret, that endeavours should be used to civilise and christianise an unpolished and savage people; yet capable of improvement, and of being made good members of society? (in Moody 1966:8)

Smith refers in a letter to the dialogue having been 'acted pretty naturally, as a real Aboriginal defended the part of the Indian' (Moody 1966:7), adding to the ironies of the situation. Unlike Eliot, then, the purpose of the dialogue could be said to give the Indian his voice, but it is still written by a white, and couched in the language of Christian philanthropy. A further level of meaning is given to the dialogue by the fact that the white is an Englishman, and one commentator, Harold Rugg, has transposed the whole exchange into the rhetoric of the revolutionary period, so that like Pontiac in Chapter 3, the Indian here is representing something other than himself. The dialogue, says Rugg, deals with 'the position of the underprivileged during the revolutionary period, the underprivileged being the Indian who, through a definite venture in type-casting, is allowed to speak for his race and its position in relation to the reactionary political and social controls we, as a people, were fighting at the time.' (Rugg 1942:56).

The most serious attempts to slough off these over-determinations, and find an Indian position not already ethnocentrically prescribed by whites have been in anthropology, in the form of objective and scientific accounts, freed from the biases of travellers or missionaries, but recent searching self-examinations within the discipline itself have thrown into question the adequacy of authoritative and closed ethnographic descriptions. This has to be seen as part of a larger development, what has been called a crisis of representation within the social sciences, which involves a questioning of the legitimacy of ruling scientific paradigms, and the methods they entail. (Marcus and Cushman 1982; Clifford 1983b; Clifford and Marcus 1986; Marcus and Fischer 1986; Ruby 1982).

The constitution of the stance of objectivity in the writing of ethnography has been shown to be a rhetorical strategy, which involves the turning of personal into impersonal, the erratic and discontinuous dialogue of fieldwork into the smooth, monologic written text. Even when the anthropologist has taken on the role of participant-observer, the textual conventions serve to contain and delimit the significance of this, since the purpose of participating is the better to gain understanding, to quarry knowledge which is then transformed into texts. The result is that the ethnographic texts present a very selective account, as the publication of Malinowski's diaries and their revelation of a private individual very different from the patient figure of the ethnographies vividly demonstrated (see Clifford 1988:92–113). The degree of immersion in native life, the degree of the loss of white Western subject in the object being studied is, therefore, always controlled by the need to come back, to re-establish objectivity, and to this end the writing down and recording is crucial. The writing subject creates himself implicitly in his writing as an objective 'man of science', by constituting his object of study (the people and their ways) stripped of the subjective and personal engagement and dialogue by which he gained what is now presented as knowledge.

In the context of American anthropology this emphasis on scientific objectivity and inclusiveness was early established and institutionalised. Faced with the imminent prospect of the disappearance of whole Indian tribes and cultures, the scientific response was a huge effort of what has come to be called salvage ethnography. This, as I tried to show in the last chapter, was an effort not so much to salvage the people and their way of life as to save and process information about them before it was too late. The early rationale for this was an evolutionary one, with John Wesley Powell and others justifying the need to know about primitive peoples because they represented a step in our development. Later, mainly under the profound influence of Boas, stress was laid on the collection of data about specific cultures with a view to understanding how elements of a culture interrelated, rather than stressing any evolutionary or hierarchical scale (Mark 1980; Hinsley 1981). Clearly, Boas' emphasis on the need to look at material in its *own* cultural context, and the consequent playing down of the ethnographer's own views and preconceptions, was of crucial importance in ridding anthropology of the blatantly ethnocentric assumption that one could easily understand a culture by casual observation or intuition or by slotting it into a pre-existing framework. His insistence on scientific objectivity, exemplified in the method of collecting and recording data through the use of informants and then presenting the findings in an objective and impersonal text, did mean, though, that the personal experiences and feelings of the ethnographer and his or her relations with any informants were screened out, as I have shown in dealing with his relationship with George Hunt in Chapter 6.

Largely due to the influence of Boas, this approach has prevailed in the ethnography of North American Indians, even finding its expression in the creation of autobiographies, as already shown. The private and subjective has been confined to letters, diaries and, in some cases, poetry, and kept rigorously separate from the scientific accounts. More recently, of course, the awareness of the political as well as the epistemological implications of turning personal experience and encounter into objective statement of truth has produced a widespread concern with reflexivity. But it would be wrong to see this questioning of objectivity as necessarily a privileging of subjectivity as a greater guarantee of truth, and this is where dialogical and dialectical approaches, which challenge the whole opposing categories of subjective and objective and the rhetorical forms which accompany them, are of particular interest. As a way of approaching these latest developments in ethnography and investigating how far they are able to offer any new solutions to the problems of discursive and textual authority raised earlier, I want to discuss two parallel themes – objective detachment versus subjective involvement, and scientific record versus literary creation – in relation to several accounts of aspects of Zuni life and culture.

Frank Hamilton Cushing is a particularly useful starting point, in that he has been seen as a problematic nineteenth-century precursor of the participant-observer, as a man who 'went native' to the extent that he neglected his duty to produce scientific texts from what he had discovered (See Gronewold 1972). Cushing himself certainly contributed to the development of a certain mythology about his activities. He continually presented his work, some of which is actually quite substantial, as prolegomena to the definitive work he was about to write (which might make his work an interesting version of what Krupat argues is the ironic mode of anthropological writing (:Krupat 1988). In addition, the ease with which he learned to practise Indian crafts, his brilliant intuitive insights, his success in being adopted into the Zuni Bow priesthood, and his theatrical appearances in Zuni dress, all made him an intriguing figure. Even the accusations and rumours which hung over him were in keeping with his image, in that they pointed to the blurring of the distinction between scientist and native, whether it was his relations with Zuni women or later the charge that he personally fabricated an item he later presented as an Indian artefact. (He himself said that he had restored it.)[2]

Assessments of Cushing have tried to cope with his peculiar relation to the anthropological establishment by treating him either as a scientist or as a literary artist (as in Wilson 1956), but as I hope to show, this is to insist on an unduly rigid division, especially when it comes to dealing with ethnographic texts. The role of experience, its relation to interpretation, and the division between participating and writing cannot be easily fixed in Cushing, and this is why he is of particular interest as a precursor, in working with the Zuni, of two very different figures, Ruth Benedict and Dennis Tedlock, whom I want to deal with in the context of a dialogical or reflexive anthropology.

As a way of exploring the ramifications of Cushing's emphasis on personal experience and its relation to the making of ethnographies and the constitution of scientific knowledge, I want to concentrate on *My Adventures in Zuni*. This was written for publication in three parts in *Century Magazine* in 1882-3, for a popular rather than a scientific audience, and has therefore to be seen in the context of his friendship with the journalist Sylvester Baxter, who publicised his work at Zuni, and his subsequent trip to the East with his Zuni companions.[3] Even so, it would be wrong to see commercial and scientific impulses as necessarily opposed in such a piece, and perhaps because of its (and Cushing's) hybrid character, it offers an intriguing way into issues only explicitly developed by theorists fairly recently.

In his introduction to Cushing's posthumously published *Zuni Folk Tales*, Powell acknowledges both sides of Cushing, but sees them as reconcilable:

> Under the scriptorial wand of Cushing, the folk-tales of the Zunis are destined to become a part of the living literature of the world, for he is a poet although he does not write in verse. (Cushing 1902:ix)

Cushing, we are told, can think like a myth-maker and speak like a priest, 'but his sympathy with the mythology of tribal men does not veil the realities of science from his mind' (Cushing 1901:ix). In other words, his sympathies, his closeness to the thoughts and feelings of the Zunis are only means to a scientific end. Since, as Powell puts it earlier in the same piece, 'the opinions of tribal men seem childish to civilised men', science interests itself in mythology and folklore because 'modern science now considers it of profound importance to know the course of evolution of the humanities' (1901:viii). Although Cushing does not himself express this developmental view and he sees culture differently from Powell, as I will show later, he is explicitly committed to the cause of the scientific method, most notably in a letter written from Zuni. Regardless of his own scholarly ability or lack of it, he says,

> my method must succeed. I live among the Indians, I eat their food and sleep in their houses. Because I will unhesitatingly plunge my hand in common with

their dusty ones and dirtier children's into a great kind of hot, miscellaneous food; will sit close to them having neither vermin nor disease, will fondle and talk sweet Indian to their bright eyed babies; will wear the blanket and tie the Pania round my long hair; will look with unfeigned reverence on their beautiful and ancient ceremonies, never laughing at any absurd observance, they love me and I learn. (Cushing 1979: 136–7)

This approach, which he calls elsewhere 'the reciprocal method' (Mark 1980:123), is clearly different from that of Matilda Stevenson, for instance, whom Cushing viewed as an insensitive bully, confident of her ability to understand the Zuni on the basis of a superficial acquaintance with the people and their lives (though see Lurie 1966 for a more sympathetic view). Still, it is worth noting the fundamentally asymmetrical nature of his relationship with the Zuni. Cushing learns not because he loves *them*, but because they love *him*. This is a strange sort of reciprocity, in which like is not exchanged for like. To be fair, in his account of his life there Cushing does express fondness for the Zuni, and he does refer to regular occasions on which they ask him about life in the East, and are seen to be learning, but his expression of his *method* here does reveal the fundamental difference in aims of both parties. Cushing's closeness to the Zuni is presented by him as a means to an end, that of knowledge:

After having secured the two necessities, the absolute confidence and the language of the Indian, I feel it my duty to use these necessities or advantages to the fullest extent of their value, toward the end which I acquired them for. (Cushing 1979:150).

This participant-observer approach, which he speaks of elsewhere as 'the personal equation' is referred to as an ordeal and a sacrifice for science, as 'my self-inflicted degradation to the daily life of savages' (Cushing 1979:140). Clearly, statements like this have to be seen in context – in this case Cushing's self-justification against the sniping of Stevenson – but they do indicate an aspect of his enterprise which needs to be integrated into the picture of his stay in Zuni presented in his published works. It is not that his letters or other documents give the lie to the picture presented for public consumption, but rather that we are able to see in the texts available the variety of conventions and rhetorical patterns which were available to Cushing. It is interesting to note that Powell, in the passage quoted earlier, refers to Cushing's 'scriptorial wand', linking up Cushing's writing to science, but also to magic and the Zuni world. Typically here the middle term for Powell is literature, with all its connotations of being able to transcend cultural limitations and communicate at an essential level similar to myth. What I want to stress is the inadequacy of any separation which ignores the activity of *writing* involved in ethnography and science, as well as literature. Cushing's 'wand' creates ethnography as well as literature.

One recurrent theme in *My Adventures in Zuni* is Cushing's reference to his note-taking and sketching. The Zuni mistrust it and it constitutes a constant barrier to friendship, but he holds on to it as if it is an essential part of his identity. He changes his mode of dress, what he eats, how he speaks, but all in order that he can better record. This becomes his defining characteristic, it creates him as ethnographer, even as it brings the Zuni into existence for the white reader. In a confrontation with two of the Zuni chiefs, Cushing refuses to leave his notebooks and pencils behind, insisting that he must carry them everywhere:

> 'If you put the shadows of the great dance down on the leaves of your books today, we shall cut them to pieces' they threatened. Suddenly wrenching away from them, I pulled a knife out ... and said that whatever hand grabbed my arm again would be cut off, that whoever cut my books to pieces would only cut himself to pieces with my knife. It was a doubtful game of bluff, but the chiefs fell back a little and I darted through the door. Although they followed me throughout the whole day, they did not again offer to molest me, but the people gathered so closely around me that I could scarcely find opportunity for sketching. (Cushing 1979:70).

The Zuni dislike of having their activities recorded implies a belief in the intrinsic connection between the representation and the thing, which ethnographers in general have always been at pains to dismiss, insisting that merely representing something or someone does not harm them, or steal their identity. Here Cushing *himself*, in his curious rhetorical figure in which he equates person and book, makes the connection usually made by the natives, but it is the identity of Cushing himself as well as the object of study which is being constituted, illustrating recent discussions of the way the ethnographer creates himself as observing an objective subject, by constituting his object (his subject of study) as other and separate. Part of the fascination of Cushing's account is the way that reversals and twists such as these take place. (His eventual means of gaining access to one of the most secret ceremonies, for instance, is, ironically, through providing some of his black *ink* (connected with the writing so disliked by the Zuni) for use in it.)

Closely related to the theme of recording is the way that Cushing's observation of the Zuni is presented. At one level, the observer must be detached, able to gain perspective, yet it is part of Cushing's self-proclaimed method, and that of later participant-observers, to be immersed in ordinary daily life. There is an interesting fluctuation in Cushing's account between being excluded, the lone figure who, for better or worse, does not fit in, and the feeling of never being alone, of being constantly watched and crowded, which is caught in the last sentence of the passage quoted above, where recording and observation are shown to be prevented by excessive *closeness* just as much as by distance. Earlier he describes the constant surveillance under which he is kept ('they were systematically watching me') until he takes on some of the Zuni ways. Only after he has symbolically lost everything that makes him white, when his party leaves without arranging for the provision of his 'coffee, sugar, flour and other necessities' and he has eaten Zuni food and worn Zuni clothing, does he achieve his implicit end, which is to become invisible to them as an alien observer, but actually to *be* one nevertheless.

The echoes of captivity narratives and adventure stories in foreign parts are important elements throughout the account, and the continual shifting of focus and of narrative style is closely linked to his varying use of these models, as well as to the actual 'adventures' in Zuni his title promises. His first experience of Zuni is alone, having ridden ahead of his companions. He views from a distance the whole landscape opened out before him, and does not at first realise that one of the hills

> so strange and picturesque, was a city of the habitations of men, until I saw on the topmost terrace, little specks of black and red moving about against the sky. It seemed still a little island of mesas, one upon the other, smaller and smaller, reared from a sea of sand, in mock rivalry of the surrounding grander mesas of Nature's rearing. (Cushing 1979:50)[4]

Entering the pueblo he finds that all the Indians are gathered on the terraces looking down at a ceremony, and after some opposition he makes his way up to join them: 'at last, gaining my wished-for position on the edge of the terrace, I came face to face with nearly the whole population of Zuni' (Cushing 1979:50).

This is an interesting situation, since he is able to watch them watching their own ceremony, so he is only 'face to face' with them in an indirect way, which is interestingly parallel to the false reciprocity discussed earlier, and also to Clifford Geertz' influential image of anthropology as 'reading over the shoulder' of the people being studied. It is also worth noting in passing that this initial view of the Zuni is a striking image of what so many later observations have fastened on: the public nature of their society, in which the most secret and fundamental areas are ceremonial rather than personal. In this context the phrase 'face to face' intriguingly combines the idea of revelation and intimacy with the idea of surfaces and masks, an idea I shall return to later with reference to Ruth Benedict.

Later that evening, after his party has camped outside the pueblo, Cushing gives us a very different view of the Zuni, one which is much more recognisably a set-piece.

> Some of us, a young officer and several ladies who had joined our party, strolled up to the pueblo, through a sandy lane and along a winding pathway that led down the hill to a well. As I sat watching the women coming and going to and from the well, 'How strangely parallel', I thought, 'have been the lines of development in this curious civilisation of an American desert, with those of Eastern nations and deserts'. (1979:54)

In the preceding paragraph he has made passing comparisons with Egyptians and Romans, and here he goes on to refer to the Pools of Palestine, and to describe the 'picturesque sight' of the water-carriers. When he and his companions go beyond this framed picture – framed by their own cultural expectations and reference points – this same cultural baggage limits them:

> We attempted to penetrate a narrow street or two, to enter one of the strange, terrace-bounded courts, but the myriad dogs, with barks and howls in concert, created such a yelping pandemonium that the ladies were frightened, and we returned to camp. (1979:55)

Gentility, then, the 'stroll' and the appreciation of the 'picturesque' puts limits on what we see, and Cushing specifically notes in a letter that the Zuni had varied a dance when it was being observed by 'a company of officers and ladies from Wingate... not only cutting it short but also casting out of it all obscenities – or rather indecent observances – on account of their presence' (Cushing 1979:136).

Clearly the Zuni had taken the measure of white tastes and limitations here, but it is far from clear whether they changed the dance out of consideration, a reciprocal fellow-feeling, fear of the distinctly non-reciprocal outrage of a powerful white official, or out of a wish to keep some things secret and private.

The various stages of Cushing's initiation into Zuni life are ways of getting *beyond* the barriers of white taste, which are also used by the Zuni in that they can retreat behind them rather than confront them, and increasingly the set-piece descriptions of places and people are from a position *inside* the community, where the perceptions are presented as shared, if only temporarily. Evoking the shared evenings and conversations in his room, for instance, Cushing dwells on the lights from the cigarettes.

> A dozen red stars glowed and perished with every whiff of as many eager visitors, or burned in concert at the end of each joke or story, revealing strange features which started forth from the darkness like the ruddy ghosts of some pre-Columbian decade. 'Shake the blazes out of the brands', one of these ghosts would say; and another, with a long cedar stick, would poke the brands till the flames would dart up the chimney anew, the cigarette stars would fade into ashes in the sunlight of the pinon, when lo! the ancient ghosts became sprawling half-nude Indians again. (1979:95)

The detached observer here is temporarily muted, while the participant reigns, and the specific historical situation is made into a timeless (pre-Columbian) moment. Though the transition from observer to participant presented in this single incident is aesthetically shaped in what we may call a comic mode (all turns out well, Cushing the detached observer is still there and in charge at the end), there is also a more tragic direction in which it could go, which would be the death of the adventurer or, in anthropological terms, the obliteration of the detached observer. The outsider could be consumed by the culture which he tries to observe, and of course this is the 'fate' of going native with which Cushing was associated, and which he partly exploited.

Jesse Green, in the introduction to his excellent selection of Cushing's writings (Cushing 1979) refers to Melville's *Typee* (1846) as one of a number of precursors of *My Adventures in Zuni*, but does not develop the comparison. The profound ambiguity running through Melville's book revolves around the intentions of the Typee themselves who, like the Zuni, never leave their visitor alone, and are apparently solicitous of his welfare. They are, though, rumoured to be cannibals, and when Melville tries to leave at the end he has to fight his way out, maiming, perhaps killing one of them. Like Max, in one of the most popular present-day children's books, Maurice Sendak's *Where The Wild Things Are* (1963) the adventurer has to leave before he is swallowed up. The ambiguous monsters of Max's dream voyage, with their thoroughly human feet but terrifying teeth, want him to stay: 'Oh please don't go – we'll eat you up – we love you so!' But Max sails away and returns home for supper. This comparison is not really so bizarre when we consider the widespread nature of this pattern of encounter with the alien or exotic other, and timely escape from its ambiguous mixture of danger and fascination. The adventure story pattern has to have Cushing survive, but it also has to have the Zuni constitute a threat to his survival; this is where the adventure format begins to run counter to another narrative direction in the text, which would logically culminate in his becoming a Zuni. Their love would not just facilitate his learning, but would claim him as their own, in true reciprocity, though this would involve the loss of his white identity – 'we'll eat you up – we love you so'.

Cushing does describe incidents where his life seems to be at risk. In his letters and elsewhere he refers to coming under suspicion of sorcery, which is punishable by death. There is an appropriate irony in the fact that, as he points out, he can be suspected of it 'on the grounds that I had become a Zuni – Americans being considered free from sorcery' (Cushing 1979:155).[5] How, then, does Cushing reconcile the contradictory directions of his narrative? The account does end with a death, but rather than Cushing's it is that of his 'adopted uncle', with its accompanying ceremonials, which Cushing uses to illustrate Zuni beliefs about the dead. When we look at these beliefs, though, we find a surprising resonance with Cushing's whole enterprise. He is himself struck by the Zuni belief that turtles are 'our lost others', and narrates at some length a myth which explains that only a part of the Zuni people arrived at the 'middle of the world', the others remaining in the lake to welcome the dead who go there. There is, therefore, for the Zuni, a world *from* which they have come, but which is still akin to them, and which is 'delightful and filled with songs and dances' (Cushing 1979: 132). That world is reached (our lost others are found) by losing our identity in *this* world. The developmental schema which sees Indians as a stage we have left behind has, of course, always been accompanied by the nostalgia which sees them precisely as 'our lost others' in a spiritual sense,[6] but Cushing's 'adventure' in becoming an Indian must ultimately skirt the question of the loss of self. By ending his account with the death of his old uncle he is able to *raise* the question of death and the lost others, but then to transfer it on to an alternative and instantly recognisable form of aesthetic and ideological closure, the death of the Indian as emblem of the inevitable death of a way of life.[7]

The Indian's death offers a resolution of sorts to the paradoxes which have been hinted at throughout, particularly the one involving the claims of the incommunicable and visionary, as against the scientific recording of data. Some years later, in a lecture on his stay at Zuni, Cushing framed his account with the recital of a dream of the return to origins:

> Fifteen years ago, one winter night, I fell asleep before my desk in the old tower of the Smithsonian Institution. I dreamed that I was far away in a country I had never seen or heard of. There the sun was brighter, the air clearer; the valleys, vast and twilit, were like cracks down to the foundation rocks of the world. (Cushing 1979:41)

During the dream, after an experience of danger and disorientation, he finds a strangely shaped little idol, which six months later he actually finds a sketch of in an exhibition, and discovers it is a Katchina dancer. Whatever the possibilities of coincidence, he insists, 'my eyes were first turned toward Zuni by a vision of the night' (1979:42). But on that particular night in the Smithsonian Institution, he wakes to find himself 'empty-handed, my head pillowed among the papers on my writing-desk'. The opposition here, of the papers and the dream, might suggest the secondariness of science and writing to the primacy of vision, but it is a conjunction as well as an opposition, and one which is central to Cushing's work, where we can see the claims of the Romantic sublime and of the developing science of anthropology never fully reconciled.

These contradictions in Cushing are not necessarily shortcomings, of course. In fact it is central to my argument that such potential contradictions and the rhetorical strategies which accompany them are neither peculiar to Cushing nor completely avoidable, and a brief look at another well-known anthropological account of Zuni, by Ruth Benedict, may help to underline this. The influence of Zuni itself, and pueblo cultures in general, on successive generations of anthropologists has been to crystallise for them a non-evolutionary and holistic way of viewing individual cultures:

> They kept a way of life so unique and coherent, that three separate times, with Cushing, with Haeberlin and with Benedict, it inspired the formulation of the modern anthropological concept of culture. (Mark 1980:114)

Here was a culture which, at a time when violent changes were destroying and demoralising other Indian tribes, or had already done so, continued to live in a coherent, ordered and apparently timeless way. Here was a whole that morally and aesthetically could be contrasted to the fragmentation of modern life, and methodologically could be used as the basis for a view of cultures as infinitely various, but equally valid and self-sustaining.

Benedict's *Patterns of Culture* makes an argument for the variety of human cultures which is also implicitly an argument about possible directions for American society.[8] To this end she describes the Zuni as 'Apollonian' as opposed to the 'Dionysian' Kwakiutl. Even though Boas himself tended to stress the way aspects of a culture are transmitted, and concentrated on recording the many aspects of a culture while postponing the description of the totality, Benedict's is a thoroughly Boasian approach in its avoidance of any evolutionary scale of complexity or morality. It is also based on fieldwork, even if its schematic contrasts of cultures, which made it so successful and influential with a popular audience, have elicited a steady stream of scholarly criticism.[9] In relation to Cushing what is immediately evident is the objective and impersonal stance. The evidences and traces of Benedict's personal experience are almost completely effaced, as is the identity of her informants, and in this way the closed and authoritative text is created. 'The Zuni have no sense of sin', we are told, and 'there is no courting of excess in any form'. Or again, 'Suicide is too violent an act, even in its most casual forms, for the Pueblos to contemplate. They have no idea what it could be.' My interest in such generalisations is not in their accuracy, but in the way they are supported and made possible in the text by the use of what has come to be called the 'ethnographic present tense' (Fabian 1983). The effect of this is to create a textual space, in which a culture is shown operating, which is *not* the same historically bound present as the one in which the reader and the writer live, a product of grammar (the present tense) rather than history (the present). Accompanying this ethnographic present tense is a generalising of individual utterances, so that they illustrate an argument, or fulfil a pattern, rather than function in the context of any dialogue, as the awkward syntax of the following sentence perhaps illustrates: 'Everyone says she must love him, they say, and all her relatives are ashamed' (Benedict 1935:78).

Even in her field-notes there is apparently relatively little about Benedict's private impressions, or her relationships with her informants, with all the emotional effects of the place and the people finding more direct expression in her poetry. Her biographer notes that she and Ruth Bunzel, 'even when they lived in the same house, shared the same primary informants and deferred, in letters, to the same professor of anthropology', saw different sides of Zuni life (Modell 1984:172). The ordered and serene life which fitted Benedict's Apollonian model was not the one which Bunzel saw, but because of the ethnographic model of writing in which they worked they were both able, even required, to sound equally authoritative. In one way, though, Benedict could feel justified in presenting an impersonal picture of the Zuni. In a society which emphasised the public and formal dimension as more fundamental than the private, the surface or the mask *is* the truth. Benedict took the idea of different and equally valid patterns of culture seriously enough to present this dimension of Zuni life without implying that to get behind the mask was to get to the truth. As Modell puts it, 'From her perspective, the placid surface constituted an accurate portrait of Zuni culture precisely because this was the way Indians chose to present themselves. She retold their story' (1984:177).

It is, of course, 'their story' transposed through an interpreter, written up in field-notes, and then used as part of a larger argument directed to Americans about *their* lives, but to say this is only to be reminded of the complex and determinate processes by which experience of other cultures becomes texts which claim to *represent* them. Benedict's account, like Cushing's, ends with a death, and here too it provides a formal patterning, as each of her case studies in the book ends with a different response to death. Each account, each narrative, effects a closure according to the rhetorical modes in which the writers are working. The closure, though, is textual, and once we start to read the text in relation to the conditions of its production, which include generic conventions, as well as the historical context of the relation of the two cultures reconciled in it, we are back in that messy and untotalisable area which it has been the function of the various rhetorical strategies to efface. The coherence demonstrated in the text, then, is as much a product of the investigation as a property of what is being investigated. Jack Goody has briefly demonstrated, for instance, how Cushing's version of Zuni origin myths, which was used by Durkheim and Mauss in order to build up a coherent classificatory scheme, was in fact necessarily based on partial information. He quotes Ruth Bunzel as pointing out that,

> There is no single origin myth but a long series of separate myths... There is not, however, any collected version which is 'the talk' because no mind in Zuni encompasses all knowledge, the 'midmost' group to which Cushing refers being a figment of his own imagination. (quoted in Goody 1977:57)

The reconciliation of disparate elements to create an integrated and balanced whole has its parallel, of course, in the development of a coherent model of how *societies* function, and in the treatment of Zuni ritual life, and in particular of those aspects of it which seem most incongruous and repellent, we can see how such a challenge to such a totality may be dealt with. The problematic elements have either been played down altogether or fitted in as release or compensatory mechanisms to maintain rather than challenge the overall equilibrium of that culture. But once we change our social model, or increase our scepticism about constituting intellectual wholes, the Zuni can look quite different.

Stephen Greenblatt, for instance, as part of his general argument about power and subversion referred to earlier, takes the disgusted reactions of Cushing's visitor, Captain Bourke, who accompanied him to a Newekwe dance, as a starting point for challenging the idea of a totalisable view of the Zuni. Picking up Bourke's comparison of it with the European Feast of Fools, Greenblatt uses Bakhtin's idea of carnival as an overturning and dialogising of official views from below to suggest that part of the meaning of what Bourke witnessed may have been a parodying of him and his authority, and that the ceremony itself was not about timeless and integrated ideals:

the elements are not fully integrated, they defy hierarchical organisation, they do not form a unified whole. Somehow the magical healing [the reason given for the scatological rites] has survived alongside all of the portentous significance of the encounter with white civilisation, and has resisted semantic organisation by that encounter. In this indifference to unity, this refusal of conceptual integration, we may grasp one of the sources of the Zunis' dogged resistance, to this day, to assimilation. (Greenblatt 1982:5)

Unfortunately Greenblatt does not develop this view of the Zuni, or substantiate it further, but his view can be seen as the latest example of the way that methodological approaches have meshed with political assumptions in describing the Zuni. His use of Bakhtin here, though, does lead us back to the issues of dominant discourses and their subversion by relativising and dialogising practices, which can usefully be approached through the work of another Zuni scholar, Dennis Tedlock, in whose work we find both a powerfully argued case for a dialogical approach and a sustained effort to put it into practice. In his fullest exposition of the case for dialogical, as opposed to analogical, anthropology he refers to Cushing, characteristically through a Zuni account of him, which he gives in the particular form (discussed briefly in Chapter 6) that he has pioneered for the transcription and presentation of oral narrative:

Once they made a white man into a Priest of the Bow,
he was out there with the other Bow Priests –
he had black stripes
on his white body.
The others said their prayers from their hearts,
but he read his from a piece of paper. (Tedlock 1983:229)

Tedlock uses this story not just to give the lie to claims that Cushing 'went native' by pointing out his crucial difference, the way he stood out from the rest. He is also giving us Cushing viewed from a Zuni perspective, or rather, in line with his dialogical approach, he is demonstrating in his reading of the story the complexities and difficulties of locating and reproducing this perspective. Since in Zuni the word for the written page is 'that which is striped' there is a joke involved in the story:

> Further, on Cushing's skin, the stripes of the Bow Priesthood made him look a little like a black-and-white striped *neweekwe*... or clown. To translate all this, what *kuushi* [Cushing] was all about was not revealed solely by the piece of paper he held in his hand. It was written all over him.

Having offered us a 'translation' here, Tedlock throws doubt on it as any sort of summary of a native point of view. He mulls over the differences (saying prayers from inside and from memory, rather than outside, from writing), and the similarities (the priests are striped too, they all say the same prayer) and as he says 'we could keep on going back and forth over this story, following its alternate black and white stripes, and that is just the point'.

His point is the difficulty of fitting such a story into the standard patterns of analogical anthropology, which seeks to present a clear picture, preferably of a 'pure' culture, one unaffected by this sort of cultural feedback. As a result, such a story would have to be relegated to memoirs, or back pages, 'the front ones being properly reserved for a pristine creation myth'. In order to constitute the subject (and this can mean both the anthropologist as speaking/writing subject and his or her subject, or topic, since in this sense ethnographers write themselves into being), the traces, or what Tedlock calls the tool-marks, need to be erased, and one of these traces is that of the native individual voice, interacting with the anthropologist. We may hear at length, of course, the disembodied and communal voice which recites myths, and elsewhere the individual telling his or her life history, but uninterrupted, as if he or she was 'one of those insufferable personalities who can only talk about themselves', and Tedlock identifies it as a law of analogical anthropology 'that the ethnographer and the native must never be articulate between the same two covers' (Tedlock 1983:324). This is because, according to his definition, analogical anthropology

> involves the replacement of one discourse with another. It is claimed that this new discourse, [the anthropologist's interpretation/translation] however far removed it may seem to be, is equivalent or proportionate, in quasi-mathematical sense, to the previous discourse. *Ana-logos*, in Greek, literally means 'talking above', 'talking beyond', or 'talking later', as contrasted with the talking back and forth of dialogue. The dialogue is a continuing process and itself illustrates process and change; the analogue, on the other hand, is a product, a result. (1983:324).

The distinction here is certainly clear enough, and his criticisms of analogical approaches correspond closely with those made by Marcus, Clifford and others, but his emphasis on process rather than product does raise the question of whether what he is describing *can* really be textualised.

(It is rather surprising that he is so hard on Paul Rabinow's work, which represents one of the few fully reflexive attempts at ethnography, and he gives no positive examples of his desired form at all.) He refers to dialogue as 'not a method, but a *mode*, a mode of discourse within which there may be methodical moments, on either side' (Tedlock 1983:323), and says that 'the dialogical path' (i.e. not method?) does not involve scrapping existing methodologies.

This raises important questions, however, about his attitude to interpretation in general. His dismissal of the 'quasi-mathematical' claims of analogical approaches seems to imply a suspicion of all interpretative approaches based on the extracting of rules and models, since they may freeze process into product, and his response to Dell Hymes' work evinces the same suspicion. The development of an 'ethnography of speaking', which stresses language in use and therefore as an element of human interaction and dialogue, will only be truly dialogical if its practitioners see it as

> something more than a mere methodological means to the theoretical ends of
> an analogically conceived sociolinguistics, a sociolinguistics that would
> systematically transform native discourse into lists of what are aptly called
> 'rewrite rules'. (Tedlock 1983:337)

There seems to be the assumption here that finding the rules by which language or language behaviour works involves a misrepresentation or appropriation of it, which comes close to a valorisation of unmediated experience over analysis or interpretation, which Tedlock would surely reject. Presumably it is a question of whether the interpretation and abstraction is then brought *back* into dialogue, or used to prevent any further dialogue, by freezing the two sides into knower and known, subject and object. Rather than constructing laws or models, Tedlock's own work is devoted to finding ways of representing in English print Indian oral storytelling performances, and if his final aim is not so different from the traditional ethnographic one of making Indian stories and modes of narration knowable and understandable within our terms, he would also want to insist on the modification of our ways of understanding and perceiving which these texts can offer us.

One of his favourite devices in his essays is the use of episodes and anecdotes, like the Cushing one quoted earlier, which indicate a native point of view, and he uses these episodes not towards the assembly of a complete account of Zuni or any other culture, or as a claim to get inside Zuni experience, but as a challenge to white assumptions that either of these things is possible. Right at the end of an early essay on the translation of style in oral narrative, in which, incidentally he criticises Cushing for his unacknowledged interpolations of Victorian moralising in his Zuni translations, Tedlock, having pointed to the 'analytic rewards' of treating oral narrative as dramatic poetry also insists on the aesthetic rewards. These latter, though, will depend on the recognition that such works, performed events more than texts, in their stripped down and almost mimimalist forms may need 'maximal interpolation by audiences'. He is reminded, he says, 'of the Zuni who asked me, "When I tell these stories do you picture it, or do you just write it down?"' (Tedlock 1971:133). Coming where it does, *after* he has made the case for his own method of presentation, the question resonates, and is meant to. The narrative needs our help in filling it out, picturing it, rather than just passively recording or receiving it, but Tedlock has just criticised Cushing and others for imposing alien styles on Zuni materials, which implies criteria of accuracy and adequacy on Tedlock's part.

The distinction is no doubt that Cushing and the others closed off the possibility of a dialogue in the form in which they presented the material, filling all the gaps, and more beside, with their own monologic voices, and allowing the reader no potentially alienating or estranging sense of the original performance or context. Tedlock's subsequent translations have all been done in close collaboration with named and fully acknowledged native speakers, so much so that the making of the translation is in itself presented as an instance of dialogue, and of rapport. In the case of his major work so far, the translation of the Quiche Mayan book of creation, the *Popol Vuh* (Tedlock 1985), which of course exists only in a written form, he recounts how he and his wife even undertook an apprenticeship under the diviner Andres Xiloj, in order to be able to use the present knowledge and cultural forms of the Quiche people to throw light on the text. The later collaboration of Xiloj is described in some detail by Tedlock as a 'three-way dialogue among Andres Xiloj, the Popol Vuh text, and myself', but the book as a whole, while it explicitly acknowledges this dialogue, does not present it. To say that what we have is ultimately a scholarly text replete with footnotes is in no way to make a cheap criticism but to point to a very real question about whether dialogue is really an epistemological and methodological as much as a political and moral issue.

The debates which have been carried on over what has come to be called postmodern ethnography have been complex and wide-ranging and perhaps partly because of the slipperiness of terms like dialogue it is hard to pin down real oppositions or distinctions. Everyone shares a rejection of scientism based on a non-reflexive idea of objectivity. There is general agreement that ethnographies have a rhetorical component, and that this has involved the transformation of a dialogical and dialectical involvement in the field into a monological text. As in the wider political world, it would be hard to find someone who thought dialogue was not a 'good thing', but the differences start to show up in deciding whether it is an end in itself or a means to a different end. In what follows, my reading of aspects of this debate will push this rather crude distinction between ends and means, as a way of clarifying the particular role dialogue has played in the debate as a whole and relating it to the concerns of this book.

Tedlock is working for the most part with an idea of voice, the idea of articulation, of self-presence and he even tries to challenge and reverse the Derridean assumptions about voice and writing.[10] This may be perfectly appropriate in someone working with forms of oral expression for which he wants to develop at the same time both an aesthetic and a mode of translation that avoid the traditional available textual forms which completely efface the oral performance and its dialogical rather than monological nature. An aesthetic object, in however revised and expanded a form we take the word aesthetic after Rothenberg and Tedlock, is the end in view. The problems inherent in his claims for dialogical approaches start to appear when we move to other forms of ethnographic work, which are concerned with presenting not an oral performance but a more general account of a cultural practice or belief, because this immediately raises the question of interpretation which in Tedlock can be contained within a concern to carry over what the speaker meant, and how the audience understood it.

Of course, at one level it could be said that anthropology in general should settle for this. It should be concerned, and content, with giving us the native view and using all its skill and ingenuity, both intellectual and literary, to make us see through their eyes, or at least over their shoulders. To do this would strike a blow against any ethnocentric belief that our way, or any one way, was right or natural, and would correspond to that political pluralism and anti-colonialism necessary to ensure the political and cultural survival of many powerless cultures in a world increasingly threatened by monoculture. The problem with his privileging of the native view comes if we view the role of anthropology, like any social science, as interpretive rather than descriptive, and if we acknowledge that in fact description cannot be separated and made prior to interpretation. In this case understanding rather than empathy is the ultimate goal, and this involves distance rather than closeness, difference rather than identity. Distance and difference are insisted upon not in order to preserve our values but because the gap between cultures and the mutual estrangement (in the sense of making strange, rather than a prelude to separation and divorce) can be used as the basis of a critique, rather than a confirmation, of the values and 'common sense' of both sides. As Steven Webster puts it, 'The gap is the foundation of understanding, not its subversion'(1982:106). To ignore this would involve, for one thing, effacing our own position, what Webster, paraphrasing Gadamer, calls 'the logically necessary priority of the interpreter's historicity', with the result that we could finish up celebrating the empathic communication of two disembodied and hypostatised subjectivities, a 'fable of rapport' with a vengeance. On the other hand too easy an acceptance of the gap fixes us in a scientism and positivism which leaves our ethnocentrism unchallenged. The paradox is nicely brought out by Webster:

ethnocentrism must underlie the profession of social anthropology insofar as we can only translate one culture into another. To put it another way, escape from ethnocentrism is our business, but a definitive escape puts us out of business altogether. (1982:101)

This movement back and forth across the gap could still be a description of dialogue, of course, and Webster does talk in terms of 'the inescapable historical and dialectical nature of understanding' and the need to 'rediscover certitude as a dialogue'(1982:101). Furthermore he refuses to come down on either side of any subjectivity/objectivity divide, insisting that they are

> equally reifying abstractions from the practicality and particularity of dialogue. Each has already assumed a meaning transparent to the world, and so has given away the dialectic on which it is based and from which it must derive its authenticity. Nevertheless, these fictions are the framework in which an elusive truth must continually be reestablished. (1982:111)

Nevertheless the fact that truth, however elusive and provisional, rather than mutality or a shared aesthetic, is the end in sight does suggest a difference from Tedlock, and the reservations implicit in Webster about too easy a crossing of cultural gaps are given a different turn in an essay by Richard Handler, who voices a recurrent criticism that stress on dialogue runs the risk of leaving intact and unquestioned what the two cultures share, their 'common sense', in the name of celebrating commonality and rapport. In dealing with issues of nationalism and ethnicity Handler points out that there may be a great deal in common between the assumptions about cultural boundaries and cultural difference held by both anthropologist and ethnic group in question, and he points out the difficulties:

> Destructive analysis of shared premises is more important than a dialogue with those who share them. Indeed in this case dialogue will amount to little more than mutually confirming, rather than critically examining each other's beliefs.... By contrast destructive analysis, because it challenges common sense, may pave the way to a more genuine dialogue, that is, to one in which both parties are led to re-evaluate their positions. (1985:178)

Strangely enough, then, what the idea of dialogue turns out to depend on, according to Handler, is a prior *assumption* of difference and otherness, and a consequent faith that the conjunction of differences will create insight. The close relation of this to a whole variety of modernist literary techniques and theories, ranging from surrealism, as sketched out by Clifford, to Brecht and Benjamin has already been touched upon in Chapter 6, but we need to look a bit harder at the way epistemological claims are being made for aesthetic forms. The most developed discussion of this is probably to be found in the writers of the Frankfurt school, and their commentators, and their extended debate with a Lukacsian model of realism.[11]

Within this debate, as in the present ethnographic one, the question is about which forms and techniques best reflect reality. That is, within a Marxist aesthetic it is assumed that art does have an epistemological role and value, and therefore a political duty to tell the truth, and this brings it very close, of course, to ethnographies. The problem is, what sort of truth? Lukács' insistence that a proper critical realism was to be distinguished from both naturalism and impressionism because it settled for neither surface fidelity nor subjectivity but presented events in an objective and historical reality may raise all sorts of questions about his privileging of narration as the sole form to do this, but it does offer a useful way of seeing ethnography as realism. The question then becomes whether the experimental and dialogical forms are a modernist form of achieving the same end, but actively and self-reflexively, as Brecht would claim for his innovations, or in fact forms of naturalism or impressionism which, far from telling the truth reflect only the commodification and fragmentation of their time. Steven Webster has used the framework of this debate, and Raymond Williams' revised definition of realism, to caution against an acceptance of an implicit naturalism in recent ethnographic debates. While he accepts that the major proponents of the new ethnographic realism 'have not themselves favoured such mystified forms of naturalism' he sees their demonstration of the limits of the ethnographic genre, fuelled by a deconstructive stress on 'writing' and textuality, as in danger of treating these limits as 'natural' rather than the product of the cultural hegemony of real, historically specific forces. By the same token, if textuality is seen as the problem, the implication is that the answer must lie there too, rather than in any larger social context.

Just as the debate over modernism and realism always threatened to slip into an idealisation of form in itself, either the fragmentation, juxtapositions and estrangements of modernism or the narrative of the realist novel, so dialogue, reflexivity or objectivity could be similarly treated. As Webster argues:

> Surely, to hypostatise genre conventions of a social science, let alone those of purely literary discourses, by raising pure form to a status which transcends history, obscures its contingent historical origins and contributes to the paralysis of history which the illusory form likely reinforces. Ethnography is not merely a genre, but also a science, in the original enlightenment sense of an emancipatory rationalism and opposed to the later sense of an instrumental rationalism. (1986:59)

Clearly, then, in terms of my earlier crude distinction, Webster would see dialogue as a means to an end, the end being an emancipatory knowledge, but his comments on the idealisation of form also provide a useful way of approaching another very relevant debate involving Marxist aesthetics, and one of the main sources for recent formulations of the idea of dialogue, namely the work of Mikhail Bakhtin.

For reasons connected partly with the vagaries of the publication of his work, partly with the circumstances of its writing under censorship, and partly with the slipperiness of some of his key terms, Bakhtin has been used to support a very wide diversity of positions in the West.[12] In particular he has been separated off from the Marxist emphasis of Voloshinov's *Marxism and the Philosophy of Language* (1973) and made to embrace various forms of deconstruction and pluralism. The idea of dialogue has played a key role in this process, being made to serve treble duty as a formal literary technique, a property of language itself and a political ideal. James Clifford's use of Bakhtin is an interesting example of some of these appropriations. Having floated dialogue as a possible tool in the dismantling of the monologic, objective and authoritative/authoritarian form of the classic ethnography, he is quick to acknowledge its possible limitations, one of which he sees as the tendency to reduce the participants to a representative role, or 'type'. With this term he clearly invokes the debates over realism, and in a footnote refers us to Lukács, Such a process, he says

> reinstates the synecdochic interpretive authority by which the ethnographer
> reads texts in relation to context, thereby constituting a meaningful 'other'
> world. If it is difficult for dialogical portrayals to escape typifying procedures,
> they can, to a significant degree, resist the pull toward authoritative
> representation of the other. This depends on their ability fictionally to
> maintain the strangeness of the other voice and to hold in view the specific
> contingencies of the exchange. (Clifford 1988:44)

This assumption that types are to be avoided is not necessarily shared by Bakhtin, whose idea of dialogisation in the novel, which effects a relativisation of all the voices including the author's, is achieved by virtue of the voices being recognised *not* as unique or idiosyncratic (which would just be naturalism), but as representative. In this way Bakhtin is quite close to Lukács and his claims that a true realism must see the specific through the general. Clifford contrasts Bakhtin's view of the novel as 'a carnivalesque area of diversity' with Lukács' 'tour de force of cultural or historical totalization', and sees him discovering 'a utopian textual space where discursive complexity, the dialogical interplay of voices, can be accommodated' (1988:46-7).

One of the main sources of difficulty and confusion in using Bakhtin has been in deciding exactly what claims are being made for the dialogical possibilities of novelistic discourse in itself, and what for the more general and inherent dialogical properties of language in any society.[13] Bakhtin's apparent faith in the centrifugal linguistic forces of common speech, which is endlessly relativising and carnivalising the centripetal efforts of monologic official language, has certainly been taken up with some alacrity as an alternative to a view of discourse as sealed and inescapable, and there has also been a temptation to assume that some particular literary form would automatically produce and nourish this carnival. What this leaves out of account, of course, are the particular political and linguistic conditions which can prevent this happening, unless one is to believe that the form itself can transcend these conditions. In cross-cultural situations this is further complicated by the status and mutual (un?)intelligibility of different languages, as I have been trying to show, and Clifford acknowledges this in his reference to Bakhtin's 'utopian' textual space. Even so, this has not stopped his critics from seeing his approval of Bakhtin as contradicting his more general claim that all forms of representation involve textualisation and rhetorical patterning, thereby undermining any claims for realism or truth. If all we can produce are fictions, why should one be seen as better than any other? Clifford's response has been to deny any wish to idealise the capacities of any one form, but to argue that in the present context some forms,including dialogical ones, are to be welcomed 'because they help create a field of explicit contexts for authority'. What others have seen as a contradiction in his position is, he says,

> a systematic ambivalence and complex location, an attempt to survey
> discrepant paradigms and to chart current contestations of authority from a
> politically and historically enmeshed position itself only partially
> understandable (because open-ended) and built on exclusions. (in Roth
> 1989:562–3)

One of the strongest criticisms of some of Clifford's claims has taken up the question of where exactly the dialogisation takes place . According to Steven Sangren 'Bakhtin and many critics of anthropology interested in textual authority conflate authority in texts with authority in society' (1988:411). This encourages them to assign liberatory or authoritarian power to a text, rather than to the total context in which it is read and used, which has the same effect as the idealisation of form already described. In the case of anthropology, Sangren sees it as a way of short-circuiting the normal institutional practices of criticism and debate, pre-empting criticism in accordance with the normal criteria of accuracy and adequacy by claiming, in stressing textuality, more of an aesthetic than a scientific status. Whether or not Sangren's is a fair account of the intentions of his opponents, his main point about the importance of the social and institutional production and reception of texts is an important one, and returns us to Clifford's 'utopian' space. Utopian thinking can be seen as either aside from, and an escape from politics, or as an essential element in critical and political thinking,[14] and no doubt Clifford would see it in the second way, with the literary text presenting an image of political possibility rather than an escape from a world of unequal and intractably complex power relations, in a wish-fulfilment world of authenticity and transparent communication.

Clifford describes 'an alternate textual strategy, a utopia of plural authorship' which would give collaborators the status of writers, not just 'independent enunciators' (Clifford 1989:51). He sees this as likely to *remain* only utopian partly because of the overall initiating and editorial position of the ethnographer, which means that 'the authoritative stance of "giving voice" to the other is not fully transcended' and more fundamentally because plural authorship challenges what he calls 'a deep Western identification of any text's order with the intention of a single author' (1988:51). But to reduce it to order and authorial intention like this seems to me to avoid the more fundamental question of whether coherence is necessary not just to preserve authority, authorial or colonial, but to create and sustain meaning. As I tried to argue in Chapter 6, systems are both necessary and constantly breaking down into other systems, but this is the precondition of understanding and interpretation. The 'utopia' of a text without coherence, without textual authority, may be only a dream of no meaning, of understanding and communication with no sign system at all, of nature before culture. Rather than thinking in terms of dialogisation taking place *within* texts, a more historically situated approach is surely to see it happening *between* texts, each of which as a methodological necessity needs to assert its own coherence and authority if it is make any interpretive or representational claims.[15]

Another approach is to stress not the unity of the intention but of the reception, in that the reader is finally the one to make sense and coherence of the text. This becomes particularly interesting in texts of multiple authorship, since Clifford's reservations about white editorial control may be less relevant if an Indian audience (itself not a homogeneous whole, of course), takes and makes what it wants from the text. Larry Evers' and Felipe Molina's *Yaqui Deer Songs/Maso Bwikam* (1987), to take a fairly recent example, combines bilingual versions of the deer songs (with an accompanying cassette) with extended discussions of their meaning and place in Yaqui culture. The book is apparently deeply rooted in the community, with continual and detailed references to the contributions of other named singers, and makes a striking contrast to the anonymous texts of Boas discussed in the last chapter. In addition, whereas Boas' texts, as I have suggested, were not intended to be read (there was literally no readership) the assumption behind this book (well founded or not) is that the Yaqui text will be read by Yaqui speakers, not just by scholars using it as a linguistic text.

The authors of this text sometimes write separately and sometimes as 'we' (which certainly raises Clifford's spectre of implicit white control), but the combination allows for an intriguing movement between viewpoints and cultures. The way that the deer songs themselves almost, but for a non-Yaqui reader never quite, become swamped by the notes, commentaries and discussions is in sharp contrast to the way in which earlier presentations of Indian songs as literature rather than ethnography felt obliged to strip them of cultural specificity to reveal their universal qualities. But of course this plethora of information suggests a white readership which needs it, or a Yaqui reader who is sufficiently far from the traditions described to be playing the part of a white reader. Evers' and Molina's discussion of the problems of translating into English some words in the songs which are not even standard Yaqui or, as they put it, 'writing song-talk', confronts this persistent problem of how much information the reader needs in order to make sense and, with modernist experimentation behind us, how much the reader needs to make sense. The authors have a dual goal, which implies in this case a dual audience: 'for the continuation of deer songs as a vital part of life in Yaqui communities, and for their appreciation in all communities beyond'. They are aware of the difficulties inherent in such a joint venture because of the inequality of cultural and political power, both past and present – what they refer to as the 'long shadows' cast by 'the historically exploitative aspects of the relationships between Euramericans and native Americans' (Evers and Molina 1987:9).

One of the shadows of exploitation cast on this encounter between a white academic and a Yaqui Indian is bound to be the presence of the still hugely popular works of Carlos Castaneda, whose encounters with Don Juan, the Yaqui *brujo*, have now run through a whole series of books. Castaneda is interesting for my purposes as one of the best known, and most controversial, examples of the cross-over between fictional and anthropological techniques, who is yet almost completely ignored in the discussions I have been outlining. It is tempting to see his neglect as a consequence of a certain degree of embarrassment. For all the talk of experiment within ethnography the lines around the profession remain firmly in place, whereas Castaneda actually thoroughly blurs them *and* is hugely popular. He was awarded a PhD from the University of California at Los Angeles on the basis of a dissertation which was published as *The Teachings of Don Juan*, but ever since there has been controversy about the existence of Don Juan and the ethnographic status of Castaneda's encounter (see De Mille 1980; Noel 1976; Murray 1981). Not only does he blur the status of the ethnography in relation to the fieldwork, he also explicitly challenges the standards of rationality which have allowed the detachment from native beliefs in the supernatural necessary to present a proper ethnographic account.[16]

It is easy to place, and therefore dismiss, Castaneda's work as a countercultural product of the 1960s and 1970s, more interested in hallucinogenic experiences and personal psychology than in other cultures. Certainly there is very little detail of Yaqui culture, and in each successive book the encounter between acolyte and master becomes more isolated and archetypal. Rather than magic being seen as inseparable from a whole set of practices and beliefs it is essentialised and mystified in talk of an unspecified power, and Don Juan's curing role, like his social connections generally, are ignored. Edmund Leach early on saw Castaneda's work in a literary Romantic tradition: 'The general tone is Coleridge-De Quincy by Rousseau out of eighteenth-century Gothick' (in Noel 1976:33). Nevertheless, in the context of Stephen Tyler's call for an occult anthropology rather than an anthropology of the occult, it is not possible just to ignore Castaneda, and the tradition of occult writing on which he draws. As I have argued elsewhere (Murray 1981) his work can be looked at in the context of literary expressions of the supernatural, which depend on a particular use of rhetorical figures to achieve *effects*, and it is the creation of effects, under the guise of a description of things that actually happened, that Castaneda is concerned with. As Todorov says, in relation to the genre of the fantastic,

> If the fantastic constantly makes use of rhetorical figures, it is because it originates in them. The supernatural is born of language, it is both its consequence and its proof: not only do the devil and vampires exist only in words, but language alone enables us to conceive what is always absent: the supernatural. (1973:82)

The characteristic textual stress here can itself be seen as Todorov's powerfully defensive and recuperative defence of rationality, whereby what we cannot describe or comprehend must be contained and understood merely as a textual effect, but it throws into relief, I think, what is at stake between Castaneda and the call by Tyler (who might be uneasy at the association) for an occult ethnography.

In George MacDonald's occult novel *Lilith*, written in 1895 the narrator encounters a book in his library, which appears to be stuck in a false wall disguised as a bookcase. He can only read fragments, beginnings and ends of lines, which make no sense. The words themselves, though, awake in him 'feelings which to describe was, from their strangeness, impossible', and he is affected by a great longing 'to know what the poem or poems might, even yet in their mutilation, hold or suggest' (MacDonald 1962: 198). The strategic use of the fragment in creating effects of the sublime in Romantic writing and since has already been referred to in relation to the presentation of Indian speeches and poetry, but here the sentence is completed, the fragment restored to the whole. The narrator of *Lilith* discovers that the other half of the book sticks through into another world (mirrors are the more usual interface). In other words, the sentence keeps disappearing into the 'other side', leaving gaps in our syntax, discontinuities, breaks of meaning.

Castaneda presents the dialogues with Don Juan as constantly revealing the inadequacies of the young anthropologist's view of reality, and of his language in trying to describe what is happening to him. The gaps and fissures in their conversations point *towards*, rather than describe the 'separate reality', in the best Romantic and occult tradition, but in refusing to label his work as fiction, in gaining an academic degree on the strength of it, he is refusing to accept the divide which has been more theoretically challenged in the continuing debate over rationality and the ruling paradigms of the social sciences.[17]

He also remains, I think, a problematic and uncomfortable figure in terms of postmodern anthropology. The debate over the incorporation of fictional techniques in ethnography has tended, as I have shown, to operate within the terms of realism using a reflection theory of art, but can Castaneda's work be handled in this framework? We do, after all, have dialogue, in which the position of the white anthropologist is profoundly relativised, and we have fictional techniques used in the interest of presenting the native view *and* reflexively showing the limitations of such effects. Why, then, is Castaneda rarely cited as an example? Unless by occult Tyler just means obscure and mystifying (which is what some of his recent work would suggest),[18] we have to ask what would disqualify Castaneda. One obvious answer is that, for all the talk of fiction, there is throughout postmodern anthropology an implicit assumption that fiction only operates *within* a text already authorised as ethnography and therefore as non-fiction, and that there are professional and unstated parameters of behaviour, which Castaneda has violated. Steven Webster, one of the few people to have really pushed the issue of the limits of fiction in this context, and to have used Castaneda, uses an intriguing passage from Clifford Geertz about the curious mixture of good and bad faith which he sees as underlying the anthropological encounter, but also ensuring the peculiar sort of authenticity it can claim. Research involving an informant, Geertz says, is

> considered as a form of conduct, continually ironic. To recognise the moral tension, the ethical ambiguity, implicit in the encounter of anthropologist and informant, and still to be able to dissipate it through one's actions and one's attitudes, is what encounter demands of both parties if it is to be authentic, if it is actually to happen. And to discover that is to discover also something very complicated and not altogether clear about the nature of sincerity and insincerity, genuineness and hypocrisy, honesty and self-deception.(quoted in Webster 1982:92)

As a very brief coda I want to use one last encounter between anthropologist and Yaqui, except that this Yaqui really *is* 'other'. In G.C. Edmondson's science fiction novel *Chapayeca* (1971) an American anthropologist realises that the Yaqui Indian in the traditional chapayeca mask to whom he is talking is an alien from another planet, and is not wearing a mask at all. Over the course of many conversations, which echo and parody the anthropologist–informant encounter, he comes up against baffling gaps in their mutual understanding, which are eventually explained by his discovery that the alien comes from a civilisation using telepathy, and in which the individual thought has been replaced by 'collective, antlike behaviour and individual stupidity' (Edmondson 1971:158). The irony here is that this parodic version of tribal identity as constituted in myths of the primitive mind is in every way superior to our culture. A few young disaffected aliens have come to earth to slum it, and try out individual thinking as a countercultural activity. As a result

Geertz' questions of sincerity and authenticity, of who is in control and why, are given yet another twist:

> 'Teta is dead. Now you are my only –' Chap [the alien] hesitated, searching for a word.
> 'Friend?' Taber suggested.
> 'No.'
> 'Protector?'
> 'Something like that.'
> 'Owner?' Taber hazarded.
> The alien was silent for a moment. 'Not exactly', he finally said.
> 'Captor?' Taber tried.
> 'It's no use', the *chapayeca* said. 'There is no word.' (1971:136)

Notes

1. Porter refers to the frequent use of the Irish as examples of primitives comparable to the Indians, and certainly the role of Ireland within English thinking offers interesting parallels to much of what I have been describing in Indian/white terms. A classic use of the dialogue form to present a monologic discourse of a particularly racist character is Edmund Spenser's *View of the Present State of Ireland* (1596), a text by the great poet and colonial administrator which is, not surprisingly seldom mentioned by the English. Bruce Avery (1990) analyses this in terms of colonialist discourse, and shows the suppression of dialogue by means of the authority of mapping.

2. The fullest account of Cushing is Brandes (1965), but see also Mark (1980). For a view based on Zuni memories and impressions, see Pandey (1972). Cushing is usefully placed in a series of visitors to Zuni in Crampton (1977) and in relation to fellow-anthropologists in Hinsley (1981).

3. Baxter published a number of articles in popular magazines, such as *Harpers* and *Century Illustrated*, as well as more specialised publications, on Cushing's work in the Southwest, and his pieces have such a marked similarity to Cushing's own views and writings that at times he seems almost like a mouthpiece for him.

4. Pratt (1985) explores the relation of landscape to inhabitants in colonialist writing in a European/African context.

5. Interestingly Cushing describes a trial of a Zuni for sorcery which ends with an acquittal in the *Adventures*, whereas in his letters he describes being present at an execution which was 'horribly violent' (Cushing 1979:527).

6. There is an intriguing reversal of this view in Baxter's account of the Zuni pilgrimage to the East coast under Cushing's supervision, when we are given the speculations of the Zuni themselves on their relation to the Americans. When Nai-iu-tchi was chosen to go to the sacred water in the East (the Atlantic) 'he repeated the ancient Zuni tradition of the people that had gone to the eastward in the days when all mankind was one, and said that now "Our Lost Others", as they were called, might be coming back to meet them in the shape of the Americans' (Baxter 1882:527).

7. Even allowing for self-aggrandisement, Cushing's anxiety that he would be 'among the last who will ever witness it in its purity' (Cushing 1979:135) because of the impending arrival of the railroad was real enough. By one of the ironies with which his enterprise was fraught, his very presence and the publicity he gave Zuni was seen later as a factor in destroying the life-style. In an impassioned letter to Ruth Benedict, questioning her enterprise of recording Zuni myths, Jaime de Angulo warns 'Don't forget that Cushing killed Zunyi' [sic] (Mead 1969:298).

8. *Patterns of Culture* appeared in 1934 at the same time as John Collier's New Deal policies towards the Indians were being formulated in the Indian Reorganisation Act. These policies were themselves based on a view of life influenced by Collier's experience of the Pueblos of the Southwest (Collier 1963:126). In Benedict's book the Zuni fulfil very much the same role as they did for Collier in his conversion to cultural pluralism.

9. Most of the criticisms have been of the partial nature of Benedict's picture, and they take issue with her exclusion of the violence and strong emotional under-currents that others have found. These criticisms, then, accept implicitly a positivist approach, and treat questions of emphasis and balance as remediable by greater scientific knowledge and objectivity, rather than as part of an inevitable rhetorical shaping of evidence. Clifford makes a general argument about the inevitability of such shaping, and the need to be aware of it: 'In this light the open allegorising of a Mead or a Benedict enacts a certain probity – properly exposing itself to the accusation of having used tribal societies for pedagogical purposes. (Let those free of such purposes cast the first stone!).' (1986:120).

10. See Tedlock (1983). Arnold Krupat has made a more careful approach to the issue (Swann and Krupat 1987b: 113–28).

11. See especially Lunn (1982) and Jameson (1971). A good collection is Bloch et al (1977).

12. See Murray (1987).

13. There is a particularly clear statement of this position, in Hirschkop and Shepherd (1989:5).

14. Fredric Jameson has made this point in a Marxist context (1976).

15. An excellent account of these difficulties, which uses a feminist perspective to emphasise the inadequacies of a postmodernist faith in changes in style and form at the expense of a concern for the political realities which constitute and reinforce 'otherness' can be found in Mascia-Lees, Sharpe and Cohen (1989). See also Roth (1989) and Taylor (1989) for a detailed critique of Clifford.

16. See Michael Harner's work for a more complex treatment of the relation of drug-induced experiences to the ethnographer's sense of priorities and emphasis in his descriptions of native belief. Harner does use some narrative techniques reminiscent of fiction, but still remains clearly within ethnographic rules.

17. The rationality debate can be said to run as an unstated theme throughout much of this anthropological debate, though its classic formulations tend to be outside anthropology. For useful collections see Hollis and Lukes (1982) and Wilson (1974).

18. Tyler's *The Unspeakable* contains passages obviously designed to produce intellectual vertigo, a putting into practice, perhaps, of the state in which 'fragments of the fantastic whirl about in the vortex of the quester's disoriented consciousness' (1987:202).

Bibliography

Abbott, D.N. (1981) *The World Is Sharp As A Knife*, Victoria, BC, Provincial Museum.

Abler, T.S. (ed.) (1989) *Chainbreaker: The Revolutionary War Memoirs of Governor Blacksnake*, Lincoln and London, Nebraska University Press.

Anderson, C.G. (1976) *Growing Up In Minnesota*, Minneapolis, Minnesota University Press.

Anonymous (1836) 'Indian Eloquence', *The Knickerbocker*, 7:385-90, repr. in Clements (1986).

Apes, W. (1831) *A Son of the Forest; the Experience of William Apes, a Native of the Forest, Written by Himself* revised 2nd edn, New York, G.F. Bunce.

—— (1833) *The Experiences of Five Christian Indians of the Pequod Tribe: Or the Indian's Looking Glass for the White Man*, Boston, James B. Dow.

—— (1835) *Indian Nullification of the Unconstitutional Laws of Massachusetts relative to the Marshpee Tribes, or the Pretended Riot Explained*, Boston, Jonathan Howe.

—— (1837) *Eulogy on King Philip, as Pronounced at the Odeon in Federal Street, Boston, by the Rev. William Apess, an Indian*, Boston, published by the author.

Ashcroft, B., Griffiths, G. and Tiffin, H. (1989) *The Empire Writes Back: Theory and Practice in Post-Colonial Literatures*, London and New York, Routledge.

Austin, M. (1970) *The American Rhythm: Studies and Re-expressions of Amerindian Songs*, (1930), New York, Cooper Square Publishing.

Avery, B. (1990) 'Mapping the Irish Other': Spenser's *A View of the Present State of Ireland*, *MLN*, 57(2):263-79.

Axtell, J. (1981) *The European and the Indian: Essays in the Ethnohistory of Colonial North America*, Oxford and New York, Oxford University Press.

—— (1985) *The Invasion Within: the Contest of Cultures in Colonial North America*, New York and Oxford, Oxford University Press.

—— (1987) 'The Power of Print in the Eastern Woodlands', *William and Mary Quarterly*, 44(2):301-9.

Babcock, B. (1982) 'Ritual Undress and the Comedy of Self and Other: Bandelier's *The Delight Makers*', in Ruby (1982).

Bakhtin, M. (1981) *The Dialogical Imagination: Four Essays*, Austin, Texas University Press.

Barker, F. et al. (1985) *Europe and Its Others*, (Conference Papers) Colchester, University of Essex.

Barrett, S.M. (1974) *Geronimo: His Own Story*, London, Abacus.

Bass, A. (1932) 'John Howard Payne's Story of Sequoyah' *Colophon* 9.

Bassnett, S. and Lefevere, A. (eds.) (1990) *Translation, History and Culture*, London and New York, Pinter.

Basso, K. (1971) ' "To Give Up On Words": Silence in Western Apache Culture', in Basso and Opler (1971).

—— (1983) ' "Stalking With Stories": Names, Places and Moral Narratives among the Western Apache', in Bruner (1983).

—— (1988) ' "Speaking With Names: Language and Landscape Among the Western Apache', *Cultural Anthropology*, 3:99–130.

Basso, K. and Opler, M.E. (1971) *Apachean Culture History and Ethnology*, Tucson, Arizona University Press.

Basso, K. and Selby, H. (eds.) (1976) *Meaning In Anthropology*, Albuquerque, New Mexico University Press.

Bataille, G. and Sands, K. (1984) *American Indian Women: Telling their Lives*, Lincoln, Nebraska University Press.

Baxter, S. (1882) 'An Aboriginal Pilgrimage', *Century Illustrated Monthly Magazine*, 24:526–36.

Benedict, R. (1934) *Patterns of Culture*, London, Routledge and Kegan Paul.

Berkhofer, R. (1970) *The White Man's Indian*, New York, Knopf.

Bevis, W. (1975) 'American Indian Verse Translations', in Chapman (1975).

Bhabha, H. (1984a) 'Representation and the Colonial Text', in Gloversmith (1984).

—— (1984b) 'Of Mimicry and Man; the Ambivalence of Colonial Discourse' *October* 28.

Bieder, R.E. (1986) *Science Encounters the Indian, 1820–1880: the Early Years of American Ethnology*, Norman and London, Oklahoma University Press.

Bitterli, U. (1989) *Cultures in Conflict: Encounters Between European and Non-European Cultures, 1492–1800*, Oxford, Polity Press.

Black, N.B. and Weidman, B.S. (eds.) (1976) *White on Red: Images of the American Indian*, Port Washington, NY and London, Kennikat Press.

Blackburn, S. (1984) *Spreading the Word: Groundings in the Philosophy of Language*, Oxford, Oxford University Press.

Bloch, E. et. al. (1977) *Aesthetics and Politics*, London, Verso.

Bloch, M. (1989) 'Literacy and the Enlightenment' in Schousboe and Larsen (1989).

Blodgett, H. (1935) *Samson Occom*, Hanover, NH, Dartmouth College Publications.

Boas, F. (1895a) *Indianische Sagen von der Nord-Pacifischen Kuste Amerikas*, Berlin, A. Ascher.

—— (1895b) *The Social Organisation and Secret Societies of Kwakiutl Indians*, Ottawa, Report of National Museum.

Boas, F. (1902) 'The Ethnological Significance of Esoteric Doctrines' *Science* 16(143):872–4.

Boas, F. and Hunt, G. (1905) *Kwakiutl Texts*, Memoirs of the American Museum of Natural History, Vol. 3.

—— (1928) *Bella Bella Texts*, New York, Columbia University Press.

—— (1930a) *The Religion of the Kwakiutl Indians*, New York, Columbia University Press.

—— (1930b) 'Anthropology' *Encyclopaedia of the Social Sciences* Vol. 2, pp. 73–110.

Boon, J.A. (1982) *Other Tribes, Other Scribes: Symbolic Anthropology in the Comparative Study of Cultures, Histories, Religions and Texts*, Cambridge, Cambridge University Press.

Bowden, H.W. and Ronda, J.P. (eds.) (1980) *John Eliot's Indian Dialogues: a Study in Cultural Interaction*, Westport, CT, Greenwood.

Boyd, D. (1974) *Rolling Thunder*, New York, Dell.

Brandes, R.S. (1965) 'Frank Hamilton Cushing: Pioneer Americanist', PhD thesis, University of Arizona.

Bright, W. (ed.) (1966) *Sociolinguistics*, The Hague and Paris, Mouton.

Brinton, D.G. (1883) *Aboriginal American Authors and their Productions*, Philadelphia

—— (1888) 'The Language of Palaeolithic Man', paper presented to American Philosophical Society, Philadelphia, McCabe & Co.

—— (1893) 'On an "Inscribed Tablet" from Long Island', *The Archaeologist*, 1(11):201–3.

—— (1894) 'On Certain Morphological Traits of American Languages' *American Antiquarian*, November.

—— (1885) 'The Philosophical Grammar of American Languages, as set forth by Wilhelm von Humboldt' *Proceedings of American Philosophical Society*, 22:306–54.

Brodzki, B. and Schenk, C. (eds.) (1988) *Life/Lines: Theorizing Women's Autobiography*, Ithaca and London, Cornell University Press.

Brotherston, G. (1979) *Image of the New World: the American Continent Portrayed in Native Texts*, London, Thames and Hudson.

Brown, J.E. (ed.) *The Sacred Pipe: Black Elk's Account of the Oglala Sioux*, Norman, Oklahoma University Press.

Brown, N.O. (1966) *Love's Body*, New York, Random House.

Brown, R.W. and Lenneberg, E.H. (1954) 'A Study in Language and Cognition', *Journal of Abnormal and Social Psychology*, 49(3):454–462.

Bruchac, J. (ed.) (1983) *Songs From This Earth on Turtle's Back: Contemporary American Indian Poetry*, New York, Greenfield Review Press.

—— (1987) *Survival This Way: Interviews with American Indian Poets*, Tucson, Arizona University Press.

Brumble, H.D. (1981) *An Annotated Bibliography of American Indian And Eskimo Autobiographies*, Lincoln, Nebraska University Press.

—— (1982) 'A Supplement to *An Annotated Bibliography of American Indian and Eskimo Autobiographies*', *Western American Literature* 17:242–60.

—— (1983) 'Indian Sacred Materials: Kroeber, Kroeber, Waters, and Momaday', in Swann (1983).

—— (1988) *American Indian Autobiography*, Berkeley, Los Angeles and London, California University Press.

Bruner, M. (ed.) (1983) *Text, Play and Story: The Construction and Reconstruction of Self and Society*, Proceedings of the American Ethnological Society.

Bush, C. (1977) *The Dream of Reason: American Consciousness and Cultural Achievement from Independence to the Civil War*, London, Edward Arnold.

—— (1988) 'Cultural Reflections on American Linguists from Whitney to Sapir', *Journal of American Studies*, 22(2):105–212.

Butterfield, S. (1974) *Black Autobiography in America*, Amherst, Massachusetts University Press.

Camp, C. (1978) 'American Indian Oratory in the White Image: an Analysis of Stereotypes', *Journal of American Culture*, 1(4):811–17.

Carroll, J.B. and Casagrande, J.B. (1966) 'The Function of Language Classifications in Behavior', in Smith (1966:489–504).

Castaneda, C. (1968) *The Teachings of Don Juan: A Yacqui Way of Knowledge*, Berkeley, California University Press.

Castro, M. (1983) *Interpreting the Indians: Twentieth Century Poets and the Native Americans*, Albuquerque, University of New Mexico Press.

Chapman, A. (1975) *Literature of the American Indians: Views and Interpretations*, New York and Scarborough, Ontario, New American Library.

Cheyfitz, E. (1989) '*Tarzan of the Apes*: US Foreign Policy in the Twentieth Century', *American Literary History*, 1(2):339–60.

Chiappelli, F. (1976) *First Images of America* Berkeley, California University Press.

Clements, W.M. (1981) 'Faking The Pumpkin: on Jerome Rothenberg's Literary Offences', *Western American Literature*, 16:193–204.

—— (1986) *Native American Folklore in Nineteenth Century Periodicals*, Athens, OH, Ohio University Press.

Clifford, J. (1980) 'Review Essay of Edward Said's *Orientalism*' *History and Theory*, 19:204–23.

—— (1983a) 'Power and Dialogue in Ethnography: Marcel Griaule's Initiation', in Stocking (1983).

—— (1983b) 'On Ethnographic Authority', *Representations* 2:132–43.

—— (1986) 'On Ethnographic Self-Fashioning: Conrad and Malinowski', in Heller (1986); repr. in Clifford (1988).

—— (1988) *The Predicament of Culture: Ethnography, Literature and Art*, Cambridge, MA, Harvard University Press.

Clifford, J. and Marcus, G.C. (eds.) (1986) *Writing Culture: the Poetics and Politics of Ethnography*, Berkeley, California University Press.

Codere, H. (1950) *Fighting With Property: a Study of Kwakiutl Potlatching and Warfare 1792–1930*, Seattle and London, Washington University Press.

Cole, Douglas (1985) *Captured Heritage: the Scramble for Northwest Coast Artifacts*, Seattle, Washington University Press.

Collier, J. (1963) *From Every Zenith*, Denver, Sage Books.

Cowling, E. (1978) 'The Eskimos, the Indians and the Surrealists' *Art History*, 1(4):484–99.

Coyle, W. and Damaser, H.G. (eds.) (1968) *Six Early American Plays, 1798–1890*, Columbus, OH, Merrill.

Crampton, C.G. (1977) *The Zunis of Cibola*, Utah, Utah University Press.

Crapanzano, V. (1977) 'On the Writing of Ethnography', *Dialectical Anthropology*, 2:69–73.

Cushing, F. (1882–3) 'My Adventures in Zuni', *Century Magazine*, 25:191–207, 500–11; 26:28–47; repr. in Cushing (1979).

—— (1901) Zuni Folk Tales, ed. J.W. Powell, New York and London, G.P. Putnam's.

—— (1979) *Zuni: Selected Writings of Frank Hamilton Cushing*, ed. Jesse Green, Lincoln and London, Nebraska University Press.

Davidson, D. and Hintikka, J. (1969) *Words and Objections: Essays on the Work of W.V. Quine*, Dordrecht, Holland, Reidel.

Davis, J.B. (1930) 'The Life and Work of Sequoyah' *Chronicles of Oklahoma*, 8:149–80.

Davis, C.T. and Gates, H.L. (eds.) (1985) *The Slave's Narrative*, Oxford, Oxford University Press.

Debo, A. (1976) *Geronimo: the Man, His Place, His Time*, Norman, Oklahoma University Press.

De Certeau, M. (1986) *Heterologies: Discourse on the Other*, Manchester, Manchester University Press.

Delaney, S.R. (1966) *Babel 17*, New York, Ace Books.

Deloria, V. (1970) *Custer Died For Your Sins: an Indian Manifesto*, New York, Avon.

DeMallie, R. (1964) *The Sixth Grandfather: Black Elk's Teachings Given to John G. Neihardt*, Lincoln, Nebraska University Press.

DeMille, R. (1980) *The Don Juan Papers: Further Castaneda Controversies*, Santa Barbara, Santa Barbara Press.

Derrida, J. (1972) 'Structure, Sign and Play in the Discourse of the Human Sciences' in Macksey and Donato (1972); repr. in Derrida 1978.

—— (1976) *Of Grammatology*, trans. G. Spivak, Baltimore and London, Johns Hopkins University Press.

—— (1978) *Writing and Difference*, London, Routledge and Kegan Paul.

Dews, P. (1984) 'Power and Subjectivity in Foucault' *New Left Review*, 144:72–95.

Diamond, S. (1974) *In Search of the Primitive: a Critique of Civilisation*, New Brunswick, NJ, Transaction Books.

—— (ed.) (1980) *Theory and Practice*, The Hague, Mouton.

Dodge, R.I. (1882) *Our Wild Indians: Thirty Three Years Personal Experience Among the Red Men of the Great West*, Chicago, A.B. Nettleton.

Dominguez, V.R. (1986) 'The Marketing of Heritage', *American Ethnologist*, 13(3):546–55.

Dorris, M. (1987) *A Yellow Raft in Blue Water*, New York, H. Holt.

Drake, S.G. (1832) *Indian Biography, Containing the Lives of More Than Two Hundred Indian Chiefs*, Boston, Josiah Drake.

Drucker, P. and Heizer, R.H. (1967) *To Make My Name Good: A re-examination of Southern Kwakiutl Potlatch*, Berkeley and London, California University Press.

Dwyer, K. (1977) 'On the Dialogic of Fieldwork', *Dialectical Anthropology* 2(2):143–51.

Dyk, W. (1938) *Son of Old Man Hat: a Navajo Autobiography*, New York, Harcourt, Brace.

Eastman, C. (1971) *Indian Boyhood*, New York, Dover, (first published 1902).

—— (1977) *From the Deep Woods to Civilisation: Chapters in the Autobiography of an Indian*, London and Lincoln, Nebraska University Press, (first published 1916).

Eastman, E.G. (1978) *Sister to the Sioux: the Memoirs of Elaine Goodale Eastman 1885–91*, ed. Kay Graber, Lincoln, Nebraska University Press.

Edgerton, F. (1944) 'Notes on Early American Work in Linguistics', *Proceedings of the American Philosophical Society*, 87:25–34.

Edmondson, G:C. (1971) *Chapayeca*, London, Hale.

Edwards, J. (1787) *Observations on the Language of the Muhhekaneew Indians*, New Haven, Josiah Meigs.

Elgin, S.H. (1985) *Native Tongue*, London, The Women's Press.

Eliot, J. (1647) *The Day-Breaking if not the Sun-Rising of the Gospel with the Indians* in *New England*, London, repr. in *Collections of Massachusetts Historical Society*, 4 (3rd series) Cambridge, 1834.

—— (1649) *The Glorious Progress of the Gospel Amongst the Indians in New England*, London, repr. in *Collections of Massachusetts Historical Society* 4 (3rd series) Cambridge, 1834.

—— (1685) *The Dying Speeches of Several Indians*, Cambridge.

Erdoes, R. and Lame Deer, J. (1972) *Lame Deer: Seeker of Visions*, New York, Simon and Schuster.

Erdrich, L. (1985) *Love Medicine*, London, Futura.

Evers, L. and Molina, F. (1987) *Yaqui Deer Songs/Maso Bwikam: a Native American Poetry*, Tucson, Arizona University Press.

Fabian, J. (1983) *Time and the Other: How Anthropology Makes its Object*, New York, Columbia University Press.

Faulkner, V. and Luebke, F.C. (eds.) (1982) *Visions of Refuge: Essays on the Literature of the Great Plains*, Lincoln, Nebraska University Press.

Fell, B. (1976) *America B.C.: Ancient Settlers in the New World*, New York, New York Times Book Co.

Ferguson, C.A. and Heath, S.B. (eds.) (1981) *Language in the USA*, Cambridge and New York, Cambridge University Press.

Fishman, J. (1966) 'A Systematisation of the Whorfian Hypothesis', in Smith (1966).

Ford, C.S. (1941) *Smoke From Their Fires: the Life of a Kwakiutl Chief*, repr. Hamden, CT, Archon Books, 1968.

Foreman, G. (1938) *Sequoyah*, Norman, Oklahoma University Press.

Foster, G.E. (1885) *Se-quo-yah the American Cadmus and Modern Moses*, Philadelphia, Indian Rights Association.

Foster, H. (ed.) (1985) *Postmodern Culture*, London, Pluto.

—— (1985) *Recodings: Art, Spectacle, Cultural Politics*, Port Townsend, WA, Bay Press.

Foucault, M. (1978) *The History of Sexuality*, Vol. 1, New York, Random House.

Franklin, B. (1784) 'Remarks Concerning the Savages of North America', repr. in Black and Weidman (1976).

Friedrich, P. (1986) *The Language Parallax; Linguistic Relativism and Poetic Indeterminacy*, Austin, Texas University Press.

Frost, R. (1972) *Poetry and Prose*, New York, Holt, Rinehart and Winston.

Geertz, C. (1976) 'From the Native's Point of View: on the Nature of Anthropological Understanding' in Basso and Selby (1976).

—— (1988) *Works and Lives: the Anthropologist as Author*, Cambridge, Polity Press.

Geiogamah, H. (1980) *New Native American Drama: Three Plays*, Norman, Oklahoma University Press.

Ginzburg, C. (1990) *Myths, Emblems and Clues*, London and Sydney, Hutchinson.

Gloversmith, F. (1984) *The Theory of Reading*, Brighton, Harvester.

Goddard, I. and Bragdon, D.J. (1988) *Native Writings in Massachusetts*, Philadelphia, American Philosophical Society.

Goldman, I. (1975) *The Mouth of Heaven*, New York, Wiley.

—— (1980) 'Boas on the Kwakiutl', in Diamond (1980).

Goldschmidt, W. (1959) *The Anthropology of Franz Boas*, Memoir 89, American Anthropological Association.

Goody, J. (1977) *The Domestication of the Savage Mind*, Cambridge and London, Cambridge University Press.

—— (1987) *The Interface Between the Written and the Oral*, Cambridge and London, Cambridge University Press.

Grace, G.W. (1987) *The Linguistic Construction of Reality*, London, Croom Helm.

Greenblatt, S.J. (1976) 'Learning to Curse: Aspects of Linguistic Colonialism in the Sixteenth Century' in Chiappelli (1976:561–80).

—— (1981) 'Invisible Bullets: Renaissance Authority and its Subversion', *Glyph*, 8:40–61.

—— (1982) 'Filthy Rites', *Daedalus*, Summer: 1–16.

Gronewold, S. (1972) 'Did Frank Hamilton Cushing Go Native?' in Kimball and Watson (1972).

Haas, M.R. (1969) 'Grammar or Lexicon? The American Indian Side of the Question from Du Ponceau to Powell', *International Journal of American Linguistics*, 35:239–55.

Handler, R. (1985) 'On Dialogue and Destructive Analysis: Problems in Narrating Nationalism and Ethnicity', *Journal of Anthropological Research*, 41(2):171–82.

Harbsmeier, M. (1989) 'Writing and the Other: Traveller's Literacy, or Towards an Archaeology of Orality', in Schousboe and Larsen (1989:197–228).

Harman, G. (1969) 'An Introduction to "Translation and Meaning" ', in Davidson and Hintikka (1969:14–26).

Harner, M.J. (ed.) (1973) *Hallucinogens and Shamanism*, New York, Oxford University Press.

Harper, F.A. (1952) *Sequoyah: Symbol of Free Men*, Irvington-on-Hudson, NY, Foundation for Economic Education.

Hegeman, S. (1989) 'Native American "Texts" and the Problem of Authenticity', *American Quarterly*, 41(2):265–83.

Heller, T.C. (1986) *Reconstructing Individualism: Autonomy, Individualism and Self*, Stanford, CA, Stanford University Press.

Helm, J. (1966) *Pioneers of American Anthropology: the Uses of Biography*, Seattle and London, Washington University Press.

Hertzberg, H. (1972) *The Search for an American Indian Identity: Modern Pan-Indian Movements*, Syracuse, Syracuse University Press.

Hinsley, C.M. (1981) *Savages and Scientists: the Smithsonian Institution and the Development of American Anthropology*, Washington DC, Smithsonian Institution Press.

Hirschkop, K. and Shepherd, D. (eds.) (1989) *Bakhtin and Cultural Theory*, Manchester and New York, Manchester University Press.

Hollis, M. and Lukes, S. (eds.) *Rationality and Relativism*, Oxford, Blackwell.

Honour, H.W. (1976) *The New Golden Land: European Images of America From the Discovery to the Present Time*, London, Allen Lane.

Horigan, S. (1988) *Nature and Culture in Western Discourses*, London and New York, Routledge.

Horsman, R. (1981) *Race and Manifest Destiny: the Origin of American Racial Anglo-Saxonism*, London, Harvard University Press.

Hulme, P. (1986) *Colonial Encounters*, London, Methuen.

Humfreville, J.L. (1978) 'The Sign Language, its Mysterious Origin and Significance' in Umiker-Sebeok and Sebeok (1978).

Hymes, D. (1966) 'Two Types of Linguistic Relativity (with Examples from Amerindian Ethnography)' in Bright (1966:114–167).

—— (1977) 'Discovering Oral Performance and Measured Verse in American Indian Narrative' *New Literary History*, 8(3):431–57; repr. in Hymes (1981b).

—— (1979) 'How To Talk Like A Bear In Takelma' *International Journal of American Linguistics*, 45:101–106.

—— (1980a) 'Verse Analysis of a Wasco Text: Hiram Smith's "At'unaqa" ' *International Journal of American Linguistics* 46(19):65–77.

—— (1980b) 'Particle, Prose and Pattern in American Indian Narrative Verse' *American Indian Culture and Research Journal* (4):7–51.

—— (1981a) 'Reading Clackamas Texts' in Kroeber (1981).

—— (1981b) *In Vain I Tried To Tell You: Essays in Native American Ethnopoetics*, Philadelphia, Pennsylvania University Press.

—— (1983) 'Victoria Howard's "Gitskux and His Older Brother": a Clackamas Chinook Myth', in Swann (1983).

Jacobs, M. (1959a) 'Folklore' in Goldschmidt (1959).

—— (1959b) *The Context and Style of an Oral Literature: Clackamas Chinook Myths and Tales*, Chicago, Chicago University Press.

—— (1960) *The People are Coming Soon: Analyses of Clackamas Chinook Myths and Tales*, Chicago, Chicago University Press.

Jackson, D. (ed.) (1964) *Black Hawk: an Autobiography*, Urbana, Illinois University Press.

Jakobson, R. (1959) 'Boas' View of Grammatical Meaning', in Goldschmidt (1959).

—— (1971) *Marxism and Form*, Princeton, NJ, Princeton University Press.

—— (1976) 'Introduction–Prospectus: to Consider the Relation of Marxism to Utopian Thought', *Minnesota Review*, 6:53–8.

Jefferson, T. (1787) *Notes on the State of Virginia*; repr. in Peterson (1975).

Jennings, F. (1976) *The Invasion of America: Indians, Colonialism and the Cant of Conquest*, New York and London, Norton.

Jonaitis, A. (1981) 'Creations of Mystics and Philosophers: the White Man's Perceptions of Northwest Coast Art from the 1930s to the Present', *American Indian Culture and Research Journal*, 5(1):1–45.

Jones, L.T. (1965) *Aboriginal American Oratory: the Tradition of Eloquence Among the Indians of the United States*, Los Angeles, Southwest Museum.

Kaiser, R. (1987) 'Chief Seattle's Speech(es): American Origins and European Reception', in Swann and Krupat, (1987b:497–536).

Kaplan, D. and Manners, R.A. (1972) *Culture Theory*, Englewood Cliffs, NJ, Prentice-Hall.

Kehoe, A.B. (1989) *The Ghost Dance: Ethnohistory and Revitalisation*, New York, Holt, Rinehart and Winston.

Kermode, F. (1969) 'The Structures of Fiction', *Modern Language Notes* 84:891–930.

Kimball, S.T. and Watson, J.B. (eds.) (1972) *Crossing Cultural Boundaries: The Anthropological Experience*, San Francisco, Chandler.

King, R. (1980) *A Southern Renaissance: the Cultural Awakening of the American South, 1930-1955*, New York, Oxford University Press.

Kingston, M.H. (1977) *The Woman Warrior*, London, Picador.

Kinsey, R.R. (1979) 'A New Vision of Sequoyah', *The Masterkey*, 53, 1.

Kirk, R. (1986) *Translation Determined*, Oxford, Oxford University Press.

Kroeber, K. (1981) *Traditional American Indian Literatures*, Lincoln and London, Nebraska University Press.

Krupat, A. (1984) 'Mythography and Dialogue in the Study of Native American Literature', *American Indian Culture and Research Journal*, 8(4):47-55.

—— (1985) *For Those Who Come After: a Study of Native American Autobiography*, Berkeley, California University Press.

—— (1988) 'Anthropology in the Ironic Mode: the Work of Franz Boas', *Social Text*, 19-20: 105-18.

—— (1989) *The Voice in the Margin: Native American Literature and the Canon*, Berkeley, Los Angeles and London, California University Press.

Langness, L.L. and Frank, G. (1981) *Lives: an Anthropological Approach to Biography*, Novato, CA, Chandler and Sharp.

Larson, C.R. (1978) *American Indian Fiction*, Albuquerque, New Mexico University Press.

Leach, E. (ed.) (1967) *The Structural Study of Myth and Totemism*, London, Tavistock.

Lenneberg, E.H. and Roberts, J.M. (1956) 'The Language of Experience', *Indiana University Publications in Anthropology and Linguistics*, 13; repr. in Saporta (1961).

Leo, J.R. (1978) 'Riding Geronimo's Cadillac: *His Own Story* and the Circumstances of Text', *Journal of American Culture*, 1(4):818-37.

Levi-Strauss, C. (1978) *Structural Anthropology*, Vol. II, Harmondsworth, Penguin.

—— (1981) *The Naked Man: Introduction to a Science of Mythology*, Vol. IV, London, Cape.

—— (1982) *The Way of the Masks*, Seattle, Washington University Press.

—— (1985) *The View From Afar*, Oxford, Basil Blackwell.

Liberty, M. (1978) *American Indian Intellectuals*, St Paul, Minnesota and New York, West Publishing.

Lincoln, K. (1983) *Native American Renaissance*, Berkeley, Los Angeles and London, California University Press.

Love, W.de L. (1899) *Samson Occom and the Christian Indians of New England*, Boston and Chicago, Pilgrim Press.

Lowie, R.H. (1940) 'Native Languages as Ethnographic Texts' *American Anthropologist*, 42(1):81-9.

Lunn, E. (1982) *Marxism and Modernism: a Historical Study of Lukacs, Brecht, Benjamin and Adorno*, Berkeley, California University Press.

Lurie, N.O. (1966) 'Women in Early American Anthropology' in Helm (1966).

Lyotard, J.-F. (1984) *The Postmodern Condition*, Manchester, Manchester University Press.

McCallum, J.D. (ed.) (1932) *Letters of Eleazar Wheelock's Indians*, Hanover, NH, Dartmouth College Publications.

McClusky, S. (1972) '*Black Elk Speaks* and So Does John Neihardt', *Western American Literature*, 6(4):231-42.

MacDonald, G. (1962) *Phantastes and Lilith*, London, Gollancz.

MacDonald, G.F. (1981) 'Cosmic Equations in Northwest Coast Art', in Abbott (1981).

McKenney, T.L. and Hall, J. (1842) *History of the Indian Tribes of North America, with Biographical Sketches and Anecdotes of the Principal Chiefs*, Philadelphia, Rice and Clark; repr. ed. F.W. Hodge, Edinburgh, John Grant, 1933.

Macksey, R. and Donato, E. (eds.) (1972) *The Structuralist Controversy: The Languages of Criticism and the Sciences of Man*, Baltimore, Johns Hopkins University Press.

McLoughlin, W.G. (1984) *Cherokees and Missionaries, 1789-1839*, New Haven, CT, Yale University Press.

—— (1986) *Cherokee Renascence in the New Republic*, Princeton, NJ, Princeton University Press.

McNickle, D. (1936) *The Surrounded*, New York, Dodd, Mead.

—— (1978) *Wind From An Enemy Sky*, San Francisco, Harper and Row.

McQuaid, K. (1977) 'William Apes, Pequot: an Indian Reformer in the Jackson Era', *New England Quarterly*, 50(4):605-25.

Mails, T.E. (1979) *Fools Crow*, Garden City, NY, Doubleday.

Mallery, G. (1880) *Introduction to the Study of Sign Language among the North American Indians as Illustrating the Gesture Speech of Mankind*, Washington DC, US Bureau of American Ethnology; repr. in Umiker-Sebeok (1978).

—— (1881) 'The Gesture Speech of Man' *Proceedings of the American Association for the Advancement of Science* 30th Meeting: repr. in Umiker-Sebeok: 283-313.

—— (1888) *Picture-Writing of the American Indian*, Washington DC, US Bureau of American Ethnology, 10th Annual Report.

Marcus, G.E. and Cushman, R. (1982) 'Ethnographies as Texts', *Annual Review of Anthropology*, 11:25-69.

Marcus, G.E. and Fischer, M.M.J. (1986) *Anthropology as Cultural Critique: an Experimental Moment in the Human Sciences*, Chicago, Chicago University Press.

Mark, J. (1976) 'Frank Hamilton Cushing and an American Science of Anthropology', *Perspectives in American History*, 10:449-86; repr. in Mark (1980).

—— (1980) *Four Anthropologists: an American Science in its Early Years*, New York, Science History Publications.

Mascia-Lees, F.E., Sharpe, P. and Cohen, C.B. (1989) 'The Postmodernist Turn in Anthropology: Cautions from a Feminist Perspective', *Signs: Journal of Women in Culture and Society*, 15(1).

Mathews, J.J. (1934) *Sundown*, New York, Longmans Green.

Mattina, A. (1987) 'North American Indian Mythography: Editing Texts for the Printed Page', in Swann and Krupat (1987b:129-148).

Mayhew, E. (1727) *Indian Converts, or Some Accounts of the Lives and Dying Speeches of the Christianised Indians of Martha's Vineyard in New England*, London.

Mead, M. (1969) *An Anthropologist at Work: Writings of Ruth Benedict*, London, Secker and Warburg.

Meserve, W.T. (1956) 'English Works of Seventeenth-Century Indians', *American Quarterly*, 8(3):264-277.

Messent, P.B. (1981) *Literature of the Occult: a Collection of Critical Essays*, Englewood Cliffs, NJ, and London, Prentice Hall.

Minkema, K.P. (1988) 'The Edwardses: A Ministerial Family in 18th Century New England', PhD Thesis, University of Connecticut.

Modell, J. (1984) *Ruth Benedict: Patterns of a Life*, London, Chatto and Windus.

Momaday, N.S. (1968) *House Made of Dawn*, New York, Harper and Row.

—— (1969) *The Way to Rainy Mountain*, New York, Ballantine.

—— (1975) 'The Man Made of Words' in Chapman (1975).

—— (1976) *The Names: a Memoir*, New York, Harper and Row.

Moody, R. (ed.) (1966) *Dramas from the American Theatre, 1762–1909*, Cleveland and New York, World Publishing.

Mooney, J. (1897–8) *Myths of the Cherokees*, 19th Annual Report of Bureau of American Ethnology.

Murphy, M.N. (1970) 'Silence, the Word, and Indian Rhetoric', *College Composition and Communication*, 21:356–363.

Murray, D.J. (1981) 'Anthropology, Fiction and the Occult: the Case of Carlos Castaneda' in Messent (1981).

—— (1987) 'Dialogics: Conrad's *Heart of Darkness*', in Tallack (1987).

—— (1989) *Literary Theory and Poetry*, London, Batsford.

Neihardt, J.G. (1972) *Black Elk Speaks*, New York, Pocket Books.

Niatum, D. (1975) *Carriers of the Dream World: Contemporary Native American Poetry*, New York, Harper and Row.

Noel, D.C. (ed.) (1976) *Seeing Castaneda: Reactions to the 'Don Juan' Writings of Carlos Castaneda*, New York, Putnam.

Norman, H. (1976) *The Wishing-Bone Cycle: Narrative Poems from the Swampy Cree Indians*, New York, Standhill.

—— (1982) *Where The Chill Came From: Cree Windigo Tales and Journeys*, San Francisco, North Point Press.

Occom, S. (1788) *A Sermon at the Execution of Moses Paul*, New Haven, CT, first published in 1772.

O'Donnell, J.H. (1979) 'Logan's Oration: a Case Study in Ethnographic Authentication', *Quarterly Journal of Speech*, 65:150–6.

Olson, P.A. (1982) '*Black Elk Speaks* as Epic and Ritual Attempt at Revenge History' in Faulkner and Luebke (1982).

Ortiz, S. (1978) *Howbah Indians*, Tucson, AZ, Blue Moon Press.

Pandey, T.N. (1972) 'Anthropologists At Zuni' *Proceedings of the American Philosophical Society*, 116:321–37.

Payne, J.H. (1977) 'Sequoyah, or George Gist, by Major George Lowery 1835, with introduction and transcription by John Howard Payne', *Journal of Cherokee Studies*, 2(4):385–93.

Pearce, R.H. (1965) *Savagism and Civilisation: A Study of the Indian and the American Mind*, Baltimore, MD, Johns Hopkins University Press.

Penn, J.M. (1972) *Linguistic Relativity Versus Innate Ideas: The Origins of the Sapir-Whorf Hypothesis in German Thought*, The Hague and Paris, Mouton.

Peterson, M.D. (1975) *The Portable Thomas Jefferson*, New York, Viking.

Peyer, B. (1979) 'Reconsidering Native American Fiction', *Amerikastudien/American Studies*, (Stuttgart) 24(2):264–74.

—— (1981a) 'The Importance of Native American Authors', *American Indian Culture and Research Journal*, 5(3):1–12.

—— (1981b) 'Autobiographical Works Written by Native Americans', *Amerikastudien/American Studies* (Stuttgart), 26(3–4):386–402.

—— (1982a) *The Elders Wrote: An Anthology of Early Prose by North American Indians*, Berlin, Dietrich Reiner.

—— (1982b) 'Samson Occom: Mohegan Missionary and Writer of the 18th Century', *American Indian Quarterly*, 6(3–4):208–17.

Phillips, W.A. (1870) 'Sequoyah' *Harper's New Monthly Magazine*, September: 542–8.

Porter, C. (1988) 'Are We Being Historical Yet?', *North Atlantic Quarterly*, 87(4):743–86.

Pratt, M.L. (1985) 'Scratches on the Face of the Country: Or What Mr. Barrow Saw in the Land of the Bushmen', *Critical Inquiry*, 12:119–43.

Price, S. (1989) *Primitive Art in Civilised Places*, Chicago and London, Chicago University Press.

Quine, W.V.O. (1960) *Word and Object*, New York and London, MIT Press and John Wiley.

Radin, P. (1913) 'Personal Reminiscences of a Winnebago Indian', *Journal of American Folklore*, 26:203–318.

—— (1983) *Crashing Thunder: The Autobiography of an American Indian*, Lincoln, Nebraska University Press, first published in 1926.

Ramsay, J. (1977) 'The Wife Who Goes Out Like a Man, Comes Back As A Hero', *PMLA*, 92(1):9–18; repr. in Ramsey (1983:76–95).

—— (1983) *Reading the Fire: Essays in the Traditional Indian Literatures of the Far West*, Lincoln, Nebraska University Press.

Ray, V. (1955) 'Franz Boas: the Science of Man in the Making', *American Anthropologist*, 57:139–140.

Remington, F. (1905), 'The Way of an Indian', *Cosmopolitan Magazine* 40(2):125–35.

Revard, C. (1980) 'History Myth and Identity among Osages and Other Peoples' *Denver Quarterly*, 14:84–97.

Richardson, L.B. (1933), *An Indian Preacher in England*, Hanover, NH, Dartmouth College Publications.

Ricoeur, P. (1971) 'The Model of the Text: Meaningful Action Considered as Text', *Social Research*, 38(3):529–62.

Rodriguez, R. (1981) *Hunger of Memory: the Education of Richard Rodriguez: an Autobiography*, Boston, Godine.

Rogers, R. (1914) *Ponteach or the Savages of America: a Tragedy*, Chicago, Caxton Club.

Rogin, M.P. (1975) *Fathers and Children: Andrew Jackson and the Subjugation of the American Indian*, New York, Knopf.

Rohner, R.P. (1966) 'Franz Boas: Ethnographer on the Northwest Coast' in Helm (1966).

—— (ed.) (1969) *The Ethnography of Franz Boas*, Chicago, Chicago University Press.

Ronda, J.P. (1977) ' "We Are Well As We Are": an Indian Critique of 17th Century Christian Missions', *William and Mary Quarterly*, 34:66–82.

Rossi-Landi, F. (1973) *Ideologies of Linguistic Relativity*, The Hague and Paris, Mouton.

Roth, P.A. (1989) 'Ethnography Without Tears', *Current Anthropology*, 30(5): 555–69.

Rothenberg, J. (1968) *Technicians of the Sacred: a Range of Poetries from Africa, America, Asia and Oceania*, Garden City, NY, Doubleday.

—— (1972) *Shaking the Pumpkin: Traditional Poetry of the Indian North Americas*, Garden City, NY, Doubleday.

—— (1975) 'Total Translation: an Experiment in the Presentation of American Indian Poetry' in Chapman (1975).

—— (ed.) (1976) *Alcheringa*, 2, (2).

—— (1981) *Prefaces and Other Writings*, New York, New Directions.

Rothenberg, J. and D. (eds.) (1983) *Symposium of the Whole*, Berkeley, California University Press.

Ruby, J. (1982) *A Crack in the Mirror: Reflexive Perspectives in Anthropology*, Philadelphia, Pennsylvania University Press.

Rugg, H. (1942) 'The Dartmouth Plays, 1779–1782', *Theatre Annual*, 1:55–68.

Sachlins, M. (1981) *Historical Metaphors and Mythical Realities: Structure in the Early History of the Sandwich Islands Kingdom*, Ann Arbor, Michigan University Press.

Said, E. (1978) *Orientalism*, London, Routledge and Kegan Paul.

Salisbury, N. (1982) *The Indians of New England: A Critical Bibliography*, Bloomington, Indiana University Press.

Sanchez, T. (1972) *Rabbit Boss*, New York, Ballantine.

Sandefur, R.H. (1960) 'Logan's Oration: How Authentic', *Quarterly Journal of Speech*, 46:289–96.

Sangren, P.S. (1988) 'Rhetoric and the Authority of Ethnography: "Postmodernism" and the Social Reproduction of Texts', *Current Anthropology*, 29:405–23.

Sapir, E. (1951) *Selected Writings of Edward Sapir*, Berkeley and Los Angeles, California University Press.

Saporta, S. (ed.) (1961) *Psycholinguistics: A Book of Readings*, New York, Holt, Rinehart and Winston.

Scholer, B. (ed.) (1984) *Coyote Was Here: Essays on Contemporary Native American Literary and Political Mobilisation*, Aarhus, Seklos.

Schousboe, K. and Larsen, M.T. (1989) *Literacy and Society*, Center for Research in the Humanities, Copenhagen, Akademisk Forlag.

Schubnell, M. (1985) *N. Scott Momaday: the Cultural and Literary Background*, Norman, Oklahoma University Press.

Seeber, E.D. (1947) 'Critical Views on Logan's Speech', *Journal of American Folklore*, 60 (April):130–46.

Sheehan, B. (1969) 'Paradise and the Noble Savage', *William and Mary Quarterly*, 26.

—— (1980) *Savagism and Civility: Indians and Englishmen in Colonial Virginia*, Cambridge, Cambridge University Press.

Silko, L.M. (1977) *Ceremony*, New York, Viking.

—— (1979) 'An Old-Time Indian Attack Conducted in Two Parts', *Shantih*, 4:3–5.

—— (1981) *Storyteller*, New York, Seaver Books.

Silverman, H.J. and Aylesworth, G.E. (1990) *The Textual Sublime: Deconstruction and its Differences*, Albany, State University of New York Press.

Silverstein, M. (1979) 'Language Structure and Linguistic Ideology', *The Elements: Proceedings From the Parasession on Linguistic Units and Levels*, Chicago Linguistic Society: 193–247.

Simmons, L.W. (ed.) (1942) *Sun Chief: The Autobiography of a Hopi Indian*, New York and London, Yale University Press.

Smith, A.G. (1966) *Communication and Culture: Readings in the Codes of Human Interaction*, New York, Holt, Rinehart and Winston.

Smith, J. (1966) 'A Dialogue Between an Englishman and an Indian' in Moody (1966).

Smith, R.N. (1979) 'The Interest in Language and Languages in Colonial and Federal America', *Proceedings of the American Philosophical Society*, 123:29–46.

Smith, S. (1987) *A Poetics of Women's Autobiography: Marginality and the Fiction of Self-Representation*, Bloomington and Indianapolis, Indiana University Press.

Sorber, E.C. (1972) 'The Noble Eloquent Savage', *Ethnohistory*, 19(3):227–36.

Sossing, B.J. (1870) 'Our Barbarian Brethren', *Harper's Monthly Magazine* 40, (May): 793–811.

Spier, L. (1963) *The Ethnography and Ethnology of Franz Boas*, Austin, Texas Memorial Museum Bulletin 6.

Spradley, J.P. (1969) *Guests Never Leave Hungry: the Autobiography of James Sewid, A Kwakiutl Indian*, New Haven, CT, Yale University Press.

Steadman, R.W. (1982) *Shadows of the Indian: Stereotypes in American Culture*, Norman, Oklahoma University Press.

Steiner, W. (1982) *The Colors of Rhetoric: Problems in the Relation Between Modern Literature and Painting*, Chicago, Chicago University Press.

Stepto, R.B. (1979) *From Behind the Veil: a Study of Afro-American Narrative*, Urbana, Illinois University Press.

Stocking, G.W. (ed.) (1974) *The Shaping of American Anthropology, 1883–1911: A Franz Boas Reader*, New York, Basic Books.

—— (1983) *Observers Observed: Essays on Ethnographic Fieldwork*, Madison, Wisconsin University Press.

Stone, J.A. (1829) *Metamora*; repr. in Coyle and Damaser (1968).

Strickland, W. (1977) 'Cherokee Rhetoric: a Forceful Weapon', *Journal of Cherokee Studies*, 2(4):385–93.

Swann, B. (ed.) (1983) *Smoothing the Ground: Essays on Native American Oral Literature*, Berkeley, California University Press.

Swann, B. and Krupat, A. (eds.) (1987a) *I Tell You Now: Autobiographical Essays By Native American Writers*, Lincoln, Nebraska University Press.

—— (eds.) (1987b) *Recovering the Word: Essays on Native American Literature*, Berkeley, California University Press.

Sweet, D.G. and Nash, G.B. (eds.) (1981) *Struggle and Survival in Colonial America*, Berkeley, Los Angeles and London, California University Press.

Takaki, R. (1979) *Iron Cages: Race and Culture in Nineteenth Century America*, London, Athlone Press.

Tallack, D. (1987) *Literary Theory At Work*, London, Batsford.

Tanner, L. and Krasner, J.N. (1989) 'Exposing the "Sacred Juggle": Revolutionary Rhetoric in Robert Rogers' *Ponteach*', *Early American Literature*, 24:4–19.

Tarn, N. (1976) 'The Heraldic Vision: a Cognitive Model for Comparative Aesthetics', *Alcheringa*, 2(2):23–41.

Taylor, A.R. (1981) 'Indian Lingua Franca', in Ferguson and Heath (1981).

Taylor, P. (1989) 'Ethnography As Genre: Are Orality and Literacy Romantically Linked?', *Southern Review*, (Adelaide) 22(3):290–300.

Taxay, D. (1970) *Money of the American Indians and Other Primitive Currencies of the Americas*, New York, Nummus Press.

Tedlock, D. (1971) 'On the Translation of Style in Oral Narratives', *Journal of American Folklore*, 84:114–33.

—— (1983) *The Spoken Word and the Work of Interpretation*, Philadelphia, Pennsylvania University Press.

Tedlock, B. (1984) 'The Beautiful and the Dangerous: Zuni Ritual and Cosmology as Aesthetic System' *Conjunctions*, 6:246–65.

Tedlock, B. and T. (1985) 'Text and Textile: Language and Technology in the Arts of the Quiche Maya', *Journal of Anthropological Research*, 41(2):121–46.

—— (1985) *Popol Vuh: the Mayan Book of the Dawn of Life*, New York, Simon and Schuster.

Todorov, T. (1973) *The Fantastic: A Structural Approach to a Literary Genre*, Cleveland, Case Western Reserve University Press.

—— (1984) *Conquest of America: The Question of the Other*, New York, Harper.

Tooker, W.W. (1896) *John Eliot's First Indian Teacher and Interpreter, Cockenoe-de-Long Island and the Story of his Career from the Early Records*, New York, Francis P. Harper.

Tracy, W. (1871) 'Indian Eloquence', *Appleton's Journal of Literature, Science and Art*, 6 (November):543–5.

Traveller Bird (1971) *Tell Them They Lie: the Sequoyah Myth*, Los Angeles, Westernlore.

Tyler, S.A. (1986) 'Post modern Ethnography: From Document of the Occult to Occult Document', in Clifford and Marcus (1986:122–40).

—— (1987) *The Unspeakable: Discourse, Dialogue and Rhetoric in the Postmodern World*, Madison, Wisconsin University Press.

Umiker-Seboek, D.J. and Sebeok, T.A. (1978) *Aboriginal Sign Languages of the Americas and Australia*, 2 Vols., New York and London, Plenum Press.

Vanderwerth, W.C. (1971) *Indian Oratory: Famous Speeches by Noted Indian Chiefs*, Norman, Oklahoma University Press.

Velie, A. (1979) *American Indian Literature: An Anthology*, Norman, Oklahoma University Press.

—— (1982) *Four American Indian Literary Masters: N. Scott Momaday, James Welch, Leslie Marmon Silko, and Gerald Vizenor*, Norman, Oklahoma University Press.

Vizenor, G. (1976) 'I Know What You Mean, Erdupps MacChurrbs: Autobiographical Myths and Metaphors', in Anderson (1976).

—— (1978) *Wordarrows: Indians and Whites in the New Fur Trade*, Minneapolis, Minnesota University Press.

—— (1981) *Earthdiver: Tribal Narratives on Mixed Descent*, Minneapolis, Minnesota University Press.

Voloshinov, V.N. (1973) *Marxism and the Philosophy of Language*, New York, Seminar Press.

Walens, S. (1981) *Feasting With Cannibals: an Essay on Kwakiutl Cosmology*, Princeton, NJ, Princeton University Press.

Walker, W. (1981) 'Native American Writing Systems', in Ferguson and Heath (1981:145–74).

—— (1984a) 'Literacy, Wampums, the Gudebuk, and How Indians in the Far Northeast Read', *Anthropological Linguistics*, 26(1):42–51.

—— (1984b) 'The Design of Native Literacy Programs and How Literacy Came to the Cherokees', *Anthropological Linguistics*, 26(2):161–9.

Washburn, W.E. (ed.) (1964) *The Indian and the White Man*, New York, Doubleday.

Watson, G. (1987) 'Make Me Reflexive – But Not Yet: Strategies for Managing Essential Reflexivity in Ethnographic Discourse', *Journal of Anthropological Research*, 43(1):29–41.

Wauchope, R. (1962) *Lost Tribes and Sunken Continents: Myth and Method in the Study of American Indians*, Chicago and London, Chicago University Press.

Webster, S. (1962) 'Dialogue and Fiction in Ethnography' *Dialectical Anthropology* 7:91–114.

—— (1986) 'Realism and Reification in the Ethnographic Genre' *Critique of Anthropology*, 6(1):39–62.

Weiskel, T. (1976) *The Romantic Sublime: Studies in the Structure and Psychology of Transcendence*, Baltimore and London, Johns Hopkins University Press.

Welch, J. (1974) *Winter in the Blood*, New York, Harper and Row.

—— (1980) *The Death of Jim Loney*, New York, Harper and Row.

—— (1986) *Fools Crow*, New York, Viking.

White, H. (1973) *Metahistory*, Baltimore, Johns Hopkins University Press.

—— (1978) *Tropics of Discourse: Essays in Cultural Criticism*, Baltimore and London, Johns Hopkins University Press.

—— (1987) *The Content of the Form: Narrative Discourse and Historical Representation*, Baltimore and London, Johns Hopkins University Press.

Whorf, B.L. (1956) *Language, Thought and Reality*, New York, John Wiley and MIT.

Wiget, A.O. (1986) 'Native American Literature: a Bibliographical Survey of American Indian Literary Traditions', *Choice*, (June):1503–12.

Williams, R. (1643) *A Key into the Language of America*, repr. Providence RI, E.A. Johnson, 1963.

Williams, T.C. (1976) *The Reservation*, Syracuse, Syracuse University Press.

Wilson, B.R. (ed.) (1974) *Rationality*, Oxford, Blackwell.

Wilson, E. (1956) *Red, Black, Blond and Olive: Studies in Four Civilisations: Zuni, Haiti, Soviet Russia, Israel*, New York, Oxford University Press.

Wilson, R. (1983) *Ohiyesa: Charles Eastman, Santee Sioux*, Urbana, Illinois University Press.

Witherspoon, G. (1977) *Language and Art in the Navajo Universe*, Ann Arbor, Michigan University Press.

Wong, H.D. (1989) 'Pictographs as Autobiography: Plains Indian Sketchbooks of the Late 19th and Early 20th Centuries', *American Literary History*, 1(2):295–316.

Wroth, L.C. (1928) 'The Indian Treaty as Literature', *Yale Review*, 17(4); repr. in Chapman (1975).

Young Bear, R. (1980) *Winter of the Salamander*, San Francisco, Harper and Row.

Index